D0929670

ENDURANCE:
CHRONICLES OF JEWISH RESISTANCE

ENDURANCE
CHRONICLES
OF
JEWISH RESISTANCE

AMNON AJZENSZTADT

MOSAIC PRESS
OAKVILLE NEW YORK LONDON

Canadian Cataloguing in Publication Data

Ajzensztadt, Amnon, 1919–
   Endurance: chronicles of Jewish resistance
(The Eyewitness series)
ISBN 0-88962-389-9 (bound) ISBN 0-88962-390-2 (pbk.)

1. Ajzensztadt, Amnon, 1919–   . 2. World War, 1939-1945 – Personal
narratives, Jewish. 3. World War, 1939-1945 – Underground movements,
Jewish – Poland. 4. World War, 1939-1945 – Underground movements,
Jewish – Ukraine. 5. World War, 1939- 1945 – Jews – Poland. 6. World
War, 1939-1945 – Jews – Ukraine. I. Title. II. Series.

D811.A39 1987   940.53'15'03924   C88-093029-2

No part of this book may be reproduced or transmitted in any form, by
any means, electronic or mechanical, including photocopying and re-
cording information storage and retrieval systems, without permission
in writing from the publisher, except by a reviewer who may quote brief
passages in a review.

Published by Mosaic Press, P.O. Box 1032, Oakville, Ontario L6J 5E9
Canada. Office and warehouse at 1252 Speers Rd., Unit 10, Oakville,
Ontario L6L 5N9 Canada.

Published with the assistance of the Canada Council and the Ontario
Arts Council.

Copyright © Amnon Ajzensztadt, 1987
Design by Edward Pickersgill
Cover by Rita Vogel
Typeset by Speed River Graphics
Printed and bound in Canada

ISBN 0-88962-389-9 cloth
         0-88962-390-2 paper

MOSAIC PRESS:

In Canada:
   Mosaic Press, 1252 Speers Road, Units #1 & 2, Oakville, Ontario
L6L 5N9, Canada
P.O. Box 1032 Oakville, Ontario L6J 5E9

In the United States:
Riverrun Press Inc., 1170 Broadway, Suite 807, New York, N.Y., 10001,
U.S.A. distributed by Kampmann & Co., 9 East 40th Street, New York,
N.Y. 10016.

In the U.K.:
John Calder (Publishers) Ltd., 18 Brewer Street, London, W1R 4AS,
England.

This book is dedicated to the miraculous sprouts of a new beginning.

My children: Miriam-Liba and Zishe-Aaron.

My grandchildren: David, Jordana, Markie and Shana.

ACKNOWLEDGEMENT

Profound gratitude is hereby expressed to:

The dean of Toronto's Jewish writers, Mr. Joachim Schoenfeld; Mr. Ben Kayfetz; Rabbi Bernard Baskin; Mrs. Channa Ajzensztadt; Mrs. Pearl Bader; Dr. David Nimmo; and last but not least, Mr. Murray Horowitz, the son of survivors, who is a worthy member of the post-Auschwitz generation with great love for his people's heritage and adherence to the Torah command not to forget what the Nazi Amalakites did to European Jewry.

All of these individuals participated in their own way, morally and practically, with both advice and deeds in making this book possible.

ראש הממשלה
THE PRIME MINISTER

Jerusalem   August 3, 1987.

Dear Mr. Ajzensztadt,

      Your memoirs are an important contribution to the literature of the Holocaust. It is a gripping story of personal courage, determination, man's will to overcome the worst adversity and to retain your faith is a real saga. The book focuses on a hitherto little-known aspect of Jewish resistance to the Nazis that deserves to be told.

      I hope this account of the modern Marrano will be read by the younger generation and give them pride in the Jewish freedom fighter who with ingenuity, faith and spiritual strength ultimately triumphed.

            Sincerely,

            Yitzhak Shamir

Mr. Amnon Ajzensztadt
630 Brock Avenue
Toronto Ontario
M6H 3P2 Canada

AMNON AJZENSZTADT

Amnon Ajzensztadt was born in Sandomierz, Poland and was educated in Warsaw where he attended Yeshiva academies and the Jewish Teachers' Seminary. He also studied music at the Warsaw Conservatory and was a contributor to the Yiddish weeklies *Unser Ruf* and *Unser Welt*.

After serving with the underground forces during World War II, he lectured in Hungary, Austria and France from 1945 to 1948. In Canada, he was co-editor of *Hemshek*, a journal for newcomers and a member of the editorial staff of the *Daily Hebrew Journal*. He has contributed numerous articles, essays and poetry to the Montreal *Canadian Eagle*. the New York *Algemeiner Journal*, the Toronto *Jewish Standard* and the *Canadian Jewish News*. He is the author of *And the Earth Did Not Cover the Blood*, the drama *The Three Lives of Adam* and numerous articles and essays.

ENDURANCE: CHRONICLES OF JEWISH RESISTANCE

Amnon Ajzensztadt

Table of Contents

FOREWORD

What Is Being Said About
Endurance: Chronicles of Jewish Resistance

Amnon Ajzensztadt has written an extraordinary book — a gripping autobiography, which is yet much more the purely personal account of a complex character's adventures amidst the horrors of World War II.

He terms himself "a self-appointed chronicler of Israel's drama among the nations," seeking to fulfil the Torah's command to tell one's children their people's story. His life mirrors in microcosm the history of Jewish suffering, struggle and ultimate survival.

PROFESSOR ELEAZAR BIRNBAUM

Some books are written to entertain us. Other volumes are supposed to educate us. Usually, the latter are dry as dust, and are put aside to be read when there is no alternative.

Amnon Ajzensztadt has written an autobiography that is educational and interesting. When you start reading it, you will find it so gripping a tale that you won't be able to leave it until you finish it.

RABBI DR. MOSES J. BURAK

Amnon Ajzensztadt has written a powerful, gripping story of a young Jew's flight from the Warsaw Ghetto to avoid his fellow Jews' tragic fate to his ultimate freedom in Russia following the War. Masquerading as an Aryan in *Wehrmacht* uniform, he evaded detection and remained alive by relying on his wits, his providential encounters with the "subterranean world of Polish Jews" in similar disguise, and, above all, his unswerving faith in God's ultimate providence.

LIBBY GARSHOWITZ, Ph.D.

Like Weisel, Ajzensztadt is not just a writer on the Holocaust. Those who know him personally see in him the personification of the Survivor. It is said of the tzaddikim that one could see the Shecinah on their foreheads. To look into the author's sad blue eyes, one sees the Ner Tamid, the constant vision of a whole generation, family, friends, civilization, etched into his thoughts.

RABBI MEIR URI GOTTESMAN

ENDURANCE: CHRONICLES OF JEWISH RESISTANCE

The soul-searing memoirs of Amnon Ajzensztadt, sheds light on one man's odyssey, both physical and spiritual, from anguish to joy, from darkness to hope. Like Yosef of old, alert to, and guided by DEYUKNO SHEL AVIV, his father's countenance, our author also "survives" because of his sainted father's "imprint". Unlike similar manuscripts on the Shoah, his are not simply poignant events loosely strung together leaving the reader with gaps to be filled by personal intuition and imagination. His memoirs constitute a revelation emanating from the innermost recesses of his heart, expressed with a straight-forward eloquence which frequently so absorbs the reader that he and writer become indissolubly intertwined and share experiences never-to-be-forgotten. The book lacks the niceties which tend to obfuscate realities. Persons and events are real and, as such, verily cleave the heart and mind. It deserves to be written; it deserves to be read and digested. Its message serves as a MATZEVET HACHAYIM, a living monument, and a tribute to the undaunted spirit of one man and, by extension, the spirit of Jews everywhere. "A little light dispels a multitude of darkness."

RABBI HENRY HOSCHANDER

His chronicle has moments of suspense and drama; wanton brutality and tender selflessness; barbaric savagery and poignant expressions of kinsship; breathless adventures and philosophical musings about the human reality. It is a veritable roller-coaster moving between the depths of despair and the heights of hope and faith.

RABBI J. IMMANUEL SCHOCHET

Amnon Ajzensztadt has written a captivating tale relating his experiences as a young Jew caught up in the events which took place during the period of the Nazi domination of Poland. In lucid, highly evocative prose, he tells the story of his life under an inhuman oppressor, and although his narrative is articulated in terms of one individual, it reflects the universal Jewish experience during a bitter period in our history.

In some of the episodes contained in this volume, the events grip the reader as though one were engrossed in a mystery novel. The author describes his firsthand encounter with Polish anti-Semitism, Nazi brutality, and the Russian "bear" in graphic terms.

RABBI IRWIN E. WITTY

PREFACE

The Memoirs of Amnon Ajzensztadt

BY EMIL L. FACKENHEIM

"It was a kind of spiritual wrestling bout between Jewish endurance, resourcefulness and the diaspora training acquired through
the millenia — namely, the capacity to turn a disadvantage into an
advantage — versus the formality-conscious, orderly, technocratic evil genius of Nazi *Puenktlichkeit*, Nazi-accuracy, so characteristically epitomized in the scrupulous utilization of their victim's possessions, including the hair of their heads and the fat of
their bodies for industrial purposes . . ."

THUS, at one point in his autobiography Amnon Ajzensztadt describes his
unbelievable struggle to survive as a Jew during the years of Nazi horror. Several things in this work are unbelievable yet true. The "Aryan"-looking son of
a Hasidic rebbe; the luck that assisted the son — the father was murdered — in
passing for an Aryan, and indeed in one way or another passing for a sup-
porter of the enemy; moments of near detection too many and varied to even
hint at here; these are enough to make a fascinating story. But most
unbelievable of all are the two facts stressed often enough in previous accounts
of survivors, but that need telling and re-telling, again and again — the two
facts stated in the quotation above: a wickedness without precedent in the
annals of mankind, made with Teutonic efficiency into a system so thorough
as to make countless ordinary, dime-a-dozen individuals into willing or even
enthusiastic instruments; and in the face of this over-powering force, a Jewish
will-to-survive of heroic proportions. This latter emerges especially clearly in
this book since the author never lets the reader forget what is a plain fact but
what is all-too-often obscured or even denied today for all sorts of reasons, all
unforgivable: the fact that Jews were Nazism's singled-out victims. As Elie
Wiesel has well put it, not all victims were Jews, but all Jews were victims.

The reader gets a clear grasp of the author's own kind of heroism in an
unforgettable scene early in the book. The father is a famous, learned, gentle
Hasidic rebbe. That such a man has an "aryan"-looking son is unlikely

enough. That the son has enough worldly enterprise to seek survival by moving out of the Ghetto and trying to pass for an actual Gentile is more unlikely still. Most unlikely of all is that the son is a follower of Jabotinsky, i.e. a Jew who does not hide and pray when the murderous enemy comes, but rather tries to get hold of arms; however pitiful, to defend himself. Yet father and son have much in common. Throughout the book there emerges the son's love not only for his dead father but also for his pious heritage. The grounds for this bond appear in the unforgettable scene. The time to part has come — with neither man having any illusions that it is forever. The father approves of the son's way though it is not his own, but gives him one admonition — that there is one thing that he ought not to do even in order to survive, namely, hide in a privy or latrine. The father has heard of incidents of the Nazis discovering Jews in such a place and proceeding — Nazi-style fun and games — to shove them in. To drown in feces, the father tells the son, is no way for a Jew to die. The son fully shares the fathers view. In this book he relates many ways in which he "turned a disadvantage into an advantage." Never did he do anything he would have to be ashamed of. This book is a glowing tribute to Jewish dignity, in the face of the enemy that did whatever was humanly possible — with a formality-conscious, orderly, technocratic evil genius" — in order to rob Jews of their humanity before robbing them of their lives.

I have the manuscript before me more than forty years after the Third Reich came crashing down. Is it not time to forget the grim past? The truth is that the world has yet adequately to bring it to consciousness, which is why distortions, evasions and out-right lies about Nazism and all its works abound, to say nothing of pornographic exploitations. A Midrash comments on the curious passage in the book of Exodus according to which, just prior to the Sinaitic revelation, a shofar was blown, and it waxed louder and louder. Shouldn't it be the opposite, for if a person blows a horn it becomes less and less loud as the person runs out of breath? The shofar at Sinai waxed louder and louder, the Midrash explains, because what was happening was so momentous that the human ear had to get used to it gradually. When after the war the world saw pictures of the murder camps it looked briefly, but then averted its eyes. Then survivors wrote their stories but few read them. Not until decades later were their voices beginning to be heard, and only now the masterful film *Shoah* has appeared . . . and it is still seen by far too few people! In the midst of the war the greatest voice of the time, that of Winston Churchill, promised to rid the world of Hitler's shadow. Inspired by that voice, those that heeded it rid the world of Hitler. But his shadow will haunt the world until it faces with utter truthfulness the unprecedented hideousness of his works. To this end this book makes a notable contribution.

INTRODUCTION

BY AMNON AJZENSZTADT
Toronto , September 1987

FOR the author of this book, Jewish history is not simply a compilation of episodes from bygone days, but a reflection of the continuous ongoing drama of Israel among the nations.

There are no fictitious characters in the pages of these memoirs. I was an eye-witness to a most turbulent and awe-inspiring period of horror and valor, havoc and gallantry, fiendishness and sanctity. Only certain names and localities have been changed. However, the individuals and incidents portrayed are genuine parts of an unusual saga of Jews who, on forged Aryan papers, managed to infiltrate the Wehrmacht forces and, from within, to engage in illegal, underground activities and sabotage.

In these days of the Ernst Zundels, Jim Keegstras, Louis Farakhans, the Aryan neo-Nazis, and the historical revisionists, the publishing of personally experienced accounts is of supreme importance.

There is yet another profound reason which compelled me to write this work. Far too many people have used the Holocaust as a pretext for peddling their own sensationalist and titillating accounts of what they claim really happened. They have used the national disaster of what happened to the Jewish people as a vehicle for their own self-advancement.

Of course, there are also authors who have written excellent books about slave-labor, concentration camps, and the resistance movement with heartfelt compassion and understanding. These books, based on interviews and research files are a thoroughly responsible attempt to place the terrible story of what happened to the Jews of Europe in an appropriate historical context.

Yet, to counteract the cynical falsifiers of history and the maligners of the miraculous escapees of the Nazi inferno, it is incumbent upon the remaining survivors to register for posterity the authentic memory of those days of anguish, agony and genocide: the truth.

And that is the aim of this narrative!

It is also an attempt to fulfil the Torah-command of: VEHIGADTA LEBINCHA — of relating to our sons and daughters the genuine truth of their people's fate under the swastika's scourge; eternalizing the gigantic tragedy in its fullest possible extent, informing them first-hand about the hitherto unknown elements in the full story of the lime-kilns and the fighting barricades of the Ghetto mutineers; the story of the martyrdom and the intrepid spirit of their ancient nation in its incessant struggle for survival.

Finally, I would like to express my profound thanks to the Prime Minister of the State of Israel, the Rt. Hon. Yitzhak Shamir for receiving me in his office, for his graciousness for reading my book and for his kindness in writing to me regarding his reaction to my work.

The Prime Minister's poignant comments in drawing our attention to the historical parallels between the Jews on forged Aryan papers in German uniforms under Hitler with the counterfeit Marrano Christians of Spain secretly practicing Judaism under King Ferdinand and Queen Isabella in the 15th century offers us a powerful perspective from which to read this work. As an author, I can only hope that this autobiographical work underlines the commonality among Jews throughout the ages to endure adversity with pride, to cling to their own faith and to resist tyranny and injustice in all ages and in all places.

CHAPTER 1

The Rebbe's Son

BEFORE the war my late father was a well-known Chassidic rebbe (rabbi) in Warsaw. Towards the end of 1941, over two years after the Nazis invaded Poland, I was made aware of his immense contribution to my spiritual life. This affected me both directly and indirectly. I was able to use the reservoir of strength he had provided me to aid in my own struggle to survive, and I realised how important a sense of history is to Judaism. It is a record that is passed down through the ages, from parent to child.

Our family was living at the time in Ostrowiec, about 160 kilometers from Warsaw, but I had returned to Warsaw and had succeeded in smuggling myself into the Ghetto. I went with a group of Polish bootleggers, who made money out of smuggling food into the restricted areas and selling it. My aim was to smuggle out as many of my father's old manuscripts as I could; which he had been forced to leave behind when escaping from the newly created Ghetto in 1940.

I returned to Ostrowiec with a huge suitcase, filled with commentaries on the Torah and the Talmud, Chassidic treatises, books on all kinds of religious and philosophical topics including the Kabbalah, and musical compositions. My father had worked on these all his life.

I had also managed to bring along a large knapsack with valuable Shtraimels, the fur-edged hats worn by rabbis and Chassidic Jews on the Sabbath and holy days, as well as a mink fur and a silver fox coat of my mother's. I was unusually fortunate to have blue eyes and a Slavic nose, so the usual police curiosity at the train stations and ticket check points proved no barrier to my passage. I arrived after midnight at 54 Sienienska Street in Ostrowiec where my parents were anxiously awaiting my return.

As the sages state, 'Those sent on a pious mission will meet no evil.' And how true that had been in my own particular case, for I was, after all, a Jew. Jews were forbidden to travel between cities, forbidden to travel on public transportation, and forbidden to walk the streets without wearing a special 'Jew badge.' For any one of these infractions I would have been put to death at once, so I could not help feeling quite proud and gratified upon successfully completing the rescue mission.

There was no time for delay, however, in finding a safe place to keep the manuscripts. The Nazis were conducting house-to-house searches on a daily basis, and it was far too risky to leave the manuscripts lying around. They were too conspicuously important to us as Jews, and we ourselves risked certain punishment for simply having such things in our possession.

We had to ensure that our hiding place would also be safe from the prying eyes and ears of our Polish neighbours at 52 and 56 Sienienska Street. Were they to see anything they would probably assume that we were hiding precious stones or valuable currency. In the early hours of the morning we sneaked through our backyard to the lower grounds of the property, where an unoccupied cottage stood. It was a modest, old-fashioned dwelling with two tiny rooms. One of the rooms was without a wooden floor, there was only a surface of hard-packed earth that was sprinkled with light-coloured sand. Here we could either dig a deep hole in the ground or utilize the little building's thick foundation walls as a vault by removing some bricks and blocks and filling in the hollow spaces with the manuscripts, wrapped in moisture-proof paper bags and tin containers.

After covering the windows with dark blankets, the unique excavation began in earnest. We knew that we were about to bury something very near and dear to us in the sandy Polish earth. We could only pray that we would one day be able to retrieve it. We were reminded very strongly of the events at the caves of Qumran when the ancient Hebrews had placed their scrolls in the Judean desert-grotto near the Dead Sea. Ostrowiec was nowhere near the Dead Sea; it was situated in a territory that was about to become the Sea of Death for almost all of European Jewry.

Surprisingly enough, though, we felt little or no despondency. We felt rather that our purpose was divinely-inspired. The secrecy of our endeavour, the fear of surprise, and the shadow play of our silhouettes cast by the flickering candles on the lime-white walls, reminded us of the Spanish Inquisition when our ancestors had likewise had to keep the fact of their Jewishness a secret. Like them, we were filled with faith in G-d almighty. Like them, we felt how important it was to maintain the thread of Jewish life, to be passed on from generation to generation.*

When we filed out at daybreak, we were in good spirits, despite having

---

* All three excavators at 54 Sienienska Street survived the Holocaust. The hardest working one of the trio, Moshe Bruker, is a businessman, philanthropist and grandfather in Borough Park, Brooklyn, New York. His younger brother and family man, Shlomoh Brukirer, lives in Munich, Germany. And I, myself, live in Toronto, Canada.

heard about the Fuhrer's announcement that the object of his European war was the complete annihilation of the Jews.

Although we had succeeded in hiding the manuscripts, we were less successful in the financial side of our escapade. We had taken an immense risk in smuggling out the furs from the Ghetto, in order to sell them and buy food, fuel, medication, and other necessities. A few days after burying the manuscripts and before we could begin to look for someone to sell the furs to, posters were put up all over the town in the name of the Governor-General Hans Frank, in Cracow. Within a week all Jews were to hand over their furs, from posh Persian lambskins to ordinary sheep skins. Everything that was hairy or which had the hide of an animal or rodent was to be brought over to the Judenrat* premises on Ilzecka Street, after which it would be handed over to the German authorities.

Any offender who was caught trying to barter or peddle their furs to the Christian citizens or anyone who withheld any kind of pelt or leather skin would be shot instantly as a saboteur.

Abraham Baumstein, well-known from pre-war days as the owner of an apartment house beyond the Jewish section, was on good terms with his former Polish concierge and the friendly janitor who had worked for him for many years. He contacted them and they agreed to store away a few expensive heirloom fur coats.

Unfortunately, the janitor's wife was vain and she could not withstand the temptation of dressing up and going to church in an elegantly tailored seal coat. Malicious and envious gossipers could not bear it either. And the S.D. (the Sicherheits Dienst), the S.S. agency responsible for internal security, law and order was accordingly notified about the working woman who had been seen wearing the apparel of a landowner's wife.

We were told about all of this by Pinchus Hoffman, who acted as a liaison between the S.D. and the Judenrat. He also told us what happened during the interrogation.

Arrested and interrogated by the S.D.'s famous inquisitorial team of Peter and Bruno, the caretaker and his spouse immediately confessed the whole story: how the Jew had contacted them and talked them into committing the transgression. "Transgression!" Peter screamed. "Verfluchter Polnischer Schweinhund! This is not a transgression! This is a crime against the Third Reich and against the victorious German army fighting the Bolsheviks! This is a rotten Partisan subversion! Kreuz Donnerwetter nocheinmal!"

---

* Judenrat: German for Jewish Council, a body heading a Jewish community, appointed by the German occupying authorities during World War II, which was responsible for the enforcement of Nazi-orders affecting the Jews, and for the administration of the affairs of the Jewish communities.

The Poles were slapped in the face and allowed to go free with a mere kick in the behind. Abraham Baumstein was put to the wall and shot. At the same time the Judenrat's warehouse was rapidly filling up with all kinds of furry articles, from caps to gloves, topcoats, neck pieces, and even ear muffs.

As soon as we heard about this, my father and teacher called us together to discuss the situation. He started out with a lengthy illuminating talk about the Tannaim* and their practical approach to life in the diaspora, according to a humane and manageable code of ethics and loyalty to the host country of our domicile. "The law of the land is binding!" he said. ("Dine demalchuse dine" — Talmud Tractate Gittin)

"Our sages taught us that we should pay taxes and fulfill all our citizenship duties in the land where we live and enjoy the blessing of being accepted as part of the general community, looked after by all the social, civil, and legislative institutions."

"Saintly Rebbes emphasized to their followers and disciples that even when sending a parcel or a letter with someone who is fortuitously travelling to your desired point of destination and who is willing to take on your consignment, you should still meet your moral obligation and affix the proper amount of postage so that the government should not lose the income needed to run its organizational apparatus."

"This is the Jewish way — honestly and willingly to contribute to the country of our habitation."

"Jewish Rabbis who performed religious wedding ceremonies and were rewarded with cash payments for their services, would naturally inform the revenue department about this extra income and would gladly pay their share of tax on it."

"These were expressions of genuine allegiance, inspired by the tenets of the Torah, to show sincere appreciation to any land where we found a home, the possibility to earn a livelihood, and the chance to serve our G-d in the tradition of our forefathers."

"Jews have never behaved like certain other ethnic minorities who would rather walk hundreds of miles on foot, than buy a ticket on the government-owned trains. Those grudge-bearers would rather use flintstones to get their cigarettes lighted, than support the government monopoly on matches. For decades they boycotted tobacco and vodka products, for the very same reason; they did not want to subscribe to the governmental sources of revenue."

"Yet there does come a moment, which the psalmist so profoundly and eloquently voices: 'It is time for the Lord to work, they have made void your law,' (Psalm 119, 126)."

---

* Tannaim: rabbis whose teachings in the first two centuries, C.E., are included in the Mishnah.

"I gathered you all at this late hour to urge you not to be intimidated by the Governor-General's scaremongering, and, therefore, that you not deliver your fur pieces to the Judenrat."

"Every single scrap of fur which will help to comfort and keep warm a Nazi on the Eastern front is a contribution to the well-being of Satan, the strengthening of evil, and is against the letter and the spirit of our Torah. The present rulers of Poland and most of Europe are unlawful, illicit usurpers, murderers, and torturers. They are absolutely not entitled to our usual obedience, fidelity and co-operation."

"The wisest of all men, King Solomon, says, 'There is a time to break down and a time to build up.' (Ecclesiastes 3:3)

"I suggest that instead of surrendering our furs to the wicked Nazi profaners of G-d and man, we should rather rip them apart and collectively fulfill a good deed, a Mitzvah, by burning them with our own hands."

My father, the amiable, good-hearted Rebbe Reb Zishe, committed with all his heart, fibre, faculties, life, and soul to kindness and charity, spoke with the decisiveness of a combat commander.

Again we felt the excitement of purpose, and the consciousness of doing something — anything — against the swastika-bearing butchers. Again we were one united team of rebellious Maccabees. We all felt galvanized into action by the Rebbe's words.

Two Jewish families, the Brukirers and the Ajzensztadts were living together in the same house. One family consisted of my parents and me. The other family consisted of Reb Eliezer Brukirer, a close disciple of my father and our host, his wife, and their four children.

The chimney at 54 Sienienska Street billowed smoke through the night. A few hundred kilometres away, in Majdanek near Lublin, an experimental, larger chimney already billowed smoke all day and all night, fed by the flames not of processed, fashioned animal-skins, but of human flesh from gassed concentration camp prisoners. The final solution was beginning!

If a foreign visitor from the free world had visited the Brukirer's house, he would have been at a loss to understand the strange scene of nine normal-looking individuals hacking away, slashing, and completely mutilating good articles of clothing. The women were separating and carving away the external materials; they used razor blades and knives. The men were using large scissors to cut the fur skins into smaller, separate pieces, easily able to be stuffed into the kitchen furnace.

It was frightening and fascinating to watch the leaping flames. The flames rose and fell as dismembered pieces of mutton, muskrat, Persian-lamb, Alaskan seal, and fox were fed into the fire. I began to understand humankind's fascination with fire and the perversion of arson. It was quite addictive to gaze at the glow of colours in the fire. I even began to understand why an older boy from our neighbourhood, a cobbler's son, had signed up on a French steam boat, working as a stoker as it plied its way up the river Seine.

Little Chajka Brukirer brought up another basket of fur chunks mixed with silk fragments. I automatically grabbed a handful to load the stove. And suddenly, in the fluffy texture of it I recognized the fine, sable collar of my father's rabbinical otter coat. I felt the melancholy of a farmer who had just encountered the remains of his beloved pet lamb.

I realized that all of our material possessions were being destroyed. Our family furs were now being consumed by fire, our jewellery had been pawned in Warsaw's city pawn-shop, Lombard, which had been taken over by the Nazis, and the family's insurance policy from Uniona Adriatica de Securita was in the hands of Italian fascists in Milan.

I began to understand the futility of the human ambition to possess. I thought of some of the middle and upper class business people holding valid foreign Polish passports who could perhaps have saved themselves from the yoke of Hitlerism by simply picking up a single suitcase and leaving the country. Poorer people could at least have tried to escape to the occupied territories of the Soviets. But they stayed on, the wealthy chained by comforts and amenities, mesmerized by their lovely apartments, beautiful furniture, expensive carpets, oil paintings, and artifacts. The less well-to-do and the proletariat were kept back by the illusion of having their own corner called home and their few accumulated belongings.

I felt sorry for my own parents. They had been torn away from their natural habitat in the capital city's Jewish district around Dzika-Zamenhofa Streets, where for a quarter of a century they had lived a fulfilling, meaningful life of Yiddishkeit, Torah and mitzvoth, always prepared to help people in spiritual or monetary need. In that district my father presided over a majestic court in the best Chassidic tradition. He reigned wisely, dispensing cheerfulness, solace, and encouragement. He was famous for his knowledge of Judaism and had many disciples. He lived among the poor people, dispensing spiritual help wherever and whenever he could.

The fire now became symbolic of Jewish suffering, past and present. I was reminded of many things: a gigantic *auto-da-fe* of books and Torah scrolls; the Nazi Kristallnacht when so many synagogues had been burned down; the Nazi bombing of Warsaw when the city was ablaze for four weeks; the Crusaders setting fire to a synagogue that was full of men, women and children; a renowned Rabbi, Hananya ben Teradyon, who had been placed on a pyre of green brushwood, his chest drenched with water to prolong the agony of his death; and a burning, desecrated Holy Temple in Jerusalem.

I raked the fire, sifted the ashes, and put the remainder of the furs into the fire. The flames receded for a moment before blazing up with ever more power. I moved away but was unable to stop looking at the glistening oven. A peculiar pressure grew in my temples and suddenly I was reminded of another scene that was symbolic of the eternal truth of Jewish survival, Moses' vision of the burning bush. Behold! How the bush burns all aflame and yet is not consumed by the fire!

After expressing his gratitude to the Brukirer family downstairs, my father came upstairs to talk to me. He spoke to me softly, with care and compassion, advising me not to take too much to heart all the deeds of death and destruction. He emphasized that I still had a life ahead of me, and that none of the things that we had lost was irreplaceable.

I looked at him. He was dressed in his maroon velvet house-coat and black rabbinical yarmulka; he had a snow-white beard, earlocks, and penetratingly beautiful dark eyes. A surge of fondness and of love overcame me.

This patriarchal-looking rebbe with the magnetic warmth and goodness emanating from all his being was my father and mentor, my teacher and guide. He had encouraged me in my earliest boyhood to write. He had believed in my abilities as a musical composer. He had taught me how to play the violin. Music, he always said, is a passageway to all that is most spiritual in man. Through him and his soul-stirring musical renditions, I had been introduced to a wondrous communion with G-d through song and prayer. He had composed the famous tune *Utzu-Eitzu*, an optimistic hymn of the Jewish refusal to submit; a tune which is sung and danced to all over the world.

It was he who showed me how to find an apt quotation in a Talmudic encyclopedia to use in my literary endeavours, and he urged me to learn our holy Hebrew language by diligently following the Malbi'm commentary as well as Rashi on Torah and scriptures.*

He introduced me to the allegorical enchantment and charm of Rabbi Nachman of Bratzlaw's wonderful stories, as well as the miracle-chronicles of our own ancestor, Rabbi Yehuda Low of Prague (16th century) who had created the Golem, a clay figure that came to life.** He urged me, however, not to build my own self-importance and self-worth on the distinguished achievements of our great rabbinical forefathers but to try to contribute something substantial of my own.

He was that wonderful parent who soothed my burning, feverish head with

---

* Malbi'm: abbreviation of Meir Leibush ben Yechiel Mikhal — rabbi and renowned Bible commentator (1809-1879), ardent opponent of reformism and prolific writer and thinker whose thoughts on the unity of Torah Shebiksav and Torah Shebalpe (the written and the oral Torah) are compelling.
** In Jewish legend, a man artificially created by the Maharal through kabbalistic rites, for the purpose of fighting the blood libels against the Jews.

the cool palm of his delicate hands, making me forget my inflamed appendicitis, lulling me to sleep with biblical legends and songs about Joseph and his brothers, Hanna and her seven heroic children,. the righteous Mordecai, and the wicked Haman.

In pre-war times, when his busy rabbinical schedule was tight, I could not simply burst into his study with my adolescent problems and a thousand and one trivial questions about miscellaneous, paltry things. When I had to see him about something serious, I had to go through the normal channels, asking his Gabbai (his assistant) for an appointment.

Now he was sitting next to me, on the kitchen bench, without any of the usual entourage. It was just father and son, face-to-face, with him talking to me as a grown-up, mature man. My father knew about my involvement in subversive anti-Nazi activities. I had obtained Aryan papers and had a new name, Adam Arendarski. For many years I had been involved with the religious Zionist followers of Vladimir Jabotinsky. I had been a camp commander and weapons instructor in the religious paramilitary youth organizations, Brith Yeshurun and Brith Chashmonaim. My father had read my article, 'For G-d and for Freedom,' in the August 1939 issue of *Our Call*, the weekly paper of the Jabotinsky movement. He knew, therefore, that I had no intention of cooperating with the Nazi destroyers of our people, or of voluntarily jumping into any extermination pit if and when ordered to do so by Odilio Globocnik, the S.S. Einsatzgruppen chief in the Lublin district.

It was, therefore, a propitious moment for a heart-to-heart talk. Both of us knew that we were confronting an unavoidable predicament when serious decisions would have to be made while we stared death in the face.

"Son!" he looked at me with his beautiful dark eyes full of fatherly concern.

"Yes, father," I replied respectfully.

"You have to promise me something; and that is: never, ever to hide in an outhouse!"

"I am quite sure that you are not going to surrender yourself to the Nazis. You will do everything possible to outwit and outfox them, if necessary with arms, in order to stay alive. I want you to know that I am whole-heartedly with you, sanctioning unreservedly your belief that it is better to fall in battle than to expire in suffering and degradation in a concentration camp. Yet the emphasis must continuously be put on life! Because, life is indeed the most precious thing the Lord has entrusted to us. And we are obliged to safeguard it with all our might and resourcefulness."

"There are times, however, when it is important not only to live in dignity but also to die with dignity. There have been cases, for example, when people hid themselves in primitive latrines, and drowned in excrement after being found and shot by the Nazis. What a terrible way to die! They had no chance even to say the Shema Yisrael. This must be avoided at all costs."

"There are two other things which I would like to draw to your attention, namely, not to let yourself become so enticed by rebellious thoughts as to question the fairness and justice of Hashem while not comprehending His mysterious ways of permitting all this to happen to His chosen people. You are most probably going to be an eye-witness to horrors on a hitherto unknown scale. And that might shock you, temporarily unbalance you, and make you vulnerable to bitterness, resentment, and perhaps rebellion."

"Don't give in, just because you cannot understand G-d's plans. Never give up your faith and heritage. Be loyal to the endurance of Daniel in the Lion's Den, and Isaac on the sacrificial altar! Then you will merit the right to add your story of redemption to the Haggadah, in the future Passovers of your life, and you will tell it all to your children and grandchildren."

"Also, stay determined, purposeful, and resolute, never forgetting what your priority and goal is! Do not become like the mythical stork in Aesop's fable, who demanded payment from the lion after removing a bone from his windpipe without appreciating the very fact that he simultaneously got his beak out from the predator's throat. Do not become involved in anything simply for the sake of fulfilling money-making ambitions. Do not become oblivious to the main task, which is the saving of life and not the possession of things."

My father stood up and put his hand on my head. Closing his eyes, he said with fervor:

"May the Lord bless you and protect you; may the Lord cause His countenance to shine upon you and be gracious to you; may the Lord favour you and grant you peace. Amen."

I felt something clogging my throat. It was not the allegorical stork's beak or the lion's wind-pipe bone. It was an accumulated anguish, a constriction caused by powerlessness and transformed into simple choking, spasmatic sobs of indignation at my complete inability to do anything for my beloved parents, other than melt into tears.

One hundred and sixty-three kilometers away from Warsaw, while punitive S.S. troops from nearby Klimontov ransacked the Jewish section of Ostrowiec in a merciless pogrom, my father, the Tzosmerer Rebbe, sat in a bunker-hide-out and proceeded to give me an outline of his thoughts on the human condition. I wrote his thoughts down and hid the manuscript above a ceramic oven. I managed to retrieve the manuscript notes four years later, after the war was over.

In essence, my father saw the world divided between an earthly, material realm and a heavenly, spiritual realm. Everything in the material realm emanates from the divine, heavenly realm but we humans tend to lose our way amidst the apparent necessities of material existence. We seek after illusory happiness. We waste our time in pursuit of trivial diversions and false goals. We are akin to lost souls, ourselves of G-dly descent but long since confused in our path. We need above all to find our way back to the 'royal court,' where we would still be under the wing of the Shekhinah, the divine presence. Our confusion can be overcome if we would only stop listening to the misleading call for more of what is immediately and materially available to us. If we could only hear the echo of the heavenly call, 'It is I who am the proprietor and illuminator of the world-mansion.' Then indeed would our eyes be opened and we would understand that everything that lives is similarly striving to be accepted back into the godly arms of the creator of the universe. Only a return to spiritual Jewish values will begin to heal a world that has apparently committed itself to self-destruction.

CHAPTER 2

Who Shall Live and Who Shall Die?

THE EXPEDITIONS in Ostrowiec by the S.S. at the end of 1941 were an ominous indication of what lay in store for all Jews in the smaller towns of the 'General Government' (the Nazi coined named for occupied Poland). At the beginning of 1942, Ostrowiec was still an open city. This meant that Gentile citizens and farmers from the surrounding villages could come into the Jewish city-quarters and buy or barter all kinds of goods like clothing, footwear, housewares, second-hand sewing machines and other pieces of used furniture in exchange for heating materials of wood and coal, potatoes, beans, turnips, eggs and flour. At the end of Sienienska Street, before Sasky's Brewery, as well as at the juncture of Koscielna Street and the Aleje Trzeciego Maja Number 2 and at the highway to Kunow, corner of Sienkiewicza and Browarna Streets, stood posts with attached white signs and black lettering announcing that any Jew who stepped out beyond this spot would be punished by death. There was not, as yet, a noticeable or intensely felt malnutrition in the open ghetto of Ostrowiec. One could function on the allocated ghetto diet for quite a while. There was, however, an acute shortage of living space, because Jewish refugees from the neighboring villages and the Jewish peasant families in the vicinity were forced to leave their rural homes and fields and move to the city proper. With the Jewish refugees brought in from Konin and other places incorporated into the Third Reich, the conditions in the ghetto section of Ostrowiec grew even more crowded. The sanitary conditions were dismal and typhus soon became rampant.

The Judenrat leaders attempted to isolate and quarantine the victims by turning the local synagogue into an improvised hospital. The dedicated local Jewish doctors, Dr. Maier and Dr. Abramowicz Junior, as well as Dr. Wajswhol, a refugee from Lodz, supervised the quickly-organized hospital. Their surgical nurse was Mania Gotlieb and their pharmacist was Mrs. Dichter, a graduate from a foreign university. For fear of catching the life-threatening sickness, people started to wash themselves daily from head to toe and smear their bodies with kerosene to ward off the lice-carriers of the dreadful illness.

Yet, life went on, despite everything. The ration was only 150 grams of bread a day per person. Daily, the German 'Arbeitsant' Manager (Nazi employment office head) Kredel, demanded more and more slave labourers to build the new highways and to do all kinds of hard manual work, from crushing stones and boulders with sledge hammers, to loading and unloading transport trucks and freight trains.

There evolved a new sense of ghetto-witticism, a brand new style of 'Gallows-Humour' — the kind of humour where the gravity of the situation is concealed behind the jest! The most popular anti-Nazi story making the rounds was the one about this Jewish chemical engineer from Berlin who was about to be deported to a concentration camp. When the Gestapo came to pick him up he mustered the courage to resist their order.

"In G-d's name, meine herren," he said, "You are making a dreadful mistake! I am a famous chemist and I can be of tremendous value to the Third Reich with my newest invention which is on the verge of completion." This intrigued the Nazis and they were curious about this invention. The Jewish chemist gave them a simple explanation. "I am about to perfect a system which will make it possible to turn feces into butter. Since the Fatherland has been at war for several years and the army and civilian population is in bad need of fats, let me make a deal with you."

"What is the deal, untermensch?"

"Meine Herren, I've been carrying the formula in my mind which could be the turning point in Germany's entire economy. I am therefore making the following stipulations: a) my wife and children are to be released to go to Switzerland; b) I am to drop the yellow badge and be given freedom to move about as I wish; c) a laboratory is to be placed at my disposal with all necessary equipment and instruments."

The authorities made all the concessions the chemist had asked for. Three months later, several important officials of the Ministry of Economics came to the laboratory of the Berlin Jew and they asked: "Well, was ist los? Where is the butter you promised?"

"Meine Herren," replied the chemist in some irritation, "Do you think this is child's play? You have forgotten what it involves. We are at the final phase of development that will take the world by surprise and such things don't happen overnight! We must be patient and carry on further experimentation for a while to be one hundred percent certain we are ready for mass production."

Three months passed.

This time an entire delegation of Nazi leaders came to see the Jew — economists, gestapomen, and propagandists from Goebbels' bureau.

"Well, where do we stand with your invention?" asked the excited fascist. "Do you have a practical program to report?"

"Jawohl," replied the chemist with an innocent smile. "We have made tangible progress!"

"It is now soft and it spreads. But it still stinks somewhat!"

Life in Ostrowiec continued. Dov Rabinowicz, the beloved articulate speaker and brilliant educator, maintained his vocation, teaching the young and adults. His most important subjects were history, Torah, Midrash and Talmudic explanation. Moshe Gutman, my colleague of the pre-war years in Warsaw's governmental teachers' seminary, wrote heart-rending verses in modern Hebrew of a mystical and metaphysical quality and in psalmist style.

Political youth organizations from the extreme left to the extreme right met in seclusion and commemorated past Zionist and socialist leaders, celebrated Jewish holidays. There were rumours that a prominent youth leader from the capital by the name of Mordechai Anilewicz was in Ostrowiec on a special mission to recruit dedicated, able volunteers willing to follow him to Warsaw for the purpose of a forthcoming special national emergency task.

The death penalty could be administered for many reasons: for leaving the Jewish quarters; for not wearing the shame-badge; for not being registered in a visible list of tenants in each house entrance; for the possession of gold and foreign currency; for travelling on the train or any other vehicle of transportation; for dealing in foodstuffs. Still, Jews from Ostrowiec dared to leave their forced isolation and risked their lives to smuggle into the city all kinds of vegetables, fowl and, once in a while, even a young cow.

Jewish tinsmiths invented a combination space heater and furnace stove, heated by available sawdust from Mr. Lederman's sawmill which he managed for his new Nazi overlords. Ghetto masons found a way to build miniature brick ovens to bake homemade bread. Mechanics constructed special hand mills to grind any kind of grain and turn it into a decent quality of flour, good for matzos and many other products.

My father's rabbinical activities ceased completely because he no longer had any contact with his followers. This meant no income for him and the family. I now became the breadwinner. I assumed the role of a Polish refugee from the village of Reichwald in the Poznan district, now officially annexed to the Fuhrer's planned new German empire. Adam Arendarski was my new name.

I now had two possible destinations for my commercial ventures. One was the city of Rozwadow on the other side of the Vistula River. There I could buy five to six kilos of live carp for a reasonable price, put them into my English-type large trousers with specially arranged pockets in the leg area, bring them back to Ostrowiec and sell them for a profit. The other route was to the capital, Warsaw. To get there I used a bicycle. Once I arrived safely, I went to a wholesaler of electrical supplies, picked up a couple of hundred light bulbs, tied them on a special contraption behind my seat and, on the way back, sold them as a wandering salesman. My clients were inn-keepers, industrial establishments, bakery shops and especially landowners of large estates.

Besides the financial aspect, this experience was my apprenticeship in the outside, non-Jewish world. It allowed me to accumulate the necessary self-assurance and behavioural pattern of a genuine Aryan. Yet, I distinctly knew that I was like a circus acrobat walking a high-wire, doing a balancing act and without a safety net under me.

However, as strange as it may sound, I began to feel a challenge and a certain gratification in flirting with danger. It certainly seemed to me more sensible than to sit quietly and subserviently in the ghetto, waiting for the Nazi solution to the "Jewish problem." This wandering salesman initiative went on for a few months, until the middle of April. On the night of April 28th, 1942, the Nazis killed 32 people and sent 72 other innocent men to Auschwitz. The S.S. declared that they were all communists! Some of the most prominent Jewish citizens were killed: Lawyer Sidel, Dr. Wacholder, a respected dentist and leading zionist, Yitzchak Kudelowicz, Alter Grinberg, Haim Stamm, Yehoshua Minzberg, Shlomo Katzenellenbogen and others, including the fifty year old wife of Yechiel Zukerfein.

A feverish, panicky psychosis overtook the Jews in Ostrowiec, cancelling most of their entrepreneurial initiatives. Nobody risked going outside the ghetto. People began to live simply from selling their own personal possessions even if they were cherished, sentimental memorabilia. I myself took my beautiful, golden Omega pocket watch and chain, which my father had brought me from a visit to his Hassids Reb Yosele Greenhouse's place in London, England and sold it to a jeweler for the sum of 700 Polish zloty.

Life became very grim. My only sunny moments were the clandestine get-togethers with the 'haverim' of the Jabotinsky movement — Alter Cherni-kowski, Yehuda Rubinstein, Pinchas Sher, Moshe Goldfiner and Tobias Eisen, the underground courier from Konin, who made my Aryan identification card as Adam Arendarski.

We received news from Warsaw about the capital city's ghetto. The 'mother' of the Jewish ghettos in the whole of Europe was in the process of being completely liquidated. I now felt very much like Amnon Ajzensztadt, not Arendarski Adam. I felt like a cornered powerless Jew pondering the perplexing dilemma, whether one can and should really attempt to run away from himself, from his adjusted destiny?

In some inexplicable way, the closer we came to the Jewish new year of 'Rosh Hashana' I thought more and more about my unique name of Amnon. I also thought of a particular liturgical essay recited amongst the High Holy Day prayers which devotedly encompasses communion with Hashem (G-d), the ephemeral nature of human life, sanctity, a poetic depiction of the heavenly court's judicial proceedings and counselling on how to avoid, through penitence, worship and charity, the stern decree of judgement.

Since my early boyhood I always marvelled about the author of this essay, the revered man of piety and erudition of the eleventh century, Rabbi Amnon of Mayence. The historical Rabbi Amnon's problem now became my very own life and death predicament, leaving me, as it left him, with a single choice: either stand upright as a Jew and perish, or go underground, hide out in the anonymity of my "Nordic" blond hair, "Aryan" blue eyes and "Slavic" nose, masquerading as a pure gentile and thus, perhaps, survive.

It was already October 1942. The Nazi-rulers of Ostrowiec did not allow us to congregate for prayers or any other activities. So we 'davened,' of necessity, without the traditional quorum of ten. Each family prayed alone in its own living quarters, shedding their tears in private, as they sobbingly recited Rabbi Amnon's 'Unessaneh Tokef,' which was as meaningful as ever.

To our relief, Rosh Hashana and Yom Kippur, with all its beseechments and entreaties, went by undisturbed, followed by a relatively peaceful Sukkoth.

It was the tenth of the tenth month of October. The moment of truth had arrived! No more reprieves, no more exemptions, no more postponements. The Ostrovetzer ghetto was to be liquidated. My father's patriarchal face reflected indescribable anguish and sorrow. He was to be rounded up like a criminal and carted off in a chlorinated cattle train to a concentration camp. Still wearing his rabbinical garb, he authoritatively told me to get dressed quickly in my leather jacket and student cap. "Son," he ordered, "Get out of the house. Make your way through the backyard bordering on the city's sports-track and the Almighty will lead you in the right path to safety."

"But how can I leave you here?"

"You must!" came his stoic reply. "There is 'Kidush-Hashem,' sanctification of G-d's name, in remaining alive, in enduring the greatest catastrophe in Jewish history, which is most probably the prelude, the birth-pangs of exalted events to come."

We embraced for the last time, hugging each other. My mother, "Libele" Ajzensztadt, stood by mesmerized, speechless, completely numbed by the startling calamity which was taking place. I grabbed her into my arms and covered her gentle, beautiful, fifty-four year old face with kisses. It was a silent goodbye.

When they led me out of the door into my perilous adventures as a modern-day Marrano, a man named Arendarski Adam, their moist, quivering faces reflected sadness and optimism, fear and hope. The kadish was off to the unknown!

CHAPTER 3

The Metamorphosis

The bizarre odyssey of Amnon Ajzensztadt, alias Adam Yanovitch Arendarski, thus began. His consciousness imbued with the Zionist ideal of Jewish pride, Jewish dignity and self-defence, he set out to outwit and survive his Hitlerite enemy. He now assumed a new role — a pure-blooded gentile from the Warta River district. Cautiously, over the next few months, he travelled from place to place becoming progressively more familiar with and at ease in his new identity.

MY FATHER, the Tzosmerer Rebbe, and my mother were murdered in January 1943 in Treblinka. My sister Tamar had been murdered by the Gestapo after I left Ostrowiec. I was alone, one of the few solitary witnesses to the continuing destruction of European Jewry by the Nazis. I knew that I had to follow my martyred father's advice, and that I had a mission to stay alive. I felt like Josephus Flavius, at the time of the destruction of the Second temple in A.D. 70 by the Romans. He felt that he could not commit suicide but that he had a moral obligation to stay alive in order to record what was happening around him for the benefit of future generations.

It was now March of 1943, about three weeks before the revolt of the last 40,000 Jews imprisoned in the Warsaw Ghetto. I had just returned from Stalino in the Don Basin, deep in the interior of Ukrainian Russia. This area was under German occupation, but I had succeeded in fully adopting an Aryan identity which I had invented long before, with the help of the Warsaw underground. I spoke German fluently. According to my papers I was a Pole from the area of Poznan. I was wearing the uniform of an S.S. front-line auxilliary worker. I was carrying regular transfer papers issued to me by Obersturmbann-fuhrer Willi Bender of the Stalino S.S. command. I had been sent on a mission to Warsaw because of my knowledge of the Polish country and language. My task was to find volunteers in Warsaw who would be willing to accompany me back to Stalino, three thousand kilometers to the east, to work as tradesmen in various German military units. I hoped to be able to find some Jews who could pose as full-fledged Aryans, as I had been able to do, with both the looks and the necessary forged identity papers.

I walked the streets of Warsaw, looking for some way to contact the Jewish underground. Obviously, this was easier said than done. I could hardly place an advertisement in the daily newspapers. The various places which I knew of as meeting points for couriers and emissaries were switched around all the time, for equally obvious reasons. So there I was, in the middle of Poland's capital, a blond-haired rabbi's son in the uniform of a loyal Nazi, with a death's head insignia on my military cap, a swastika on my arm, looking for some link with the Jewish community that was being exterminated *en masse*. My situation reminded me of the legend of King Solomon, who was once lost in a remote city, unclothed and unshod, without any way of revealing his true identity. Only my situation was probably worse, as I would be exposed to ridicule at best and certain death at worst if I told the wrong person who I really was. It would hardly help that I was wearing the uniform of the Nazi elite.

Instinctively, my feet led me to the ghetto wall at the corner of Leszno and Zelazna Streets. But I didn't dare walk up to the actual ghetto entrance. I stood across the way, beside the new Polish courthouses and stared at the wall and at the stone-faced Polish police who kept watch to see that no one moved out of the ghetto without proper permits.

After some time the broad gate topped with barbed-wire opened up. Who knows? Would I see someone I knew? After all, I had lived on Zamenhofa Street in the heart of Jewish Warsaw for over twenty years. It might be a neighbor, a relative, a Chassid, a follower of my father the Rebbe. But only a Judenrat official stepped out. His papers were closely scrutinized and he, no doubt, had some official business to transact with the German administrators in the city.

I stood staring for a while in full sight of all, a smile on my lips, but with an indescribable agony inside.

My intuition had foretold what was to be the bitter end. I could not tear myself away from the territory where I had grown up. It was as though someone were to be standing over the bed of a fatally sick person, quite aware of the patient's certain prospects. But every moment is still precious and he keeps observing and scrutinizing the features of the sick man, still hoping for an unlikely miracle suddenly to occur.

I stood for the last time across from the sixteen-mile long Ghetto wall and in my thoughts I was close to those nearest and dearest to me. At that moment, in cellars and secret laboratories, they were preparing bombs and grenades, home-made mines and molotov cocktails which 23 days later would be used in the heroic and desperate Warsaw Ghetto uprising, which remains a glorious chapter in modern Jewish history.

My path led me along familiar Warsaw streets from the market to Ciepla Street, to Przechodnia Street, and to Januszynska courtyard, where I saw the many Polish retailers enjoying the profits resulting from inflated prices. Some of these newly established merchants were clearly selling goods stolen from Jews.

A fence had been thrown across the courtyard. Behind it I could see young Jews with the blue and white 'Bands of Shame' on their arms standing in torn clothes and outsized shoes. Some of them were sawing wood, no doubt for their German guards who were standing by.

I walked over to the Krakowskie Przedmiescie section. I stepped through the gateway with the two lions in front of the university where before the war I had seen Polish students cracking Jewish heads, and where I had heard them shouting their slogans aloud about a Poland free of Jews.

Their wishes were being granted.

A little further on there stood the aristocratic Bristol Hotel, now a billeting place for German officers and their administration. Crossing the road I returned in the direction of the Swietokrzyska, Holy Cross Road. Looking in the windows, watching the faces, and reading the notices plastered on the walls, I kept searching for my goal. There was a theatre with a rounded entrance in which the well-known Polish quartet, the Dana Choir, was offering a musical program of song and humour. I bought a ticket and walked in, thinking of the star of Polish humour, the comedian Michael Znicz, who turned out to be a Jew and whom I last saw in the Ghetto playing a similar theatre on Novolipie Street. I did not stay long as I felt uneasy and did not want to waste any time. I left the theatre to resume my lonely walk, exploring the streets and alleyways of Warsaw. Young street hawkers offered me cigarettes: "Good flavour, Pan! Kaufen Sie! Ja, Ja, Gut!"

There was at least one of them that I could have sworn was a Jew. He had a semitic face with sad brown eyes. But his loose, vulgar street language did not correspond to his face. At a tram stop I observed a middle-aged man with a miniature Swiss flag in his lapel. I stopped next to him, as though I, too, were waiting for a tram.

I began a conversation.

"I see you're a Swiss citizen."

"That's right," he replied politely.

"Tell me, please, do you happen to know a Herr Domb, who is also Swiss?"

He looked at me rather oddly and answered that, yes, he knew this Herr Domb quite well. He said that Domb was a Swiss citizen, but of the Jewish religion. As far as he knew, this Herr Domb was in prison now for having improperly transferred Jewish properties to his name.

I walked away with an unpleasant taste in my mouth. So that's what had happened. The devout young Swiss Jew, Shlomoh Domb, who used to pray in my father's synagogue and who had helped my sister Tamar to escape from the Warsaw Ghetto to Sandomierz, was now behind bars, imprisoned by the Nazis.

It was getting dark and I hadn't even arranged for a place to sleep. I did have a letter from Jozef Wengrzyn, a Pole serving in Stalino, which he had asked me to deliver to his relatives at 42 Panska Street. He had given me a note introducing me as his close friend, praising me as a patriot and as one of his own, and asking that they extend every courtesy to me.

I felt uneasy about spending a night in the protection of unknown Poles. Who knew what might happen at home with my compatriots, in a house which I knew was formerly occupied by Jews? I proceeded in the direction of the main railway station, Warszawa Glowna.

At the corner of Chmielna and a side street not far from the station, I noticed a group of soldiers standing near a building with a red lamp hanging from it. Coming closer, I read: "Vergnügungstätte und Zimmer zu Vermieten" (Entertainment post, rooms for rent)! It was clear that this was a brothel for members of the 'master race.' I could hear sounds of drunkenness and boisterous beer-drinking mingled with the loud tones of a hoarse, over-worked piano.

For a moment a strange association of ideas ran through my mind: the scouts in the Book of Joshua, and the walls of Jericho which housed the quarters of Rehab the harlot.

I decided to go in and rent a room just to stay the night. This would be the last place anyone would think of to look for a concealed Jew.

A moment later I was inside the door and was immediately greeted by a surprise — the military police!

"Ihre Papiere, bitte (Your papers, please)."

Across from me stood a bear of a sergeant in full regalia, armed with pistol, helmet, and cartridge-belt, asking for my documents.

I coolly took out my marching orders and he began reading out loud: "Bauleitung der Waffen S.S. und Schutzpolizei Stalino den Zwanzigsten Marz 1943.

"Adam Arendarski, Fieldpost Unit #18743 is proceeding to Warsaw. Purpose of trip: Leave and recruitment of available labour personnel according to the enclosed requirements. All military and civil authorities are asked to permit the above-named to proceed and in case of necessity to provide all necessary help. Heil Hitler! Obersturmbannfuhrer of the Waffen S.S., Willi Bender."

"Comrade, are you crazy?" the sergeant began to lecture me. "This pig sty is not for you! This is only for the Wehrmacht lower ranks. You should try the special entertainment house reserved for the S.S. on Shucha Avenue, where a German doctor will give you the proper injection and where only German girls are available."

"Jawohl, Herr Feldwebel. Heil Hitler!" And raising my hand in the Nazi salute I clicked my heels, turned about and went to deliver my letter to Stanislaw and Marian Kaminski.

That night, at 42 Panska Street, I suffered the mental torture which was a daily feature of life for every escapee from the Ghetto living in forced submersion in Polish society. I realized once again that it was no accident that the

Führer had chosen Polish territory for his factories of murder.

Stanislaw and Marian Kaminiski, active members of the Polish Underground Land Army (Armia Krajowa), like most average Poles were bitter enemies of the hated Schwabs, the Germans, but their pathological hatred of the Jews surpassed even this!

After obtaining an oral report about their cousin Jozef Wengrzyn in Stalino, after putting all their questions on how he was getting along, what he was doing, questions about the Russian woman he had married, how many children he now had, and questions in general about the Poles who had settled in Stalino and how they were getting along, the younger Marian Kaminski lit a cigarette and shot this question at me:

"Tell me, my dear Adam, what about the Jewish vipers in your area there? Have they been cleared out and destroyed, and are you now free of them?"

The merit of my fathers must have come to my aid, for although I was tormented inside myself I managed to quickly improvise a vivid scene in which various Jews were being led to their deaths. And my hosts simply ate it all up, sitting in perverted delight as they drank vodka, toasted each other's health, and exulted in the destruction of the Jews.

At night in bed I was terribly afraid lest I betray myself with a revealing word, with a superfluous gesture, a groan, or a Jewish sigh.

In my dreams I saw the personal tragedy of the elder Stanislaw Kaminski as he had told it earlier. A Drozhki carriage drawn by a black horse pulls up to his home. Two men bring in his son's body, sewn in a sack like a load of potatoes, give him a military salute, and announce that his son fell in the service of his country, for Poland's independence.

"Adam!" he pleaded with me, "Tell me, wasn't his sacrifice quite useless? Did he give up his life for something worthwhile, something honourable?" Then his voice changed from a muffled, tragic note to a jarring, strident and vitriolic tirade against the 'filthy Jews' who were responsible for all of Poland's misfortunes.

"Yes, the stinking Zydy controlled the poor Polish nation, holding the entire economy in their greedy hands. Like an octopus, their tentacles were everywhere. In literature they had a Julian Tuwim, in the theatre a Krukowski, in the press a Slonimski, in finance a Szereszewski."

"Every aspect of our life was flavoured with garlic and onions! It is simply impossible to credit the diabolical conspiracy concentrated in their super-clever hands."

"This is one thing for which we must be grateful to Hitler! He freed us from the accursed parasitical Yids by solving this problem once and for all!"

I lay on the cot in this former Jewish home where I could see on the doorpost the outline of a Mezuzah that had been removed. I mumbled to myself, "Hamalach Hagoel Osi M'kol Ro (May the redeeming angel free me from all evil)." I could see in the opposite room several manikin forms snatched from plundered Jewish businesses. In the darkness they resembled frozen figures of tortured martyrs. I left as soon as I could the next morning. Just opposite Number 42 on the sidewalk, I saw a group of Polish boys and girls surrounding a young blond woman. I walked across the road and became a witness to one of perhaps hundreds of blackmail scenes which occurred in Warsaw every day.

Seeing my S.S. uniform, the gang moved off a bit and pointed to the girl. They shouted, "Jude! Jude!" One look at the pale face of the woman told me everything. Her dyed blond hair did not match her aquiline nose. Her painful expression and her look of despair, told me immediately what she was.

"Was ist hier los? (What's wrong here?)" I barked out like a true Teuton, pretending not to know what the young informers were saying. Everyone turned to me. The spokesman, a young hoodlum, tried to tell me in broken German that he thought this woman to be a Zidowka, a Jewess. She quickly took advantage of everyone's diverted attention, dashed off into a doorway and vanished.

Shouting "Donnerwetter Scheisse Nochamal!" I walked off, thinking that the survivor of this traumatic confrontation would never have thought for a moment that this slow-thinking, confused S.S. man was, like her, a Jew.

A taxi took me to Warsaw's main street, Marszalkowska Street. I walked past Hirshfeld's elegant pastry bakery, which still served coffee with the usual assortment of delicacies. I suddenly recalled that even before the Ghetto wall was sealed off, on this aristocratic avenue signs had appeared with the unambiguous warning, "No admittance for Jews and dogs."

I could not restrain myself from going up to number 131, where until the outbreak of the war, I had worked in the office of Keren-Tel Chai, under the leadership of Levi Yungster.

The building had the same front and balconies, the same broad steps to the landing, just as when the Jewish tenants had left.

I crossed to the other side of the boulevard, where the fourth floor at number 136 had been the club house of the N.Z.O., the New Zionist Organization, founded by Zeev Jabotinsky, which later became a food dispensary for the poor operated by the Joint. Here, too, I felt the anguish of the present.

I felt like a creature from another planet. Through a strange quirk of fate I had now dropped in from a totally different point in time and space, living incarnation of another world, unreal, yet in full and unrelenting existence.

I then made a turn. I saw a familiar face, as surprised as I was. It was someone I knew in the Ghetto as a refugee from Konin, a friend of my dear comrade, Lutek Eisen. The tall well-dressed gentleman, wearing a German-style hat with a feather in the band, stared at me.

He greeted me warmly, took me by the arm, and we walked into a side street. Kozakiewicz, as I learned, did not belong to an underground fighting group. In his words, he was the leader of his own private underground, consisting of three younger sisters and two younger brothers who were living in a hide-out on Wolska Street. He was their provider, guard and commander.

I was impressed by his good appearance, energy, and zest for life. He showed not the slightest symptom of despair or depression. His sense of enterprise, vitality, and sheer Jewish Chutzpa knew no bounds. He proposed to take me to a Polish dealer with a store by the iron gate, where he would collect a payment due and at the same time raise his prestige by my presence.

"Heaven itself sent you," he said, not letting me go, but insisting that I accompany him to the municipal housing office. "You see, whenever someone applies to the bureau as a single unmarried person, they're quite suspicious of him and give him the special 'once-over' from head to foot, to make sure he's not some kind of anti-social or criminal type, or even a runaway Jew. But if I show up with someone as important as you, you'll see the respect they'll show me and how quickly my request is looked after."

In both places we were a resounding success and received the attention and immediate cooperation of the persons we approached. We then walked along Krolewska Street, near the Saxon Gardens, and Kozakiewicz outlined his philosophy, the same philosophy of most Jews living on Aryan papers in 1943: to survive despite everyone and despite everything.

"You must acknowledge," he excplained to me, "that even the high priest when he entered the Holy of Holies addressed a prayer first for himself and his family. I feel that my first loyalty belongs to my younger sisters and brothers in hiding, for whom I am morally responsible. I don't claim to be a hero."

It seemed to me that any Jew who used whatever means and devices to stay alive despite Hitler's death warrant was by this fact alone a heroic champion, full of courage and endurance.

To induce Kozakiewicz to come with me to Stalino seemed pointless. He was too settled to make a move. I listened with sympathy to his excuse for not inviting me to his quarters, understanding the logic that he would not want to place himself under suspicion among his neighbours of having dealings with an S.S. man.

"If you think I can be helpful in any way," he smiled in embarrassment, "come to the Opera House entrance tomorrow afternoon. I'll meet you there at exactly one o'clock." He gripped my hand by way of a warm farewell, and whispered in Yiddish, "May G-d protect you!" He turned and rushed off.

I went back to Marszalkowska Street. I walked uphill in the direction of the large Roxy cinema house where before the war I had seen a film starring Paul Robeson, the theme of which had been racial discrimination. I walked slowly, my head in a whirl, but overlooking nothing and no one. I watched the passengers on passing trams, the hawkers at newsstands and flower kiosks, the street cleaners, the porters and carriers — everyone who passed me, on both sides of the street.

Walking this way for some distance, I saw from across the road a man whom I knew. He was standing and talking to two others. It was Wolfovicz, whose Aryan name was Janek Wilczynski, the very same man who had come up with my own Aryan papers. Just five months before it was he, at the Rozwadow railway station, who had urged me not to go to Russia.

Our eyes met and immediately Yankel was at my side. He embraced and kissed me and practically dragged me to the other side of the street where two other men were waiting patiently.

"Please meet . . ." he introduced me.

"Adam," I mumbled.

"Wojciech," said the darker man, with a moustache.

"Andrzej," said the second, a blond young man, as he gave me his hand.

"You see, gentlemen, this S.S. man is a Jew on an underground mission!"

Hearing Janek burst out with this, I thought, "Is he mad?" How did he dare to reveal my secret, or had he become an agent provocateur in the service of the Gestapo? Before I had a chance to give it a second thought, Andrzej and Wojciech both seized my hand once more to shake it with open admiration. Andrzej said in a solemn tone: "Adam, if we had more like you, our common fight against the Nazis would have a different look."

Having said this, both these mysterious men whom I had met only by their pseudonyms turned and left.

"Let's go," Janek called out, and led me to a house on Aleje Jerozolimskie where we entered through the back and went up a stairway.

"Have you taken leave of your senses?" I chided him. "How can you risk my life by telling two strange Poles who I really am?"

"Don't be silly!" he assured me, "You've just spoken to two high officers of the Armia Ludowa, the Polish left wing underground army, who are actively providing arms for the Ghetto uprising that is going to break out soon."

Suddenly I felt ashamed and silenced, seeing Janek polishing his automatic Belgian revolver with his handkerchief.

"Janek, how about throwing over this whole bloody country and coming back with me to Russia!" I showed him my iron-clad movement orders which he glanced over in an instant.

"No, Adam, although I thank you warmly," he replied. "I am too closely involved in matters which to my mind will mean a turning point in Jewish history."

"As far as my personal safety is concerned, I can assure you that I have undergone plastic surgery and have been totally deJudaized insofar as my circumcision is concerned."

"Besides, I have authentic Aryan documents with the corresponding duplicates in the town registry. as you know, my father was shot in the Ghetto. But I get letters regularly from my mother and two sisters, who are working in Germany as gentiles on a farm."

"So speaking in all honesty, I see no reason for me to leave Warsaw. It is my armoury and arsenal, and in a short time something of tremendous importance will break out, so why give it up for a tedious existence somewhere in the don Basin in Russia?"

"But I'm ready to give you a list of names of Jews with Aryan papers who are burning to go, and you'd do them an enormous favour if you would take them out of the Polish General-Government and save them from the Nazis."

That same evening, sixteen skilled labourers marched in fours, led by a rabbi's son in an S.S. uniform. We marched to the main railway station of Warsaw. After taking travel rations and Wehrmacht movement orders, we mounted the railway carriage reserved for Reichsdeutsche only, in the train heading for the Eastern front.

∽

ABOUT six weeks after our arrival in Stalino, we were forced to abandon the whole scheme. The trouble began the day I was summoned to the office of the chief of the Schutzpolizei, Major Werner, for a conversation concerning 'official business.'

I was quite sure that the call was in connection with some work to be done on the Major's office complex or private living quarters and I felt quite confident as I strolled into the police chief's office and greeted my superior officer with the Nazi salute. The police chief was elegantly uniformed but hunchbacked. He lifted his steel-grey eyes from the papers on his desk and kept his gaze on me throughout the ensuing conversation.

"Where do you come from, Herr Arendarski?" asked the little man, responsible for law and order in this front-line territory and the arbiter over life and death there.

"I am from Reichswald, near Posen, in the Warta River District," I replied.

"Why do you speak German so well?" he suddenly asked.

"I am a high school graduate and German was a compulsory subject." I was still unperturbed by the Major's inquisitiveness so I explained to him that as the majority of the population in Reichswald were Volksdeutscher, ethnic Germans, every Pole who lived there spoke at least some German. It also helped to be bilingual in the conduct of everyday business. "I am especially good at German because of my two years' practice in the auxiliary forces."

"Yes, that is quite possible," the Major mumbled to himself. He then lit a cigarette while continuing to study my facial expression. Pensively he leaned back in his padded swivel chair, inhaling the aromatic Dutch tobacco, and laconically, with the special courtesy peculiar to interrogators trying to trap a suspect, he said, "May I please ask you just one more thing? And are there any Jews amongst you as well?"

My instinctive response was to burst out into a giggle. "What do you mean by that, Major?"

"Don't you know that the Jews, the cursed Jews, they wanted the war in order to ruin the German nation!"

I burst out laughing. Sincerely and convincingly I answered, "There's nothing like that amongst us, there are no Jews in my unit!"

"Lieutenant!" the Major called loudly to his provision master who immediately came in from the back room. "We know that the Poles are our enemies! But as long as they are a disciplined part of the Wehrmacht they should get exactly the same rations as we ourselves get. Give Mr. Arendarski the appropriate amount of brandy, wine, cigarettes, and tobacco to distribute among his men."

I thanked the Major profusely and left the office with a large box full of all kinds of good things. Outside in the fresh, free air of the tree-lined street, I realised just how wrong I had been in my assumptions about the Major's intentions. I thought that he would arrange for the installation of a new electrical outlet, additional file shelves, or some more wooden packing cases in which to send to his family in Germany a new load of pork fat and smoked Kolkhoz salamis as he so often did. I suddenly understood the full seriousness of what had just transpired and the predicament I had just been in. I started to perspire profusely, despite being lightly dressed. "Daniel in the lion's den," I thought to myself. And I had so far emerged unscathed. Nevertheless, our situation was perilous. The serious Nazi interest in the birthplaces and backgrounds of the working batallion's members and especially in their Aryan pedigrees had to be more than a passing episode. It was bound to be part of a new policy from above, with the object of searching out and destroying any remaining Jews who had somehow managed to sneak into the auxiliary force and survive until now.

As I handed out the cigarettes to my sixteen compatriots, I told them of my interview with Major Werner, interpreting the whole affair as utterly distressing. "We are sitting on top of a volcano which will erupt anytime and drag us down to our doom. We must make some contingency plans within the next few days before these dialogues become even more drastic and turn into formal Gestapo interrogations! The Ubermenschen are getting wiser," I concluded with some bitterness.

I and my comrades had a terrible time that night. The simple, depressing fact was that the whole plan of our posing as loyal S.S. front-line workers was falling apart — and with it would go the tangible possibility of our being saved by a Red Army offensive or pincer encirclement. Here we were a couple of months after the Warsaw Ghetto uprising, about three thousand kilometers away from that scene of destruction, with our own dream of doing something to halt the machinery of Nazi destruction. Everything had looked so promising for a while, and now we were once again facing catastrophe.

The next day, as I walked into my little office in the workshop of the Bauleitung, I found Unterscharführer Brunner waiting for me. With a written order in his hand he asked me to accompany him to the S.S. headquarters located in Stalino's prestigious Eighteenth Street. There, the main network of the security apparatus occupied six floors, with all kinds of different departments from economic management to transportation, propaganda, and the infamous Sonderkommando, with their dark green panel trucks — the mobile gas chambers.

"This is it," I thought. "This is no social call; probably some more questions in the same vein as Major Werner's, trying to investigate the possibility that there are Jews in the Polish auxiliary forces."

It was hardly a joyous walk, although Brunner tried to make conversation about the usual trivial things that men in uniform talk about. "Hey, Adam! Don't be so downhearted! Tonight we'll see a play at the theatre followed by dancing and fun. You lost your money, you lost nothing! If you've lost your courage, you've lost everything!"

I looked at Unterscharführer Brunner's physiognomy. His features were typically semitic, like one of Julius Streicher's caricatures in *Der Stürmer*. His full round face was adorned by an aquiline hooked nose, dark eyes with pitch black brows, and a red-pinkish birthmark on his right chin like a mistaken patch of second-hand pigmentation. I thought what an irony it was that if there were such a thing as authentically Aryan stock, then Brunner was probably it. While I, on the other hand, with my excellent Nordic looks, faced the distinct possibility that my two years of supposedly authentic Aryan life were about to be unmasked. All they needed to do was check to see if I were circumcised.

The battlefields were not far away, and the booming echoes of exploding artillery shells and Katyusha whistles could always be heard. Up until now I had loved the noise made by the advancing Red Army's weaponry, as it announced my likely freedom. Now, however, the noise sounded more like the screams of men and women who were being cruelly tortured.

As I made my way to Obersturmbannführer Willi Bender's office I silently prayed to G-d almighty to watch over me. I prayed that the faith, dignity, and simple chutzpah of a Jew, who by the grace of G-d had made it thus far, would not be lacking now. I prayed to G-d for enough wisdom, intuition, and insight to avoid provoking the bloody assassins I was about to face.

To my surprise Bender was no longer there. In his place there sat Obersturmbannführer Bregman, who was now in charge of the Bauleitung der Waffen S.S. und Schutzpolizei Stalino. He was a tall man in a green leather coat and he was accompanied by a sizeable entourage of lower-ranking Schutzpolizei and Wehrmacht officers. They stood in a semi-circle around the office walls, like uniformed university students intent on catching every single word of their professor's lecture.

Obersturmbannführer Bregman came straight to the point.

"I am really puzzled! How on earth did you and your men surface in Stalino without the involvement of the normal intermediaries in such cases, the Reicharbeitsamt or the 'General Government' employment office? The truth is that I am not complaining about the quality of your work, which is completely satisfactory. However, the irregularity of your presence in this war-zone without properly documented personnel files perplexes me. I want you to explain how you came here and how you arranged with my predecessor, Obersturmbannführer Bender, to form this unit and import the people from as far away as Warsaw. Why would qualified young Poles — electricians, carpenters, mechanics, and locksmiths — prefer to travel 3000 kilometers to the front-line in the east rather than stay on in your own country and wait for the war to end?"

Positioned in the center of the room, I was now the focus of everyone's attention. The skull-and-crossbone insignia of the S.S. peered at me from all three sides. I turned to look at the new Obersturmbannführer and noticed a portrait of the Führer himself on the wall behind him. His hate-filled satanic eyes seemed also to be thoroughly examining me.

It was an amazing scenario. A chassidic rebbe's son from Poland's capital, an ex-Yeshiva boy imbued with the two thousand year old spiritual ethos of Rabbi Hillel, 'love thy neighbour as thyself,' I was forced to match wits and fight for my survival against over a dozen officers of the Nazi elite,* (bloodthirsty conquerors of Europe, psychotic members of a so-called 'master race'

---

* It was a kind of spiritual wrestling bout between Jewish endurance, resourcefulness and the diaspora training acquired through the millenia — namely, the capacity to turn a disadvantage into an advantage — versus the formality conscious, orderly, technocratic evil genius of Nazi puenktlichkeit (Nazi-accuracy), so characteristically epitomised in the scrupulous utiliza- tion of their victim's possessions, including the hair of their heads and the fat of their bodies for industrial purposes.

and a 'thousand-year' Reich, every one of them a participant in an unequalled and utterly evil reign of terror.)

"Herr Obersturmbannführer," I began, "I am willing to tell you in detail the whole story of how I got together with engineer Willi Bender and the subsequent ordeal which started at his request, albeit for our mutual benefit."

Obersturmbannführer Bregman nodded his head in approval and I began to relate the whole saga.

"I met Obersturmbannführer Bender in the beginning of March 1943, when I was living and working in Dniepropietrowsk. We happened to be sitting at the same table in a military tavern. Herr Bender was dressed in civilian clothing and I did not know of his S.S. rank or professional status. Our conversation began with the engineer enquiring whether I was German. No, I told him, I am a Pole from the Warthegau (Warta River District) who moved with my family to Warsaw.

" 'But you speak German pretty well,' he complimented me, adding, 'I badly need a man like you.'

" Overtaken by curiosity, I asked him to elaborate and tell me for what purpose he would need me. He simply explained, 'shortly, the war will come to an end. I would like to contribute to the Vaterland's efforts and make some money in the process as well, by building and repairing some living quarters for the military behind the front line. However, since all the male population up to the age of 65 years was evacuated from my territory because of its proximity to the battlefields, I have no tradesmen to go to work with and do my job properly and on schedule.' "

" 'So where do I come in and in what capacity?' I was intrigued.

" 'Well,' Herr Bender replied, 'Your job would be to go back to Poland, specifically to Warsaw, and to bring back professionally qualified bricklayers, concrete formers, glaziers, painters, roofers, plasterers, plumbers, and any other kind of craftsmen you can get a hold of, who are willing to work hard and get well-paid for their labors. As incentive for you personally you would be rewarded fifty marks per head for each man you return with. You would also hold the position of permanent foreman which makes you the highest paid wage-earner in my building company.' "

" 'But how can I leave my own outfit of the Kuzyk construction firm right here in Dniepropietrowsk? We're busy putting up an office building for the Luftwaffe on the other side of the Dniepr River in Nishny-Dnieprovsk.' "

" 'Don't worry about this at all. I will take care of everything in the most legal and orderly fashion! I assure you that my company and the people I work for have priority over everybody else.' "

"And so Herr Bender won my confidence. At midnight, we met at the railway station where for the first time I saw him in his impressive military regalia as Obersturmbannführer of the Waffen S.S. We boarded the train and I went along with him via Charkov and Yassi-Novataya to Stalino as his newly-engaged recruiting emissary in my country's capital. The train journey took us two whole days and two nights."

"The very same day of our arrival in Stalino, Engineer Bender took me out for lunch and made me take a bath in the official local Entlausungsstelle (delousing chamber). Then he walked me over to the Bekleidungskammer (quartermaster's store) and dressed me in the S.S. Frontarbeiter (front line workers uniform), I am wearing now, handing me a special identification book in which the military apparel which I had received was registered. Wishing me good luck he also gave me 200 marks on account and a Marschbefehl (marching order) of the construction administration, clearly stating that the reason for my trip was to take a short holiday and to recruit unemployed workers and artisans as per an attached list. I was to fill in their exact names, birth dates and numbers of the personal identity cards they were holding."

"And so after a couple of weeks in Warsaw, I managed to convince some of my friends and acquaintances to come along with me back to Stalino. I promised them top wages and first class food as foreign imported labour, who are paid ten times as much as the local workers."

"Now, in reference to your question, Herr Obersturmbannführer, of why young Poles would come so far away from their own home to earn a living, I must tell you quite candidly that they had an ulterior motive which was the catalyst in their coming here. Simply and truly they were attracted by the much better conditions of employment, the higher wages, and the better quality of life that they would have here. You see, their peers in Warsaw are caught almost every day on the streets and boulevards in police dragnets and shipped off to Germany in locked-up freight trains, with the probability of some of them ending up in coal and iron ore mines or in other hard labour enterprises. In Stalino, they knew that they would walk around as free men, well looked after, with a sense of adventure as part of the establishment — very much enjoying life after a hard day's work."

"In conclusion, I must honestly tell you, Herr Obersturmbannführer, that I personally suffered, however, quite a setback in my relationship with my own close family. Not all of them were enchanted with my role as recruitment-agent for an S.S. institution, and they have openly looked upon me with resentment and suspicion. But the peculiar thing is that after I fulfilled my mission to the best of my ability and brought my compatriots over here — where they are indeed very much needed and where they really proved themselves as dependable, skilled tradesmen regularly doing an excellent job — I did not become any favourite here, nor am I looked upon with appreciation and understanding. In reality, it seems that I have estranged myself from my people at home as a collaborator, and now I am being given the third degree by my superiors who seem after all to be displeased with what I have accomplished. Thus, de facto, I remain ostracized from both sides — treated with contempt by many of my own Polish relatives and unrecognized and given a cold shoulder by my German associates as well."

"What a bind I have put myself in." I lowered my head in pained disappointment. My voice was faltering, vibrating with choked emotions to the point of involuntarily weeping; I was quite unable to hold back the sobs which came spontaneously and naturally as a consequence of feeling so deeply hurt. Taking out my handkerchief, I wiped my eyes, swallowed hard, straightened myself up, and remained standing erect in front of Obersturmbannführer Bregman in silence, looking directly into his inquisitive brown eyes without the slightest nuance of fear.

There was a tangible atmosphere of suspense when the Obersturmbannführer left his chair, walked over and shook hands with me.

"Herr Arendarski," he put his arm around my shoulder in a gesture of good fellowship, saying, "Take care of your people, as you have done until now. I will see to it as soon as possible that all the technicalities in this matter are resolved and we will officially install all of your group as a worthy auxiliary unit assisting in our effort to vanquish our mutual communist enemy. Heil Hitler!" He raised his arm in salute.

I responded appropriately and left the room unhindered. I walked down the six flights of stairs, wishing to be away from all the soldiers in the overcrowded elevator. I knew that my saintly father's virtue had helped me in my hour of desperate need. After that encounter with the diabolical 'Prince' of the S.S. and his murderous henchmen, I experienced some of what the psalmist David must have felt after his encounter with Goliath. G-d almighty alone knew that my tears and spasmodic sobs had been not artificial but a genuine outburst of despair at the calamity which had destroyed my people.

When Unterscharführer Brunner, the liaison man between the Bauleitung office and the workshop, showed up in the morning with the usual work-orders and assignments, he found empty walls and nobody to talk to. There were no 'Poles,' no foreman, no tools, no bedding in the adjoining living quarters; only the small iron field-beds with the straw mattresses standing there as silent witnesses to a well-executed, orderly pull-out.

In the middle of the night I and my men had sneaked out of the compound and smuggled ourselves back fourteen kilometers to the main freight-train depot in Yassi-Novataya. Our connections with patriotic, civilian railway workers helped us to find and board the appropriate empty boxcars on their way to the Ukrainian hinterland where each of us would continue his struggle to survive.

CHAPTER 4

Dniepropietrowsk

AFTER MY abrupt departure from Stalino I worked my way back to Dniepropietrowsk. I felt completely at home there. I knew every nook and cranny of the countryside, every valley and hill from Pushkinskaya Yama (the Pushkin pit) to the mountainous terrain of Checelovka and the Szewczenko Park near the city hospital. I knew the back alleys, the bomb shelters, the botanical garden, the church cemeteries, the saloons and bars, the bootleggers and 'moonshine' distillers. Above all, though, I knew some local underground members who asked few questions and who were willing to help in times of need.

The physical skyline of the proletarian city was unaltered. But in the subterranean world of the Polish Jews on aryan papers there was quite a change! Of the more than 200 of them on forged Christian papers, approximately twenty percent had been denounced and picked up by the Gestapo. About thirty percent had voluntarily given up city life and the chance of living like normal human beings. They had joined the wandering Soviet partisans in the surrounding forests — freeing themselves of the unbearable burden of leading a double life as alleged Catholic Poles in constant fear of their own compatriots and of being unmasked as Jews. The majority, some 80 souls, went into hiding and made all kinds of arrangements with their keepers and protectors.

Only the ones with perfect Nordic looks and an immaculate command of the Polish language still dared to hold onto their managerial positions and ordinary jobs with the auxiliary forces and still wore the uniforms of the Wehrmachtsgefolge.

I found out about all of this from my friend Mishko Kapustiak. He was a westernized liberal Ukrainian with an affinity for the underdog and the ambition to be a contemporary historian. We had been friends for quite some time and he told me what had happened in Dniepropietrowsk during my absence.

"It started out with the secret initiative of a few morally degenerate hoodlums: Marian Hycel, Stephan Bydlo, and Antek Zemsta, who created their sort of private detective agency to uncover Jews among their own rank and file for the purpose of blackmailing them. They began to observe the behaviour patterns of their dark-complexioned co-workers. They looked for such signs as not crossing themselves before eating or while passing a church, speaking Polish ungrammatically or not showing enough taste for drinking and carousing. The most tell-tale sign was their would-be victim's tendency to avoid company, and avoid looking someone straight in the eye with defiance and challenge.

Once such an individual was detected, they followed him secretly to find out where he lived. Then they paid him a surprise visit. First they ransacked the place, turning everything upside down, looking for valuables which they immediately confiscated. The victim's passivity was automatic proof that he was, indeed, a disguised Jew. After picking up and bundling together everything that could be sold in the local bazaar, they told him that from now on he was to hand over to them half of his earnings every two weeks, as soon as he received his wages. If he did not do so then he was finished. He would be denounced to the police.

The victims knew that they had no choice. It was either pay up or face almost certain death in the gas-van. Antek Zemsta, Stephan Bydlo, and Marian Hycel acted like Mafia chieftains sitting in their beloved restaurant and nightclub "under the red lantern" on Sheroka Boulevard. Terrorized Jews would sneak dejectedly into the cabaret restaurants, pay the blood money extracted from them, and quickly disappear in order not to draw excessive attention from other brigands.

However, after the Warsaw Ghetto rebellion the infamous triumvirate suddenly disappeared. Nobody knew where or why. Rumours floated around that after the Jews had shown their capacity to fight, taking on the Wehrmacht and the S.S. troops and valiantly holding out for over six weeks with many Nazi casualties, it was no longer so easy to bleed the Jews and take their possessions and money. There was clearly a risk that they would not be so willing to take any more abuse. There was even talk of a mysterious underground cell which had targetted them as Fascist scum and collaborators with the enemy who deserved to be 'hit' and eliminated. The whole general attitude of the 'Polacks' somehow changed after the 19th of April, 1943. There was now talk of a united resistance movement of all Polish citizens regardless of faith and different religious persuasions.

Unfortunately, some of the Gestapo people knew of these antics and they themselves took over the initiative, turning it into a well-organized operation. Without warning and at random, they would surround a construction company on pay day, line up all the foreign workers with or without uniform and walk between the standing rows of workers seeking 'Yiddish' looking faces. The moment they sniffed someone out who did not look to them like a bona fide Aryan, they simply told him to step forward and to let down his trousers and show his genitals in everyone's presence. If there was any sign of circumcision, he was instantly taken out, handcuffed, and put into the black Gestapo van waiting right there on the spot.

"You know, Adam," Mishko said with regret, "you cannot imagine the look of those poor young men ferreted out from the line like useless weeds."

"Those bastards, those low-life, vile extortionists, they opened a pandora's box which destroyed some of their own finest people. There was a pure-blooded Polish engineer, Valerian Kuczynski, an ex-major in the Polish army, an excellent architect and construction specialist with a diploma from the University of Munich. Kuczynski spoke German masterfully and won a contract to repair and refurbish boats in the shipyards of the Nikolayev port on the Black Sea. Knowing the terrible slaughter his Jewish compatriots were going through, he wanted to help them as much as he could."

"So by word of mouth he let it be known through special trustworthy messengers that Jews who looked like 'good Christians' with any kind of identification could find employment and safety as uniformed tradesmen in the auxiliary services of the German naval forces. Within a short time, he assembled eighty people, some with their wives, who were put to work in the kitchen and as office staff wearing the navy blue apparel of the German navy."

"Everything seemed to be fine. They were all Jews, from the craftsmen to the bureau-personnel to the door-man at the dormitory. The only non-Jew was their mentor, protector and saviour — Valerian Kuczynski. A true and genuine Catholic Pole, he was obsessed with saving this unique conglomeration of desperate survivors, from many different cities. It appeared as if they might have a good chance for a new lease on life. They even started to sing and chat while hanging on the rope-ladder outside the boats, washing, scraping or painting. This miniature foreign legion of disguised Kuczynski Jews found shelter, sustenance and hope for eight months."

"And then a mean, debased son of a bitch, who happened to pass through Nikolayev and loitered around the port streets, recognized his Jewish schoolmate from Lwow (Lemberg) and followed him to the dormitory. The treacherous parasite felt, with his underworld instinct, that here was a chance for some extra income. So he posted himself in a doorway across the street, continuously observing the place. After a while, he decided that there was a true bonanza here and there must be more Zydys (Yids) inside to barter away for a substantial, hefty reward."

"At supper time, when they were all seated around the dining tables with Major Kuczynski at the head, he came back with the Gestapo. They surrounded the premises and rushed into the building. What went on inside, the beatings, the whippings and head bashing, could only be imagined from the frightful screams heard down below on the street. Stevedores and port workers, who happened to be there, told how, one by one, they led out seventy-six men, sixteen women, and seven children of the Bauleitung der Seeflotte Nikolayew. The last one to leave the massive stone dwelling was Major Kuczynski — handcuffed with a large paper bag over his head on which was inscribed in red: 'I hid Jews!' "

"A hundred lives were delivered to their deaths in exchange for one hundred bottles of whisky and a hundred kilos of sugar."

Mishko was normally quite self-controlled and cool-headed. Now, however, he had become really worked up while relating the story. "Adam," he said, "it was a massacre, a pogrom! Perniciously caused by a bestial vagrant who did not think twice about murdering Jews for a profit."

"I happened to witness the end of the whole mess. Four of the men were absent at the last Nikolayev supper, and one of them, Ignacy Polanski, was right here in Dniepropietrowsk proposing a deal to Kuzyk's company chief, Mr. Tkacz, about building, together with the Major's outfit, a huge storage facility for marine supplies."

"The blueprints, drafts and specifications were still lying spread out on the conference table when the Gestapo stormed in. They walked straight over to Polanski, most probably having had a picture of him, because they pinpointed him immediately from among all the others present."

" 'Good morning, Mr. Polanski,' the Polish speaking agent greeted him ironically. Polanski was so bewildered that he replied in accent-free Polish: 'I don't understand.' "

" 'So you answer in pure Polish that you don't understand your own native tongue?' the Gestapo man chided him sarcastically. 'Where is your wife?' he asked the confused Polanski.

"This time Polanski responded sadly, in fluent Polish: 'I am not married!'"

" 'Oh yes, you are not married, you are still an eligible bachelor, you pig!' screamed the Gestapo man. 'Bring in Frau Polanski!' he ordered."

"And sure enough they brought her in from the van outside, especially imported from Nikolayev. She was a beautiful young brunette in her twenties, handcuffed, and with an indescribable despondency in her frightened blue eyes."

"Adam," Mishko said as he lit a cigarette, "I will never forget the way they led them both down the staircase. They looked really pitiful, walking the path of the condemned."

Mishko invited me for a much-appreciated home-cooked meal at his new apartment. It was on the eighth floor of a relatively new building with a beautiful terrace. Communist party officers had lived there under the Soviet regime. Although I had known Mishko for some time and respected his passionate love of stamp collecting, I did not know of his other love — gourmet cooking.

We had a full Ukrainian menu of borscht with cabbage, sour pickles, beets, beans, and other vegetables, pierogis, and a side dish of sour cream with sugar.

In the course of the evening we emptied a litre of German brandy. We became quite sentimental. Mishko played some sad and nostalgic Ukrainian folk music on his record player, sang some nationalistic songs, and recited some of his favourite poetry about the victims of Soviet cruelty. I was so moved by his recital that I responded with a lament that I myself had written.

> The ones we love
>   Usually don't love us
> The ones we could love
>   Died young
> The ones who would love us
>   Were not yet born.

> So, we wander around
>   Dwarfed giants
> Pathetic financiers
>   With our precious
> Emotional treasury
>   Bolted up with ourselves
> Trapped
>   Like one
> Of those Rothschild barons
>   Trapped in his own
> Steel vault
>   Able to count
> His pure 24-karat gold coins
>   But unable, ever, to spend them.

It was already late when we called it a night. My Ukrainian host put me up on the living-room sofa. He hung his military Wlasow jacket on the back of a chair, emptied the pockets of their contents on the dining room table, and retired to his own bedroom. As I drifted down into sleep, a stream of images passed through my mind. I saw incarcerated Jews being led off in chains for interrogation in Nazi torture sessions. I saw the execution of that noble Polish aristocrat, the righteous Major Valerian Kuczynski — how he stood proudly against the chipped red brick wall of the Gestapo yard, refusing his killers' "gracious" offer to blindfold him as an ex-military man — and his fearless stare straight into the faces of his slayers. I saw the accursed parades of young men who had been ferreted out as hidden Jews and forced to expose their private parts. I saw the Polanskis walking down the staircase of the Kuzyk company on their final journey before their disappearance into the black van of the Nazi butchers. I saw the seven children of the Nikolayev construction outfit, bound together with rope like innocent little lambs, mercilessly driven into the slaughterhouse. The muscular Mishko Kapustiak appeared with the curly blond forelock and "Taras Bulba" Cossack moustache; the man with the rough exterior but with the tenderness of a saint, who becomes more intoxicated on poetry than on alcohol.

What an enigmatic character this friend of mine is, I thought. On the one hand, he is an ultra nationalistic, haughty spirit despising anyone who is in the way of Ukrainian sovereignty, staunchly anti-Soviet because the Communists oppress his people and have sent his father and mother, brothers and sisters away to Siberia. On the other hand, he is sentimental and soft, sincerely sorry for all the fallen victims, the maimed invalids, the orphaned children and bereaved widows, even for the inhuman extermination campaigns against the Jews. Officially, he considers the Germans as comrades in arms and allies in the task of thwarting the dark forces of Bolshevism. Officially, he is the top man in the Dniepropietrowsk Wlasow recruitment office, making fiery speeches against the enslavement of the Ukrainian homeland by the Kremlin and calling on young freedom-loving people to join the ranks of the German Wehrmacht in its struggle to defeat the dictatorial, Marxist bosses. And underneath it all he hates the Nazis as much as I do. What a unique character he is, I thought to myself as I drifted off.

I awoke early the next morning. Dawn was still hovering over the proletarian city and the air on the terrace was fresh and crisp and the horizon transparent, so that I could see far beyond the city limits, right to the surrounding collective farms with their golden-headed cornfields. The view was breathtaking and tranquil.

Down below was the winding Dniepr River with its bridges, slow-moving barges and fishing boats. There was no indication in this wonderful blend of urban and rural beauty, architectural novelty and harnessed energy called Dniepropietrowsk, of the dramatic struggle being waged by a few surviving Jews, leftovers from the attempt to make the city Judenrein, free of Jews.

I walked back into the dining room and sat down at the table. Mishko's wallet was lying right in the center, with the edges of photographs of friends and family protruding from it. I opened the wallet and began to look more closely at the pictures. There were all kinds of them. School groups, soccer teams, the Ukrainian fraternity in Lwow to which Mishko belonged, the military unit he was attached to. Suddenly something came into my hand that reflected more about Mishko's origin and background than a hundred pictures. It was a very peculiar document addressed 'to whom it may concern,' officially stating that Mishko, the son of Agata Oleniuk and Stanislaw Kapustiak, was baptized and was from pure Aryan descent. It was signed by Cardinal Novotny, the head of the Roman Catholic Church in Lwow.

What is this? I wondered. Why does Mishko carry around such a paper in his wallet, like an identification card? Why is there such an emphasis on his Aryan origins? It just did not make any sense. Would a decent citizen carry around a police certificate stating that he is not a thief? Would a respectable lady have in her purse an attestation of the crown attorney's morality squad that she is not a prostitute? Why this ostentatious emphasis on Mishko's Aryanism?

The door opened and Mishko came into the living room dressed only in his pyjama pants. His hairy chest was exposed and wet. He carried a bath towel on his right shoulder with which he began to wipe and rub himself diligently.

"Good morning, Adam," he said cheerfully.

"Dobre utro!" I responded in Ukrainian and our gazes met.

Mishko walked over to the dining room table and noticed the church letter. Without chastizing me for being so nosy he simply asked, in his deeply modulated bass voice, "Adam, what do you think of me? Did you believe that I was a Jew?"

I looked at him with warmth and admiration, replying, "Not until now! But I've got news for you! So am I!"

There was a moment of intense silence. Two Jews, straight-jacketed into images they had never really been, took off their veils, shook off their facades and revealed themselves to one another for what they really were: Jews, brothers of the same faith.

After the bloody Gestapo raid on the premises of Kuzyk Construction, the future security of the firm was somewhat doubtful, but Mishko advised me to accept the offer of Mr. Tkacz, the company president, to go back to work as foreman for Kuzyk Construction in Nizhny-Dnieprovsk! As far as he knew, my high reputation among the foreign workers was still untarnished.

"The Poles," he told me, "know that you are not Polish, although you claim to be a Poznaniak. As a matter of fact they are quite convinced that you are actually a Volksdeutsche, a very astute ethnic German who has figured out already that Hitler is not going to win this war and therefore decided to switch allegiance to the Polish people and better share his future lot with them."

That suited me fine, and I accepted the offer. I began to commute again from Dniepropietrowsk proper to the other, much quieter side of the Dniepr River where I became the Kuzyk Company's representative at the construction site of the Luftwaffe office building. The exterior of the building was finished and there was a great bustle of activity inside. Nobody really believed, however, that the impressive edifice was going to remain permanently or even for very long in Nazi hands.

My job was to sign each employee's working card itemizing the specific hours of work he put in and the overtime he made during the whole week, which was then sent back to the Kuzyk office for payment on Friday afternoon. I also saw to it that the specially installed kitchen had a warm lunch each day for the Kuzyk company men. I also had the task of obtaining the necessary foodstuffs for the kitchen chef.

The man who checked and signed my requisition order to the Luftwaffe supply center was Sergeant Hans Reichner. The diminutive Reichner, only five feet tall, was an ultra fanatical Nazi, a bellicose character who looked at everyone with suspicion. Hans already lived in the finished wing of the fourth floor offices, keeping an eye on everything as agent of the Bauleitung der Luftwaffe Rostov 26.

In collusion with the Kuzyk office and with the verbal encouragement of Mr. Tkacz, the company president himself, I still managed to outwit the Nazi-bureaucrat, and obtain the highest grade of rations for my workers, by the little trick of Polonizing the Russian and Ukrainian names with the addition of "ski" or "wich" at the end.

The racist occupation administration had a discriminatory pay-policy towards the locals, who were paid and fed according to the prewar Soviet standard of living. A local worker was officially paid only about 15 karbowantzy (Nazi money printed for the Ukraine) a day, while the imported Poles were paid 150 karbowantzy a day. The same two-tier approach was applied in the distribution of dry foods and cigarettes. The Poles and all the other imported foreigners were given German military rations including six German cigarettes per day, while the locals were given a cheaper type of food and kolkhoz-grown makhorka tobacco.

I took many Ukrainian and Russian names and changed them from "Turko" to "Turkowich," "Lubov" to "Lubowski" and transferred them to the Wehrmachtgefolge Verpflegungsliste — and the Luftwaffe quartermaster's stores delivered more and better quality grocery products to the huge Kuzyk pantry. In consequence, all Kuzyk workers received additional and better nourishment. Mr. Tkacz, who quietly organized this system on all his multiple building projects, himself received considerable extra income.

Although Sergeant Reichner never caught on to my scheme he treated me with conspicuous disdain. That still did not keep him from utilizing my services in translating his orders to the larger group of local women he personally employed to clean up the finished part of the huge fourth floor offices intended as the communication center for Rostov 26, as they called themselves. Every morning after signing the Kuzyk construction men's cards and assigning them their duties for the day, I had to walk up to the fourth floor and help Hans in putting his "ladies" to work. In return, the Sergeant grudgingly allowed me to use his little white German scale to weigh out some of the dry products for the Kuzyk men at the end of the week.

The piercing and unfriendly looks never left his grim, truculent face. A great part of Reichner's antipathy towards me stemmed from his conclusion that every Pole was an incorrigible religious Catholic always going to mass or to the priest for confession and absolution. In his subjective and hate-clouded mind, he thought that he had seen me on a Sunday morning coming out of services at the Sheroka Boulevard church together with a group of other Poles.

The following Monday morning he accosted me, "What are you doing in the church?" Without waiting for my reply he fired away indignantly: "Don't you know that Jesus was a Jew?"

Before I could respond and explain that he had mistaken me for someone else, Hans left fuming in disgust and utter disrespect for a uniform wearer of the Luftwaffe showing such respect for a Jew.

Among the sixty or so Kuzyk craftsmen and labourers working at the Luftwaffe Rostov 26 building I knew of only one disguised Jew on Aryan papers. He, Kasimir Nowacki, was lucky to be endowed with perfect Nordic features. Light complexioned with a thoroughly slavic face and upturned nose, he really looked like a prototype of a pure-blooded Pole. His command of the Polish language was excellent as well. The only trouble with this fellow was his talkativeness and his propensity to show off his bilingualism whenever he could. A simple carpenter by profession with a limited public school education and inadequate scholastic training, he butchered the German language and grammar by using the Yiddish dialect verbally underlined with a continued "ah" vowel — which gave him the illusion of conversing in the Deutsche Sprache.

Hans Reichner needed a special medicine cabinet in his bathroom and he called up Nowacki to the fourth floor pointing out the spot over the sink where he wanted it installed. Temptation was too much for Kasimir who immediately showed off his linguistic ability saying: "Ja — Ja. Ich alles verstehen, Ich machen ganz genau! gut Arbeit! Jawohl Herr Feldwebel!" (Yes, Yes! I making exactly! Good work! Yes sir, Sergeant!)

The sniffing bloodhound in Reichner must have detected something instinctively because he brought him immediately down to my office. "Arendarski," he said, "Fragen Sie ihn was fur ein Landsman er ist?"

I instantly comprehended the inauspicious situation, but having no choice I asked officially: "Mr. Kasimir, from where do you come?"

"Ja jestem ze Lwowa."

"Aus Lemberg!" I translated to an angry, red-faced Reichner.

"Yes, my dear fellow. There are many Jews in Lemberg," Hans Reichner said derisively and stormed out of the Kuzyk office.

The next day Nowacki did not show up for work anymore and when I came into Reichner's quarters to borrow the little scale to weigh the day's produce for my men, Hans refused to loan it to me saying instead with a hate-contoured mouth: "Jews, get out to Palestine!" He watched my reaction intently, perhaps expecting shock and total loss of control.

But I remained cool and unimpressed, showing no sign of nerves. I fired right back at him. "What kind of dumb jokes are these, Sergeant?"

"Well, the Gestapo will surely find everything out tomorrow," Reichner hissed threateningly, and turned his back on me.

There was no point in arguing with him so I left. As soon as I shut Reichner's door I mounted the newly installed bannister and slid down the whole four floors in seconds. I knew that I had to get out fast.

On the main floor, I hastily went to my office, took out of my desk drawer the lists of local and foreign workers, the Kuzyk seal and stationery, my private, miscellaneous belongings and off I went through a back exit into the street where I quickly mixed with the passersby.

However, when I reached the Dniepr I decided not to cross the regular way on the main bridge, but walked two kilometers using a less frequented bridge to arrive at the other side. Once I came to the city I boarded a passing streetcar to think things over and decide the next step of action. And here came a second shattering surprise. Passing the downtown's busy section near the local military command, on the corner of Konolenko and Komsomolskaya Streets, I noticed from the tram-window the tall figure of Obersturmbannführer Bregman with Unterscharführer Brunner trotting behind him like a sexton behind the church pastor. They must have arrived in Dniepropietrowsk as a result of the so-called "strategic withdrawal" of the Nazis from the Don Basin terrain.

I did not go straight home, but took a couple of streetcar rides in opposite directions. Then through side streets and back alleys, I slipped into Mishko Kapustiak's office, briefing him on what had happened.

Mishko calmed me down. Jokingly he even teased me by saying, "What is the matter with you Adam? Have you gone soft? Where is your sense of adventure, your joy in flirting with danger?" But then he became serious, gave me the key to his own apartment, and told me to wait there for him to talk things over. I followed instructions, halted a passing horse-cab and twenty minutes later was indulging in Mishko's poetry collection. Soon Mishko arrived, smoking his pipe, which he did only on special occasions of importance demanding concentration of the mind. He arrived in good spirits, with smiling eyes and whistling the popular tune Lili Marlene. Washing his hands and face he walked over to the cupboard, took out the good stuff and poured half a tea glass of Schnapps for each of us. Humorously he reassured his distraught friend that there was no better anti-depressant than a bit of fire-water. He then made two huge omelettes for us with warmed up fried potatoes and sour pickles.

"Now we can talk and concentrate properly," he winked mischievously at me meaning to cheer me up. "Before we go any further," Mishko stressed, "I want you to know that there is really no imminent danger to your person at all. They don't have your address, so, they don't know where you live. They have no picture of you or fingerprints, so, they cannot issue a warrant for your arrest. Even the Kuzyk office, as far as I am informed, does not know where you reside, right?"

"Right," I replied.

"And most importantly," Mishko went on: "They are so busy with the influx of tens of thousands of defeated soldiers and administrative personnel that they are in no mood to search for Adam Arendarski, who is perhaps of an unpopular ancestry."

I looked at him as on an older brother projecting authority, logic, and a pragmatic sense of reality and listened attentively to his arguments about the situation.

"There are three options," Mishko continued, billowing smoke out of his curly fancy pipe and pouring another drink for each of us. "One, you can go underground, like Wladek Starorzynski and Stefan Michnik did after the viciously spread rumors about their being Jewish, which means shutting yourself completely out of social life, and to call a spade a spade, voluntarily imprisoning yourself."

"You can join the partisans in the surrounding forests as many of our compatriots already have, which is, truthfully speaking, only a fifty-fifty chance of staying alive and keeping all of your limbs, given all the accelerated anti-Nazi activities that are now going on. Besides, I am not exactly sure that as the sole survivor of your whole family — which makes you an endangered species — I would like to see you maimed or dead even for the noble, heroic cause of expediting and winning the war against Hitler."

"And last, and what seems the most reasonable solution to me is: to leave Dniepropietrowsk and look for some greener pastures in some smaller place, not in a big city, where there is no Gestapo, no local military field police, no S.S., and no Schutzpolizei. A locality where small scale construction is still going on. With your qualifications and experience of the past, and speaking Ukrainian, Russian, and German — you will be an asset to a smaller firm which will probably grab you and pay you an arm and a leg to work with them in a managerial capacity."

"Well, that is all very true and it makes a lot of sense. But where does one find such a dream territory on such short notice?" I interjected.

"This is exactly what I am about to conclude with," Mishko grinned and the dimples in his cheeks became much wider. "I have a good Ukrainian friend working in the office of Beton und Monierbau Kompanie in Dolgintzevo, who will, I am sure, accommodate you with a little written introduction from 'yours truly' in Dniepropietrowsk . . ."

"Listen Adam," Mishko stood up, "from what you told me, I understand that you have some stationery and a seal of Kuzyk Construction. Well, give me a couple of official-looking letterheads of the company and I will go back to my office where I have a German typewriter with all the necessary umlauts and I will type out a Marschbefehl. It will state that you are going as an emissary of the Kuzyk outfit for consultations and job arrangements in Dolgintzevo.

After Mishko left, I went out on the terrace to observe the city of which I had become so fond. I looked down at the bustling streets and remembered striding along the sidewalks with so much hope of salvation. I said a silent farewell, a bitter-sweet goodbye to this metropolis where I, once destined for the gas chambers, had been given a second chance. I remembered the joyful meetings with fellow-members of the underground and the tears we all shed for our fallen comrades. There had been about two hundred of us Jews in Wehrmacht uniforms, doing all that we could to cause trouble for the Nazis. And now it was over for the time being; I was back to square one, a Jew on the run from the Nazis.

In the oncoming twilight I abruptly felt a compelling urge for communion with G-d. I went into the kitchen, washed my hands, and in the privacy of Mishko's terrace I tried to recollect the dusk Mincha prayer. Anyone observing the scene would have been surprised to see a blond Luftwaffe uniformed man swaying back and forth like a Chassidic Yeshiva-boy with his face turned to the east. As amazing as it might have seemed, I still remembered the eighteen benedictions of the Shemoneh-Esre, and felt an upsurge in courage when I said: "Behold, please, our affliction, take up our grievance, and redeem us with a complete redemption speedily for your name's sake, for you are G-d, the powerful redeemer. Blessed are you, Hashem, redeemer of Israel."

Even more inspiring was the mood into which I fell upon devotedly reciting the blessing of the ingathering of the exiles: "Sound the great Shofar (ram's horn) for our freedom, raise the banner to gather our exiles and speedily gather us together from the four corners of the earth to our land. Blessed are you, G-d, who gathers in the dispersed of his people Israel . . ."

When Mishko came back I was in a happier frame of mind. The Marschbefehl looked genuine, especially with the round seal of the Kuzyk company and with the little eagle and swastika in the center, which gave it undeniable, bona fide legitimacy.

Mishko put on his apron and made garlic bread with a sweet and sour salad and Lithuanian sardines. After supper and the traditional piece of apple strudel and tea, followed by a shot of Schnapps, we went to my apartment on Komsoholskaya Street Number 14. When we reached the building, Mishko told me to wait outside at the corner of Korolenko Street while he went ahead and checked if everything seemed in order and undisturbed. A little while later he came back and we both walked up to my bachelorette on the second floor. Within fifteen minutes, all my things were bundled up into my knapsack and large duffle-bag and off we went by streetcar to the small freight station at the eastern end of the city.

The little depot at the edge of the metropolis was crowded with Kalmuks, Asian people, with features like Tatars, who, after deserting *en masse* from the Red Army to become German prisoners of war, joined the Hitlerites in their fight against the communists. The Wehrmacht accepted them into their ranks and used them to combat partisans, as railway guards as well as for punitive actions which they conducted with extreme cruelty. However, they showed considerable deference to the two German-speaking blond gentlemen and especially for my grey Luftwaffe uniform.

The Ukrainian station-master was very cooperative and informed us that a train would soon come through and leave for Krivoy-Rog, which was not too far away from Dolgintzevo.

Mishko was dressed in civilian clothes, in order not to arouse the excessive curiosity of my neighbors. However, the European tailored light grey suit with the fancy hat decorated with a colorful feather in its band was convincingly German.

I looked at Mishko with a profound feeling of gratitude for everything he had done, and especially for keeping me company until the puffing locomotive with the dimmed front lights and darkened, blacked-out carriages pulled into the station. Somehow, I felt myself to be very privileged to know this unique man, whom all the foreign workers including the Poles venerated as a genuine humanitarian, sometimes even jokingly calling him the defender of the Jews.

When we embraced saying, "Auf Wiedersehen," I could not find the proper words of thanks and praise. Somehow they all sounded so superficial and cliched. So I simply whispered into Mishko's ear: "Shalom! Ulehitraoth!" — "Peace and see you again!"

"Shalom vederech tzleycha!" — "Peace and bon voyage!" Mishko whispered back, jumping off the already moving train, but remaining on the platform.

I stood at my compartment window as Dniepropietrowsk and Mishko Kapustiak gradually faded away into the distance.

CHAPTER 5

Dolgintzevo-Krivoy-Rog

IT WAS a gorgeous Sunday afternoon in late summer when I arrived in Dolgintzevo. Like an Alpine village hidden away in the Swiss mountains, Dolgintzevo was concealed in the green plains of central Ukraine, surrounded by picturesque orchards and story-book settlements of painted little cottages. In contrast with the pulsating rhythms of the big city, Dolgintzevo, as if sedated by its natural beauty and pollution-free, sunny skies, was possessed of a leisurely pace, creating its own rhythm of life. Located fifteen kilometers from the city of Krivoy-Rog and about fifty kilometers from the main railway junction of Apostolovo it was an island of tranquility for me after my close call in Dniepropietrowsk with Reichner's denunciation and the potential confrontation with Bregman and Brunner.

As Mishko had foretold, there were neither Gestapo nor other Nazi security personnel here. Law and order was maintained by the local Ukrainian militia, who stepped aside for every German uniform with great awe and reverence.

There were, however, thousands of ordinary, mostly middle-aged, Wehrmacht soldiers. They were quartered in almost every house, giving the impression that they constituted a reserve for a second line of defence in some future battle with the Russians, who were continually advancing. Fortunately for me, they seemed to have only one interest, a gluttonous love of food and feasting.

As usual for a new arrival, my first priority was to find a room or at least a place to sleep, perhaps as a subtenant in a house, preferably owned by some elderly babushka. As most male members of their families had been either mobilized into the Red Army and labour battalions or forcibly sent away to German factories, these elderly ladies lived poorly. They were genuinely pleased to accommodate someone — especially a foreigner who spoke their language — knowing well that they would be paid not only in money but also in foodstuffs and other normally unobtainable items.

Grandma Natalia Ivanovna Romanova was the ideal landlady for me. She was widowed and childless, and her only brother lived in far-off Siberia. Her chicken-coop was almost empty and she was down to her last three geese, thanks to the merciless gorging of the soldiers. She was overjoyed to rent the room adjoining her own living quarters.

"At first, they came and took away my cow," lamented the elderly lady. "They just led away my 'krasnienka,' my beautiful provider of cheese and butter and everything, claiming that I have to make the sacrifice for the good of mankind's future in its fight against communism — and they gave me a paper entitling me to collect a milking cow right after the war's end. Then they came with motorcycles in the middle of the night, like ordinary bandits, brazenly taking their booty and disappearing. Then came the more civilized ones, the 'respectable' ones, who demanded eggs and chickens, paying with all kinds of junk and trinkets like buttons from the First World War, nail clippers and belts and tarnished purses made from artificial leather. Now I can only stay alive by selling different household items, which I accumulated only by years of hard work."

"Babushka," I told her soothingly, "I am not a German! I am Polish! My name is Adam Arendarski, and here are two hundred karbowantzy which I am willing to pay you per month as your tenant. However, if you agree to clean and cook for me as well, I will supply you with everything you need, including coal, firewood, oil and kerosene."

"Holy Lord," the grey-haired babushka exclaimed, pleasantly surprised by my offer. "You are sent to me from above!" She pointed her bony finger heavenwards. "Not only will I cook and clean for you, I will also wash your laundry and iron and mend your shirts and socks. I will keep you here like a prince, as if you were my own son!"

I left my things with Natalia Ivanovna and went out for a walk to familiarize myself with the neighbourhood and to see who was promenading in Szewczenko Park near the railway station.

Despite all the atrocities and the continuous killing going on at the front, the peaceful, relatively large park was full of strolling people. There was laughter, lively talk and even singing by school children, who, under the guidance of their teacher, sang as a choir for the public. Though in the fourth year of war, with most of their clothes worn out, the people still tried to look presentable on this day of rest and recreation.

Ordinary potato sacks and military blankets dyed various colours were now the materials of which most of the people made their clothes. The most popular colours were navy blue and dark brown. It was encouraging to observe the ingenuity of the seamstresses who made themselves skirts and jackets and even dresses from the only available woven fabrics and wore them with the dignity and grace of big city models. The menfolk were not far behind with their own inventiveness. To show their own constructive imagination and their entrepreneurial spirit, they cut old rubber tires to the size of their feet, and then nicely stitched up the openings on both side, and, presto! A new kind of footwear was on the market, guaranteed to last for quite a while.

With no self-consciousness at all and with their heads held high, the people danced with the verve and carefree ease of millionaires on the huge wooden stage in the center of the park where a harmoshka accordion quartet, accompanied by flute, guitar and violin, played waltzes, fox-trots and sentimental tangos.

"We both met in life coincidentally — thus by chance we parted. We were not aware of each other's happiness, thus by chance we parted." A young mezzo-soprano in a fine silk gown and high-heeled shoes crooned with professional know-how and feeling to much applause from the audience. There were no ice cream booths, no chocolate bars, no candy, and no lollipops. Everyone munched sunflower seeds and elegantly spat out the shells into their hands so as not to litter their beautiful park.

"A cheerful people, these Russians!" commented a Wehrmacht corporal who joined me in my tour of the flower-lined paths. "No wonder that Napoleon lost his war with them!" he continued. He had a full round face and a large paunch. "You can't conquer people with such an indestructible pride. They can endure almost anything. I'm not so sure as I used to be that we are going to win either!"

I heard the pessimistic conclusion like a prophecy of Nazi doom. I looked at the grandfatherly figure of this corpulent man and, not wanting to sound defeatist myself, I just mumbled in agreement. As it turned out, a farmer from a village near Dresden, had just come back from his two weeks' leave at home and was deeply shocked by the devastation that American bombers had caused in his region. He spoke with great alarm about what was happening in Germany proper, where nothing and nobody was safe from the Allies' air attacks.

Unable to restrain my curiosity, I asked "What do you think? When will this game end?"

The Unteroffizier stopped for a moment and then continued walking, as he said, "You are young, perhaps you are a National-Socialist. But to me it doesn't matter. When it will all stop, unfortunately I don't know. However, when the war is finally over, you won't find the name of Germany on the map anymore!"

I returned from my reconnaissance tour in good spirits. I had seen nothing to dispel my peace of mind. Babushka Natalia Ivanovna had prepared my lodging place with great care. Everything looked neat and clean. The mattress was filled with fresh straw which still exuded the fragrances of the fields. A needle-point tapestry hung on the wall next to the bed. The linen, blanket-cover and pillow cases were snow-white and hand-embroidered with all kinds of blossoming plants. There was even a bouquet of her garden flowers in a glass vase standing on the little square table in the center of the room.

I spent a relaxing, peaceful night without any of the unpleasant incidents or worrisome nightmares which had so often robbed me of my sleep. The barking of the neighbourhood dogs and the whistle of passing locomotives did not disturb me at all. On the contrary, they reminded me of the good old days when the Ajzensztadt family was still alive and used to travel by train to our birthplace, the shtetl of Sandomierz on the banks of the Vistula River in Poland. It also took me back over two decades to the times of my own childhood vacations in the exquisite pine forests of Ozarow, Ostrowiec and Falenica near Warsaw, where I had experienced a little boy's joy and wonder in learning first-hand about nature and animals. I soon fell asleep.

Beton and Monierbau's construction office was two short blocks away from my new abode. There were only three people in it on that Monday morning when I walked in, dressed in civilian clothes, to deliver my letter to Trofim Stepanovich Bojko, Mishko Kapustiak's trusted friend.

A few moments later, two of them left with surveyor's equipment under their arms, and I remained alone with a lean young man with an intelligent face, who matched Mishko's description of his old school friend.

Bojko read the note from Dniepropietrowsk with curiosity, looked benignly at me, as if to check that this was the fellow so highly recommended and then, without any bureaucratic ceremonies, simply asked me: "Would you be willing to take over a position as foreman on a new project in the village of Glinko three kilometers away, where we are putting up a supply warehouse for the Deutsch Reichsbahn (the German railway system)?"

"You will have about thirty local men there, a heavy cement mixer, a small bulldozer for excavating and grading prefabricated footing forms, scaffolding, a three-ton truck for hauling the materials from the company's yard and a very capable Polish construction master craftsman. He is sure to be happy to have your help in dealing with the numerous engineers and dignitaries from Headquarters in Berlin."

I accepted at once, although I felt very uneasy about the unknown compatriot whom I was to help. Trofim seemed extremely pleased because he stood up from his desk, shook my hand, and said: "Welcome aboard Beton and Monierbau in Dolgintzevo." He returned to his chair, pulled out a side drawer in his desk and took out a special identification certificate bearing the emblem of the German Reich's railway system. He typed in my name, and then also gave me a separate tag certifying that I was a foreman of Beton and Monierbau in Glinko.

"Here are some foreign workers' ration cards," he said, handing me a few sheets of coloured ration coupons. "You can go to the 'Reichsbahn' canteen, the red brick building across from the station, and pick up your supplies, cigarettes, and tobacco for a whole week."

"Since you are a newcomer," Bojko considerately concluded, "take the rest of the day off to make your own arrangements, but be here at a quarter to eight tomorrow morning and we will take you out to the job site."

"It was a pleasure to meet you, Mr. Bojko," I said appreciatively. "Dosvidanya! Auf Wiedersehen."

On the way home I assessed my situation. I was once again a legally appointed civilian management employee of the well-known firm of Beton and Monierbau. But for how long? I could not help wondering where the next bit of trouble would come from. Who could the boss on the building site in Glinko be?

I suffered from constant stress, which wore me down. I was always afraid of a sudden change for the worse, inevitably a problem for any Jew living on forged Aryan papers. I was torn between feeling thankful to have made it alive to Dolgintzevo and worrying about the next encounter with mortal danger. "Sufficient unto the day is the evil thereof," that old Jewish saying came to my rescue. I managed to stop worrying for the time being, and determined to cross each bridge as I came to it. What really gave me courage, though, was the memory of my saintly father's promise that I would survive. I accepted that completely.

The next day I arrived half an hour early. At a quarter past seven I was already in front of the Beton and Monierbau office — in the huge yard which looked like a building supplies wholesaler specializing in all kinds of construction materials.

Two workers dressed in brown leather jackets and aided by two middle-aged villagers in soiled rubashkas were already busy walking around the compound and filling out requisition orders for the different jobs. Despite their gutteral Berlin accents and the Nazi party swastika pins in their lapels, Paul and Bruno did not seem to have that quality of menace shown by Sergeant Reichner and Obersturmbannführer Bregman. They greeted me with a friendly "Guten Morgen" and "Wie gehts?"

Paul and Bruno were the directors, overseers, surveyors, the "outside" men officially responsible for all the Beton and Monierbau projects in the vicinity within a radius of fifteen kilometers. Trofim Stepanovich, who had been a high school teacher of the German language — before joining the company — was the "inside" man, responsible for the administrative and technical work of bookkeeping, payroll, hiring and firing and the provision of ration cards. At exactly a quarter to eight, he arrived unpretentiously on a bicycle, greeting me as well with Zorastwuytye, the Russian equivalent of "hello." Then four trucks pulled in, from which labourers jumped out and started to load the different materials prepared by Paul and Bruno's men. By five minutes to eight, everybody was ready to leave the yard with the necessary supplies, Trofim and I joined the Glinko driver. Paul and Bruno went into the cabin of another truck and the motorcade set off in various directions from the yard. The only person remaining behind was Tatiana Grishina, Trofim's secretary and office girl, who cheerfully waved goodbye.

The Glinko vehicle drove along the railway tracks until it had left Dolgintzevo. Then it took a shortcut through a narrow field path over a primitive but sturdy bridge and within five minutes it had reached its destination.

"So far, so good," I thought, as we all alighted near the tool shed. We walked towards the building's foundation, which was already above ground level. I could see my new boss, the project manager, on the other side of the future storage facility. He was dressed in grey overalls, high rubber boots, and a large straw hat and seemed to be busy instructing some of the local masons where to start bricklaying. I just had time to wonder if he would be a friend or a foe before Trofim called out.

"Alexander! Come over and meet your new man!"

My heart was pounding. A familiar face was coming towards me! It was none other than the gentle, refined president of the Kuzyk firm in Dniepropietrowsk, now dressed in the ordinary garb of a construction supervisor.

"Meet Mr. Adam Arendarski," Trofim said.

The senior job manager extended his hand saying, "Alexander Chitka. But call me Alex." He formally shook my hand as if meeting me for the first time.

"O.K. you Pollacks," Bojko announced humorously. "I have no time to socialize with you. I've got too much work to do. Take care!" And he went back to the truck, picked up his bike and pedalled off to his office duties in Dolgintzevo.

"It is good to see you, Adam," Alex said, taking out his cigarette pack and treating me to a smoke. Inhaling deeply he then added, "Now with no superiors around I don't have to pretend anymore."

"It is good to see you too, Mister . . ."

"Chitka . . ." Alex corrected me, and then continued, "This is my present *nom de plume* under which I officially function. A lot of things happened since I last saw you on the Nizhny-Dnieprowsk job. But here is not the place to discuss it. Let's wait until lunch time. We will eat together and I will fill you in on the details of what has transpired in the last couple of months."

"In the meantime, do me a favour and make some order in the toolshed. What I mean specifically is: an official inventory list of everything we have from wheel barrows and shovels to pick axes and chisels and hacksaws and trowels and hammers and iron bars — the works! It has to be in German and in duplicate with one copy attached to the inside of the entrance door, and the other to be fastened down in a properly visible place on the wall so that it is noticeable to everyone and everybody can read it. That is the way some bigshot of the head office wants to have it, so we underlings have no choice but to please him. Now here is my key. I will have another one especially made up for you. By the way, underneath the improvised little table there is a cupboard with some homemade punch. Please feel free to treat yourself anytime. Welcome to the fresh air and clear horizon," Alex winked at me significantly and in a friendly fashion.

At twelve o'clock on the dot, Alex came into the shed, picked up his duffle bag with food plus a few bottles of punch, told me to stop working and to lock up the stall, as he called the tool-shed, and off we went to a nearby ravine, where we could enjoy complete seclusion.

Michael Tkacz, or, as he called himself now, Alexander Chitka, was a handsome, intelligent gentleman. He had obviously been through the mill despite his relatively young age of thirty-five years.

I had always considered him to be a basically good person, perhaps even with a certain compassion for the downtrodden and victimized. As far as I could recollect, I had never heard from the Jewish underground leaders, Wladek Starorzynski or Richard Lis, or from the living encyclopaedia called Mishko Kapustiak, that he ever took any money for accepting Jews into his Kuzyk outfit. And, in a world of bloody blackmail and atrocious complacency, this alone earned him the title of "righteous gentile."

"You know!" Alex said after consuming his lunch sandwich, while I was still chewing on Babushka Natalia's potato pancakes with jam. "We two are now in exactly the same boat, precariously waiting for salvation. Therefore it is logical, nay, let me better rephrase my sentence, it is rather incumbent on both of us in the interest of self-preservation, to watch out for one another's safety, as it says in Ecclesiastes: 'Two heads are better than one.' "

"That's fine with me," I wholeheartedly agreed. "I will be glad to participate in any plan to safeguard our common well-being and security."

"As I promised you earlier," Alex continued, "I will now tell you the story of my fall from grace, from a glorious career as chief executive of Kuzyk Construction with hundreds of employees and scores of prestigious building project to the insignificant job of superintendent of this architectural monstrosity in Glinko. Officially, this ugly ten thousand square meters of concrete and bricks is going up as a Reichsbahn parts warehouse. But, in reality, it is one of a chain of hurriedly built huge storage arsenals for artillery shells, electronic missiles, and other rocket weaponry already being prepared for the upcoming last stand in this region, which will, I think, take place relatively soon.

"Well, about two months ago I received a note from the Gestapo to come to their office on Korolenko Street at my own convenience. To be honest with you, Adam, after the Polanski case, the Gestapo suspected that there were many more disguised Jews amongst the Kuzyk crews and they kept pestering me to give them a list of possible candidates for interrogation. Unwilling to jeopardize all the lives of the over fifty men on Christian papers who worked all over the city on my different projects, I was forced to make up a list of five names, telling beforehand the people involved to go into hiding because their lives were in danger. The brand new invitation to visit the Gestapo was, I thought, perhaps a repeated attempt to brainwash me and intimidate me into delivering another itemized series of names of suspected, possible Jews."

"However, when I was finally ushered into the office of a Gestapo man, it did not take me very long to find out that I myself was in much deeper trouble than I had expected. The stone-faced man behind the desk was a prosecutor who took out a file and officially accused me of avoiding military service in the Wehrmacht, to which I was liable as the son of a German mother; secondly, he announced that the judicial system of the Third Reich charged me also with the crime of cheating the army of extra rations in wartime by fraudulently changing and switching the names of local employees to the lists of Wehrmachtsgefolge and perhaps of being involved in a conspiracy in collusion with the underground to save Jews."

"I was told to empty my pockets and put all my possessions on the table. For the next three days I was locked in a basement cell until the morning of the fourth day, when I was brought up to a second floor room. There, three black-robed characters sat behind a polished, oversized walnut desk with a gavel and a bunch of dossiers on it — seemingly in the capacity of judges. My stone-faced interrogator was also present. He read out the accusations against me, but more elaborately this time."

"One hour later, it was all over without my being allowed to say a single word in my own defence. I was found guilty as charged and sentenced to eighteen years of hard labour in an institution for rehabilitation through work. I knew very well that this euphemism meant some stinking, degrading slave-labour in a mining shaft, gunpowder factory, or perhaps even the quarry in Mathausen itself. I decided to risk an escape, choosing rather to be shot than to suffer as a convict, having my freedom taken away from me. An armed plainclothesman took me to the train station, where he was supposed to deliver me to a whole transport of other condemned deserters, to be taken over by the military police. Luckily, an air-raid alarm was sounded and pandemonium erupted. Anti-aircraft guns started to fire away with loud explosions, passengers began to run for cover into bomb shelters. It's now or never, I said to myself. As an incoming train approached the station platform, I suddenly jumped down to the tracks at the very last moment, managing somehow to pull myself up to the second platform where I got onto a slow moving freight car heading in the opposite direction, and disappeared from the sight of the confused guard."

"Naturally, I could not return home, or go to my office, so I went to Marusia Nikolayevna, my elderly cleaning lady, who had a spare key to my apartment. I confided to her my situation, beseeching her to go quickly to my place as if to do her usual, regular chores, and told her to bring me a couple of suits, a light topcoat, some underwear, shirts, socks and from underneath my desk drawer a large, closed envelope with marks, karbowantzy and other currencies which I always kept there for an emergency."

"The loyal, dear Marusia Nikolayevna threw away her knitting needles, grabbed her overcoat and shot out of her little house to fulfill her mission. Meanwhile, to be on the safe side in case something happened to her, I hid among the green bean stalks in her garden to wait for her homecoming. It was the longest three-hour wait in my whole life. It seemed like an eternity. But, finally, in a night lit only by the moon, I saw her bent silhouette carrying a double bed blanket cover stuffed to the bursting point and filled with almost everything I possessed, except of course the furniture."

"I hardly took anything with me. I tied the money around my belly, packed only a single suit, a topcoat, a pair of pants, some undershirts and underpants, a couple of pyjamas, a few shirts and a half dozen socks and handkerchiefs. I left everything else to the brave Marusia Nikolayevna as reward for her unhesitating willingness to help me."

"Early in the morning when her rooster Pietka crowed in the backyard I began my pilgrimage to the unknown, which coincidentally, by sheer luck, or perhaps by divine providence, brought me here, to this lost paradise called Dolgintzevo, where Trofim introduced you to me as my new associate."

"Well, Adam! This, in a nutshell, is the story of my odyssey and metamorphosis from Michael Tkacz to Alex Chitka, from the big-city socialite, elegant dresser and high flying entrepreneur to a low profile, provincial hick in overalls. Despite my general optimism, however, I must tell you that sometimes I think that I am in even worse shape than you and your fellow Jews. You see, you and your people have actually only one enemy, the Nazi regime, which will soon definitely collapse. Alex Chitka, alias Michael Tkacz, though, is *persona non grata* to the 'brown' and 'red' totalitarian regimes. The Hitlerites would surely kill me if they caught me. The Russians will certainly accuse me of collaborating with the murderous fascists and building offices for them, probably sending me off to Siberia for a lifetime. Anyhow, I am not the type to commit suicide out of despair! So let's live and see what happens."

On the way back to the job I asked my rediscovered ally point blank if he had already known in Dniepropietrowsk that I was Jewish. "No!" Alex responded without even turning his head. "I always thought you were a genuine 'Poznaniak' who had not jumped on the bandwagon of Nazism, pretty much aware that the illusion of a thousand-year Reich would shortly end in ruins and fade away like a mirage. But when I saw you coming up to Glinka, in Trofim's company, your semitic ancestry emerged as a possibility. Still I have news for you my dear fellow! You are not alone here. There are three more Jews working in managerial positions for Beton and Monierbau on different projects in the vicinity. I only heard their first names; Henryk, Stefan, and Jurek. They are obviously not very eager to strike up new acquaintances, and I don't blame them for that. If and when we bump into them I will discreetly point them out to you. Perhaps they will intuitively grasp the kinsmanship and try to contact you on their own."

When our day's toil was over the newly formed A and A team (Alex and Adam) decided to meet right after supper in front of the Beton and Monierbau office in order to go to Krivoy-Rog to celebrate our new partnership. "Don't you dare take lightly our little confederation," I jokingly warned my boss, Alex Chitka. "Homer said, millenia ago, that great is the strength of feeble arms combined."

Paul was supposed to give us a one-way lift into the city which he often visited himself. But for some reason he did not appear. So, armed with our credentials as Beton and Monierbau employees of the Reichsbahn, we started out on foot.

About a kilometer eastward out of Dolgintzevo, a huge square of land cleared of stumps, brush, and shrubs — but surrounded on all sides by pine thickets, like a solid, impenetrable, natural fence — obviously served as a depot for all kinds and types of fuels. Soviet prisoners of war in their shaggy brownish-grey coats rolled full barrels of fuel to waiting tank-trucks, and picked up the syphoned-off empties with wheel barrows and piled them up in a corner near a newly built railway siding. The air was saturated with heavy oil fumes, which would probably explode into an inferno from the slightest spark of a lit cigarette.

Before we could continue any further we were suddenly stopped by a sergeant with a machine gun who screamed, "Halt! Freeze! This is restricted terrain. Damn Ruskies! What are you doing here?" he asked threateningly, with blood-shot eyes.

Coolly and self-assuredly, Alex replied in his finest polished German, "We are not Russians, Sergeant! We are Reichsbahn employees and here is our identification to prove it."

The infuriated sergeant read our documents. He reluctantly let us off the hook and ordered us to retreat the way we had come. A few hundred metres back, though, we discovered an opening in the wild, tall hedges and walked across a potato field to the main road. Unperturbed by the incident with the excited, suspicious sergeant, we did not intend to give up our trip to the city for sightseeing and entertainment.

Within a short time we were offered a lift by a uniformed member of the Todt auxiliary forces, who was driving a dark green Volkswagen. We looked distinctly West European which obviously helped. Fifteen minutes later we were let off in the centre of Krivoy-Rog.

The city looked impressive and modern, with private initiative in full bloom. Restaurants, coffee-houses and commission-stores advertised their wares in the display windows. But it was really poor and anemic in appearance. In the fifth year of war and with all the industries geared for the military effort of the Third Reich, only second hand items were exhibited which people wanted to exchange mostly for foodstuffs and important, rare medicines for sick members of their families.

Even high class restaurants had none of the exquisite special dishes expected in such classy places and their version of a Wiener Schnitzel was a baked chicken breast dipped in egg and bread crumbs. For the traditional last course dessert they served improvised crushed apple dumplings in starchy sauces, instead of real French pastry, frozen sherbert, and all kinds of puddings.

Alex knew a café on Danilova Street, which he called the Literary Cabaret where, for the entrance fee equivalent to the price of two packs of cigarettes, one could receive a delicious piece of cheesecake with sweetened tea. There was also live entertainment; gypsy music played on violins and guitars as well as folk-singing.

The owners of that amusement spot were a refugee from Dniepropietrowsk and his enterprising and talented daughter Zina, whose husband, serving in the Red Army, was Jewish. Her three children were thus half-Jews — Halb juden — meriting treatment as subhumans, according to the Nuremberg race laws. To avoid complications and possible vicious gossip which might have endangered the youngsters' lives, they had moved to Krivoy-Rog, rented a dilapidated dance hall, and engaged the whole family and many close friends in refurbishing it.

Zina had a beautiful voice and was a member of the Ukrainian National Theatre ensemble, well-known in the artistic world. So they put together a number of little round tables and chairs, decorated the place as best they could, and as usually happens under such circumstances, organized an Artyel (Cooperative) consisting of various musicians and performers, each of them obtaining an agreed upon percentage of the net receipts. Needless to say, the Vinogradovs — with the daughter functioning officially under her maiden name (which was her father's Aryan name) — were not 'Germanophiles,' although publicly like everyone else, they paid lip service to the redeeming Nazi liberators.

Alex had been their longstanding friend from before — the senior member of the family being his personal, private tailor. And the then chief of the Kuzyk firm had reciprocated with generous quantities of the best quality food at his disposal, and had become a frequent visitor to the appreciative Vinogradovs who regularly invited him to join them on festive occasions.

In the loneliness and anonymity of self-imposed exile in Dolgintzevo, Alex was thrilled to run into the old man one day. The old man had immediately brought him home and re-established the close association, now even stronger because of their sharing a common enemy. Since then, Alex not only visited the 'club' but stayed over afterwards with the Vinogradovs, who treated him like their own flesh and blood.

When he walked in with me, Zina noticed us instantly, and hurried over to greet Alex with the warmth of a close relative, kissing him on both cheeks.

"This is my partner and friend," Alex introduced me. "he is one of us," he emphasized in a special tone as if to convey a specific message. Zina took a second look at me, saying politely, "A friend of Alex's is automatically a friend of mine." She then invited both of us to be her guests after the show, and apologized for having to go to prepare for the evening's show.

The dark-eyed, olive-skinned Zina with her make-up, large gold earrings, and pitch black hair adorned with two red roses on each side of her temples looked convincingly genuine when she sang her medley of gypsy songs and ballads. She had the emotions and virtuosity of a gifted opera star. Only a few people in the audience could know how personal were the sorrows that she sang about. They were in her very bones, part and parcel of her own being. Zina's late mother, Tatiana, was herself a gypsy from Budapest, with whom her father fell in love before the Revolution while visiting relatives in Franz Josef's Austro-Hungarian Empire. The tall, good-looking Yevgeni-Dimitrovich brought her over to what was then the city of Yekaterinoslav where he married her officially in a church wedding and they had a completely harmonious life until she died in an automobile accident when their only child Zina was a little girl, seven years old.

The nostalgia, anguish and lamentation were authentic. It was a call of her own blood, and her own family's misery. In some whimsical surrealistic manner it also appealed to the "Heimweh" feelings of the large German audiences who applauded her wildly with calls for an encore and shouts of Bravo!

It was quite something to watch the odd clientele in the various Wehrmacht uniforms singing the famous Russian national song, "Volga, Volga Mat Rodnaya." I thought to myself how sadly ironic it was to hear these plump and well-fed Germans amiably singing along under the baton of a half-Gypsy conductor while their compatriots fed her kinfolk from all over Europe into the gas ovens at Birkenau and Auschwitz.

Around half past nine, Zina and her entire ensemble and four-piece orchestra gave the finale of the evening which was greeted with a standing ovation. It was a sentimental, schmaltzy war hit in German, stressing the return to normal life and the pursuit of personal happiness and love.

"Once again will you be near to me!

"Once again will you be true to me!"

Zina probably had in mind her own husband in the Red Army whom she dearly loved, when she so superbly sang the song. With her charming and heartfelt grace she added a special meaning to the words, reminding me of the celebrated Jewish soubrette and vocalist Channa Grosberg of the renowned prewar experimental Young Yiddish Theatre in Warsaw, under the direction of Dr. Michael Weichert.

By a quarter past ten we were already back at the Vinogradov's to find their little bungalow overrun with combat troops. An S.S. division had occupied the whole neighbourhood, taking every house without exception, and making themselves comfortable as if they were in their own reserved lodgings for the night. Zina's sixteen year old twin daughters were almost hysterical with fright and were shivering like leaves in the wind when their mother, grandfather, Alex and I arrived.

Alex immediately comprehended the situation, that it was not a police dragnet of any kind, nor a punitive expedition or round-up of labourers for deportation to Germany. He told this to the distraught Vinogradows. Then he boldly went over to the non-commissioned officer who was apparently in charge and greeted him with a vibrant "Heil Hitler!", introducing himself as Baumeister Alex Chitka of the Beton and Monierbau firm, who was visiting his relatives Yevgeni-Dimitrovich, Zina, and the three children.

The rough looking Unterscharführer looked at him in surprise, "Are you an ethnic German?"

"That's right!" Alex responded without batting an eye, and told him their hardship story as lugubrious Fluchtlinge (refugees) from Charkov and Dniepropietrowsk — and how they all had to keep running from the murderous Bolsheviks, who had taken their father William Hoffman as hostage, dragging him off, most probably to his execution.

It was a combination of Alex's glib statesmanship and his perfect command of German which influenced that butcher wearing the skull-and-crossbone insignia to relinquish the main bedroom to the Vinogradov family. Alex and I were given the honour of bedding down with the Unterscharführer and his S.S. thugs in the living room — on green army blankets spread out on the floor, and "pillows" consisting of our clothes. Exhausted from the day's ordeal, I tried to fall asleep but couldn't, feeling a bit like a minnow in a sea of sharks.

Despite the Unterscharführer's long monologue about the strict moral race-discipline of the Sturmstaffel (S.S.) units in not fraternizing with Slavic or other females, the S.S. men went out after midnight and rounded up all the young women they could find.

All his boasting to Alex and me about the important and wise concept of Germans limiting intimate relations only to German women of their own kind and his talk of the death penalty for contracting a venereal disease was apparently just talk, like all the so-called 'race theories' of the Nazis.

That night Yevgeni Dimitrovich Vinogradov's bungalow was turned into a brothel of the lowest order in order to satisfy the lowest cravings of Heinrich Himmler's disciples who were to leave at daybreak for the front line and further duty as Nazi killers.

Alex and I waited until the S.S. Men had left to ensure that none of Zina's family were violated by the sex-starved S.S. men. Zina opened the barricaded door as soon as Alex told her it was safe to do so.

The mess was indescribable! The stench of sweat, body-odour, alcoholic beverages, urine, and excrement in a plugged up toilet was nauseating. Porcelain dishes in the kitchen were broken, pots burned on the gas stove, the imprints of fat fingers and unwashed hands were all over the walls. The floors were littered with all kinds of garbage — spilled drinks, food leftovers, ration cans, and in some places torn lingerie smeared with the blood of deflowered innocence.

Zina and her daughters cried. Their ten year old pale-faced brother, Misha, followed Grandpa Yevgeni who went to see if his sewing machine was still there. Fortunately it was. Everyone present soon realized how lucky we all were. The Vinogradovs were deeply grateful to us for protecting them. As we left for work they renewed their invitation to visit them any time.

CHAPTER 6

Partners in Distress

THE EXCURSION to Krivoy-Rog was an indelible experience that further cemented my friendship with Alex. We tried to work out some special security measures to signal that everything was fine before we entered each other's abodes. If, for instance, the window curtains were drawn together in normal fashion, it was a sign that the coast was clear. If they were pulled apart with a dishtowel or socks hanging in the middle of the rod, it indicated that something was wrong and one should stay away from the place. Even in Glinko, we also introduced security precautions, with one of us working and managing the job, while the other was scouting around keeping his eyes open for possible evidence of trouble.

Within weeks of my arrival, Dolgintzevo began to lose the peacefulness of a small regional village with tree-lined, shady streets, breathing placidity. It turned into a noisy, military camp, inundated with multitudes of soldiers.

With the late summer rains, most of the unpaved Ukrainian roads changed into muddy quagmires and clogged bottlenecks of stuck military vehicles, blocking the way to and from Krivoy-Rog for several kilometers. As adequate tow trucks or crane equipment were not available, the Wehrmacht soldiers had no choice but to band together and use their own physical force, which meant jumping into the slime and morass of marshy ground, to push and pull. In the process, they became covered with muck while helping one another to get the trucks out of the large potholes. Aggravated, exhausted, and covered in filth from top to bottom, they no longer looked like triumphant victors but dirty, vanquished refugees, in dire need of a hot bath and a cot to rest their weary bones.

Even at the railway station, acute blockages developed, as railway tracks were continuously clogged with all kinds of freight and passenger cars. Apparently, they could no longer reach their destination, which had already been captured by the advancing Russians. And so they stood there like the unused limbs of a paralyzed body, taking up space, but completely useless.

One time I was talking to a Wehrmacht corporal and I asked him how things were going.

"We are a defeated army," he replied. "I have been cooped up in this train compartment for months since our defeat at Stalingrad, and it's a miserable existence in this cubicle on wheels which goes nowhere and is always exposed to Bolshevik air attacks."

These words of despair from the disappointed Wehrmacht soldier were a general reflection of the plummeting Nazi spirits. They certainly gladdened my heart, sounding like a message from an oracle that the dream of salvation was about to come true.

In the meantime, the corporal's forecast about a visit from the Russian air force became reality. The Vanka pilots, as the Germans called them, began to show up in small numbers, two or three at a time, in planes which appeared to be small, proletarian aluminum boxes with wings, but without any ostentatious adornments; just a number and a five-pointed red star on its belly where the incendiary bombs would come out reaping havoc and destruction. The stranded rail freight cars, the caravans of trucks on the highways, and especially the gasoline tanker cars became their favourite targets. The Russian bear was alive and had apparently begun to awaken from its hibernation, regaining more and more of its fighting ability despite the heavy casualties and the many prisoners of war lost to the Hitlerites since the first days of their surprise attack following the 22nd of June, 1941.

The Russians continued to pay a heavy price in blood and lives, waging an heroic struggle to take back their territories overrun by the stubborn Nazis. The Führer had ordered the Germans to hold onto their positions, and had sent division after division of S.S. reinforcements.

I had seen a Soviet airplane shot down in a field near Glinko. The pilot, hit by shrapnel, had apparently tried to land his plane to save himself and the lives of his crew. But the anti-aircraft guns kept on firing away even when he was twenty meters from the ground, causing an explosion which ripped the plane apart at the very last moment just before impact.

It was a pathetic sight to see the limp bodies of two Soviet Air Force officers strewn in three different directions around the aircraft wreckage. Neither of them was disfigured or mutilated by the sudden collision with the ground. The captain, still wearing his pilot's headgear, had a thin strand of blood oozing from his mouth. The navigator, with his radiophone wires around his neck, looked as if he had been sleeping peacefully without any signs of violence to his body. Only the third officer in an ordinary long military coat with the epaulet of a lieutenant showed some signs of life, moving his head slightly although his eyes were closed. He wore high leather boots with special fur-lined protectors at the top. His face was dark and handsome.

I was overcome with pity when I saw his left leg broken off at the ankle, with the bone sticking out, and with the sole lying nearby still attached to the foot by some thin strips of flesh. A Wehrmacht truck took him away, while the captain and navigator remained prostrate on the ground near their wreckage of the airplane. Nazi soldiers and their girlfriends loitered around and watched the shot-down 'Ruskies,' as if this were an exotic sight at an exhibition.

The Russian aerial attacks increased day by day. Broken power lines, blazing ammunition trucks and supply warehouses lit the surrounding landscape, turning the darkness of night into the clarity of day. The 'Vankas' kept on coming not only by air but on land as well, gradually converging on Krivoy-Rog and Dolgintzevo. The terrifying shriek of the Katyusha missiles scared the wits out of the Nazi troops, who called it the Russian war organ; it played a fearsome tune of horror and death.

The Glinko project was almost completed, with only the woodwork trimmings and the doors to be installed, when chaos suddenly set in. The whole undertaking was abandoned and the local labourers helped themselves to such materials as were still available which they happily carted away for their own private use.

Days of mounting disorder and confusion followed, attesting to what seemed initially true, and then became an increasingly undeniable fact: that the whole region was surrounded from three sides by the Red Army, and that the Germans might be forced at any moment to evacuate and pull out through the only corridor left — the area administered by Rumania.

It was a sight which gladdened my heart despite the real danger of the falling bombs and the exploding shells, falling closer and more accurately by the hour. I felt like an expectant mother in the last month of her pregnancy, not knowing when the delivery would take place nor what complications might arise.

With limited transportation at their disposal, the Reichsbahn storage depots were opened to everyone who spoke German or wore a uniform. It reminded me of the sad days of the liquidation of the Warsaw Ghetto when whole streets were emptied of their inhabitants and all their possessions were left to anyone willing to come and take them. Now, by poetic justice, the Nazi rulers of Dolgintzevo were in a similar position, forced to abandon their plundered supplies of clothing, shoes, canned food, cigarettes, and all kinds of miscellaneous items from cards and office equipment to razor blades and cosmetics, underwear, coveralls and underpants — all of which would be taken away by scavengers who would not have to pay a single penny for it.

The scene brought to mind a prophetic Kabbalistic warning pronounced by Rabbi Solomon Alkabetz in the sixteenth century and contained in a rapturous Sabbath evening poem, *Lekha Dodi*: "Those who despoil you shall become a spoil, and all who devour you shall be far away."

The next day, work stopped completely and Paul and Bruno called an emergency meeting of all the foreign employees, which was attended by Henryk, Stefan, and Jurek as well. The Beton and Monierbau representatives did not make any long speeches, simply stating that the Bolshevik offensive made it necessary to evacuate to a safer place. Bruno said that in the afternoon four box cars would be marshalled into the company's railway siding. "There will be enough food and drink on them to last us for a long time and — under the circumstances — relatively comfortable folding beds to rest in at night, until we reach our destination, where we can assume our building activities again. Go home, pack your possessions, and bring them back today with your name and home address written on the special tag attached to the metal handle. Paul will be here to assign you your travel places."

Once Henryk, Stefan, Jurek and I were left alone with Alex, Alex did not lose any time and invited everyone to his home to plan what to do at this critical hour. He started out succinctly and wittily introducing me as a man whom he had known for well over a year and whose unpopular ethnic background he had legalized while employing me as foreman on a Luftwaffe building project in Nishny Dnieprowsk, when he himself was president of Kuzyk Construction. "Adam, originally from Warsaw," Alex stated, "is, as well, a son of your ancient nation. In the last two years he went through trials and tribulations which are so dramatic that they should be written about."

Henryk, Stefan, and Jurek looked at each other, ill at ease, astounded and in disbelief. But Alex did not mince any words and came immediately to the point, explaining that he never had any notion of bringing up the subject of nationality or religion for derogatory purposes. "I knew of your intrepid struggle since I arrived in Dolgintzevo. Yet I respected your anonymity and did not pester you with my curiosity or need for company. That is why I did not try to interfere with your detached, private life and force you to associate with Adam and myself. However, now, for the first time, it is essential for all of us to make a collective decision on an issue which equally concerns our whole group. I am going to put my cards openly on the table and tell you candidly that I myself and Adam are not going to be on the avacuation train when it leaves Dolgintzevo tomorrow. Whatever I have said until now was meant to let you know subtly that we must not unilaterally do something which might jeopardize the chances of freedom for the rest of us."

"So what do you propose?" Henryk, the oldest one, asked apprehensively.

"Well, I propose," Alex responded, "that for as long as possible, we should avoid antagonizing Bruno and Paul and partially follow their instructions to fill wooden suitcases with whatever rags we can lay our hands on, padlock them, bring them back and put them into their box car. This would make them believe that we intend to go along on the trip, thus giving us a chance to hide away overnight. And the way things look, within a couple of days we should be liberated by the Red Army and become free Polish citizens again."

Alex's frankness was a total surprise to Henryk and his peers. It confused them, but at the same time, the tangible sincerity of his bold statement disarmed them.

With Alex's landlady out of the house, I joined in and began to speak to them in Yiddish and Hebrew. That instantly dispelled all vestiges of their suspicion, and we held a very warm reunion of four marrano Jews and one righteous Christian on the threshhold of anticipated salvation.

As it turned out, Henryk, Stefan, and Jurek were all brothers from Cracow. They had even succeeded in rescuing their 72 year old father and bringing him to Dolgintzevo where he masqueraded as a deaf mute who could not speak or hear a single word.

Beton and Monierbau directors, personnel, equipment, and office files left the following morning, accompanied by five padlocked wooden suitcases without their owners, who had remained behind.

Dolgintzevo was now a non-man's land and militarily a front line territory beginning to look more and more like a true battlefield in the making. Beautiful Shewczenko Park was desecrated and reduced to a battered, ploughed-up mass of earth, serving as a staging point for General Guderian's Tiger tanks which were readying themselves for action. The flower beds were trampled, the glazed hot houses with exotic botanical plants smashed, the gorgeous shrubbery and winding grape vines wrecked and demolished. Overturned, crumpled vehicles, locomotives scorched by direct hits, uprooted blackened telephone and telegraph poles and the deafening, ceaseless howling of deadly flying projectiles created an atmosphere of gloom and doom as civilians avoided the streets. Staying out of sight, huddled together in their little houses, they hoped to survive the imminent bloody confrontation.

In the afternoon, German Schutzpolizei and black-clad Ukrainian Cossack collaborators arrived and began a meticulous house-to-house search, checking attics, garrets, cellars and basements — looking for "young" men and women, up to the age of 65, whom they led away to an unknown destination.

I noticed them over the fence in a neighbouring courtyard and decided to meet them head on, as a German speaking Reichsbahn employee. Straightening my navy blue uniform I did not wait until they opened Babushka Natalia's kitchen-door but strolled out of the house, intercepting them in the little alley. I was the first to speak, in my best German: "What is going on here?"

The uniformed men looked at me respectfully, "Are there any Russians hiding here?"

"Concealed Russians in my place?" I looked at them in incredulous disbelief.

"Excuse us, please," the Schutzpolizist mumbled and with a "Heil Hitler" left the premises to continue his task.

Playacting is still part of my life, I thought, and decided to go up and see what Alex was up to. Alex lived on the other side of the tracks, past the railway station square and I had to maneuver my way around artillery encampments and concrete bunkers surrounded by concertinas of barbed wire. They were guarded by steel-helmeted Wehrmacht soldiers armed with rifles with fixed bayonets, apparently ready to repel any attack on their stronghold fortifications.

I suddenly found myself in the middle of an S.S. trap, encircled by savage, ugly looking "demons" with death written all over their angry faces. Their pistols uncocked, yelling and gesturing wildly, they were grabbing just about anyone passing by to dig trenches as defensive anti-tank pits and carry ammunition right up to the front line beyond Dolgintzevo.

"I am not a Russian," I screamed at the top of my voice holding out my Reichsbahn certificate, as an unruly character, wearing a skull and crossbones started to walk towards me.

However, the infuriated demon in uniform passed me by, grabbing instead an elderly villager of about fifty whom he hit over the head with his rifle butt and marched off to the pick-up truck with the other people seized as labourers. He did not so much as ask to see his identification papers.

Instinctively, I turned around and made my way back home to Babushka Natalia's abode. It was too much of a risk at this stage of the game to continue any further, without knowing what other snares and pitfalls might lie ahead.

Natalia Ivanovna was happy to welcome me back home. She wept with relief as she saw me opening the little wooden gate door and stepping into the yard. She grabbed my arm and led me into the house to show me what had happened during my short one hour, absence. A stray heavy mortar shell had rammed through the roof, torn down part of the ceiling in my room and cut into my pillows with such force that the whole place was, as it were, spray-painted with a mixture of feathers and straw.

"Son," she said, as she put her hands together as in prayer, "they are guarding you from above! You are a man with exceptional luck, destined to survive this bloody war. This horror occurred only minutes after you left the house." And then, without asking my consent she started to carry my things over to her own apartment, consisting of two rooms and a narrow kitchen.

I gave her a hand in moving my belongings and then helped her to clean up the debris and rubble, throwing all the broken plaster, roofing paper, and pieces of dried tar into an outside garbage heap near the chicken coop. Afterwards, I went up to the roof and blocked the hole with plywood which I had once brought home from Beton and Monierbau, putting a few cement blocks on the edges to hold it down. While on the roof of the house I was able to see for quite a distance — far beyond the railway station and the Shewczenko Park — up to the places where the various roads leading to Krivoy-Rog merged. This spot, I thought to myself, and especially the nearby chestnut tree, would be an excellent vantage point from which to look around and identify the incoming Red Army troops. I would be able to watch the liberation of this beautiful haven with its tiny minority of four Jews and one persecuted Gentile.

Alas, things did not turn out as we had hoped. The terrifying and ear-splitting noise lasted the whole night. The battle scene was lit up by a myriad of blazing dwellings, grain silos, Kolkhoz barns, screaming live torches of burning cattle, and floating flares sent up into the skies by both sides in order to spot each other's positions. Perched on top of a branch I distinctly saw at some distance the Russian tanks with their five pointed Red stars.

They did not manage to break through the Nazi lines. I was in complete shock as I watched the Russian forces pull out in disarray, leaving behind some of their huge T-34 tanks, their caterpillar tracks broken and their turrets shot up. It was a living nightmare. Not only was I disappointed to see my projected future collapse before my very eyes, but I realised that my life was in grave danger as well. I felt what it must be like for a bridegroom whose wedding unexpectedly turns into a funeral, complete with attendant Nazi executioners and undertakers.

I tried to console myself with the thought that the Russians were regrouping before renewing the offensive. As the saying goes, "One must draw back the better to leap ahead." I did not feel very hopeful and my mood bordered on complete despair. The day passed and nothing happened. Nazi reinforcements kept pouring in and they put up new fortifications, forcing all remaining civilians to labour from dawn to dusk to make the new Wehrmacht front line positions impenetrable for the Red Army tanks.

By the second and third days, I was already on tenterhooks. I tried unsuccessfully to contact Alex and the three brothers by using Babushka Natalia Ivanovna as courier. But she could not find the places I described to her. At night, the bombardments began again and it was not only unwise but perilous to walk around in the blackout in defiance of the curfew regulations requiring all civilians to keep off the streets.

On the fourth day there was a change — but it was for the worse. Trofim's mother, Ludmila, a kind-hearted lady of aristocratic bearing, and, like her son, a professor of foreign languages, came to warn me. She brought the news that her boarders, Bruno and Paul, were back and that they were in a murderous disposition claiming that all the Poles were treacherous partisans conspiring to join the Bolsheviks. "They are burning to take revenge," she said, "because the wooden suitcases caper made them feel like fools. At first they thought that maybe the Poles had not made it in time because they were involved in some sort of an accident or perhaps they had got drunk celebrating their return closer to home. But when they pried open the suitcases and found garbage, rags, bricks, and, in Jurek's valise, moldy, rotten food and a couple of dead chickens, they got the message that the Poles had pulled a fast one over them and that they obviously never intended to come along in the first place."

"Adam! You have to get out of this house," Ludmila pleaded with me. "Bruno and Paul are searching for you and your compatriots. They swore that the moment they find you, they will kill you all without ceremony as traitors and subversive saboteurs. They claim that you, Alex, Henryk, Stefan, and Jurek were the malicious, clandestine criminals who set an ammunition train on fire, while it was parked behind the Beton and Monierbau complex. For G-d's sake, don't stand so calmly, as if you had diplomatic immunity! Do something to save yourself," Ludmila concluded tearfully and, wishing me good luck, she hurriedly left Babushka Natalia's place to try to warn the other Poles of the sudden ill-omened development.

Ludmilla's visit only added to the already nerve-wracking situation that I was in. I felt trapped in the middle of a minefield and watched by sadistic enemies who could not wait to see me destroy myself.

"My Lord and G-d of my forefathers," my lips spontaneously broke into prayer, "Do not allow my adversaries to corner me like a hunted animal. Thwart the plans of my tormentors to extinguish my life on the threshhold of freedom. Do not permit them the evil pleasure of annihilating the last member of my family after so many years of struggle to survive, when the beckoning ray of salvation is so close by. Merciful father in heaven! My soul is confounded and I stand here perplexed, bewildered at this moment of unavoidable, forced choice. With only two alternatives: hiding in a half-destroyed house, or picking up again the wanderer's staff and trying to go via Apostolovo to Rumanian held territory — what shall I do?"

Babushka Natalia Ivanovna stood by in discreet, silent respect like a dedicated close relative willing and ready to serve in any way possible. She knew by now that Adamchyk, her tenant and adopted son, was in deep trouble and she wanted only to be helpful, waiting for me to make up my mind and take some action. When she saw me opening my duffle bag and again putting on my grey Luftwaffe uniform, she knew that my mind was made up.

It was too late to build a proper place to hide in as Henryk, Stefan, Jurek and Alex had already started to do, even before Beton and Monierbau's evacuation. I had a psychological aversion to hideouts and bunkers as it was too much like putting all one's eggs into one basket, a basket which was all too often discovered, confiscated, or destroyed. My parents, the Tzosmerer Rebbe and his wife, had been discovered by the Gestapo in an improvised hiding place between two adjoining roofs. They were brought down, physically abused, and marched off to the cattle trucks bound for Treblinka. My cousin Luba Brukovich and her fiancé Herschel Birnbaum sat for months in the bell chamber of a church steeple, until they were betrayed by a janitor and shot. Eighty neighbours of my native city, Sandomierz, had hidden in a labyrinth of underground basements which they had built themselves underneath a small park, with enough food and water to last them for a long time. For almost a year they existed there undetected. And then hate-ridden anti-semites noticed that the snow in the little garden turf was steaming and melting in the middle of January. The Nazis were notified and, one by one, they were fished out and executed publicly in the market square.

In the recesses of my mind, I saw hiding as a trap for oneself, even ambushing oneself, especially if there still existed the alternative of masquerading again — although in much more precarious conditions — as a Wehrmachtgefolge, a member of the Nazi auxiliary forces.

"Wish me luck," I told the sobbing Natalia Ivanovna who accompanied me to the gate and with motherly tenderness handed me a bag containing sandwiches and her specialty, sweet potato pancakes.

Once again I plunged into the stream of a hazardous and illegal existence, determined to breathe fresh air and walk in dignity as a human being for as long as I possibly could. The spectre of exile, and of being on the run, had reappeared in my life. Dolgintzevo — like Stalino and Dniepropietrowsk — had become one more scar on the path of agony; the long, long road to liberty.

CHAPTER 7

Birth Pangs of Freedom

APOSTOLOVO was the only neighbouring train junction on the way to the Roumanian-held territory of Transnistria with Odessa as its largest city and only port on the Black Sea, after the capture of Nikolayev by the Russians. It was like a ghost-town. There were almost no civilians visible in the streets, despite the relative calm, and no reverberating echoes from the front line whatsoever.

In contrast to the raging sounds of detonations, explosions, ambulances wailing, and constant cannon booms in the Dolgintzevo and Krivoy-Rog region, Apostolovo was tranquil and quiet. But it was the peacefulness of a cemetery, a deserted community with empty houses and their owners mysteriously absent.

I arrived in a freight train's box car which was returning from delivering ammunition to the battlefield. The locomotive pulled only five carriages in the back and pushed in front of it two large, empty flat car platforms for security purposes so that if partisans had mined the tracks it would absorb the first, lethal consequences of the explosion.

The puffing steam engine slowed down to a crawling pace before entering the depot. I stepped down and slipped away unnoticed into the night.

In the darkness I found a little storehouse with plenty of straw. I took off my Luftwaffe uniform and changed back into my navy blue Beton and Monierbau clothes, becoming once again a civilian who had just returned from his leave in Poland and could not find his evacuated building company. This had been my idea to justify my sudden presence in Apostolovo, in case I were to encounter any complications.

In the morning, I hid my knapsack and duffle bag under the straw and cautiously left my temporary shelter, making my way to the station building. There was nobody around to ask for help — an eery idleness of vacant houses greeted me from all sides. Only when I arrived at the station did I notice that the red brick building was bombed out. From afar, the remaining side and front wall gave the building the appearance of a regular train terminal. Nearby, and for the first time, I saw a group of labourers working with pick-axes and shovels, straightening out the crushed stones between the tracks.

"Good morning," I greeted them.

"Good morning," they replied, looking at me the way local people do when a total stranger creeps up on them unexpectedly.

I came straight to the point and asked them if there were any place or outfit where one could obtain a job. This time their look had a mixture of curiosity and pity as well. They explained to me that there was absolutely nothing to be found here, that everything had been taken away and evacuated together with the population. I was on declared front line territory, and if an often passing military patrol were to catch me without proper documents and justification for being there, they would shoot me on the spot.

I still pursued the question of legalizing myself and inquired who the boss and overseer of their own activities was.

"If you want to take a chance and play poker with your life," a grey-haired man told me as he pointed to a caboose standing isolated on a siding about a thousand meters away, "over there Herr Muhr has his office. He is the station master, regional commander of all traffic and whatever other official business there is to be taken care of."

I knew very well that there was no way back. All the bridges left behind were burned. With a carefree attitude and whispering David's sixth psalm, "O Lord deliver my life once again; save me because of thy grace. For in death there is no thought of thee," I went to Herr Muhr's caboose, opened the door, and said: "Heil Hitler!"

A medium height, blue-eyed, muscular blond man in a high-ranking Reichsbahn uniform peered at me inquisitively and asked, "Are you German?"

"No sir," I replied. "I am Polish, originally from Poznan in Warthegau. My family has resettled in Warsaw, where my father was born and where we now reside."

"What has brought you to my office and what would you like me to do for you?" the man questioned me in a no-nonsense tone, but without malice.

"Well sir," I told him, "I just got back from my month's leave in Poland and could not find in Dolgintzevo the Beton and Monierbau firm I used to work for as construction foreman. Apparently they evacuated back to Germany. So I am sort of marooned without provisions or money and I badly need a job."

"Have you got any identification papers?" Herr Muhr asked.

This was the critical moment. Silently I pulled out my Beton and Monierbau letter and a forged birth certificate stating that Adam Arendarski was born on the 29th of April 1919 in Reichwald, the district of Poznan.

Herr Muhr took the papers, looked at them with a smile and put them in the center of his desk, telling me to come back in two hours.

"That's it!" I thought to myself. "Now I have absolutely nothing to show anymore in case I am stopped and asked to identify myself." It was not the best of situations to be in in a battle zone. But somehow I did not fall apart, feeling confident that something good might still come out of this daring approach of walking straight into the office of the top man around.

Just in case, I decided not to go back to my storehouse hideout in order to avoid unnecessary exposure in the open, sunlit streets. Examining the surrounding landscape I noticed a bushy little garden of tall sunseed flowers, red berries, and raspberry plants. This will be my waiting room for the next 120 minutes, I mused, as I ducked in amongst the foliage and sat down on the stump of a cut down tree.

As usual, when one wants time to fly, it moved slowly, bureaucratically and formalistically, changing from seconds to minutes, to quarters of an hour, to half hours , to full hours . . .

At eleven o'clock I stood again in Herr Muhr's office with a palpitating heart, like an arraigned man waiting for judgement. The station master was on the telephone, but smiled at me and pointed to a chair. I sat down obediently and listened in surprise at how fluently Herr Muhr spoke Russian, with a genuine Slavic accent. There was something about him which rang a bell, but I could not as yet pinpoint what it was.

Herr Muhr finally finished the telephone conversation and handed me a whole bunch of papers, ration cards, coupons for clothing and uniforms and identification legitimizing my stay in Apostolovo.

"Adam Arendarski, I assume that you can communicate in Russian as well," he said, looking benignly at the visibly dumbfounded, happy Pole who he said was from now on officially employed as foreman of local Ukrainians and Russians. "Your job will be to travel with them by hand car and check and repair the telegraph and telephone lines on both sides of the station up to a ten mile radius."

"Before you leave I want you to know, Adam, that I have just taken you under my wing out of sentiment for the city of my own birth. You see! I myself was also born in Warsaw on Karmelicka Street, although most of my years were spent in Heidelberg, where I grew up and got my engineering degree."

"Well! Welcome to the Deutsche-Reichsbahn in Apostolovo. I have assigned you an empty furnished little house. I've written down the address for you. Put the military requisition order on the door and nobody will bother you. Be here tomorrow at eight in the morning and I will introduce you to your men and tell you your mission for the day. Auf Wiedersehen." Herr Muhr concluded his short initiation and I left the caboose in great spirits.

As a free man I walked the empty streets of Apostolovo, carrying the Reichsbahn supplies allotted to me by my unusual new benefactor. I felt a new surge of vitality regenerating my entire being. I knew that G-d Almighty had answered the prayer I had recited from the psalms, and I knew that my saintly, martyred father's promise would surely be kept. I was going to survive!

Lying in bed that night in my comfortable new living quarters, I relived in my mind the events of the last few days. I found myself concentrating on Herr Muhr's unbelievable magnanimity and the cue called Karmelicka Street which he had planted in my mind.

Herr Muhr's casual disclosure that he was born on Karmelicka Street triggered a series of memories going back to my teenage years of continuously frequenting that street, which was within walking distance of my own family home. I knew that short thoroughfare like the palm of my hand. It was a main street in the northern part of the inner city, for streetcars, automobiles and horse-drawn wagons coming down from the main train depot on Chmielna Avenue and fanning out to the industrial parts of the metropolis including the area on the other side of the Vistula River called Praga. At number seven Karmelieka my landsman from Sandomierz and renowned humorist, Barach Rozenfeld, dwelt in a second floor apartment, writing his entertaining columns for the Jewish afternoon paper called *The Radio*. At number 23 there was the headquarters of the leftist zionist laborites, Poalei-Zion, with their firebrand leaders Shachna Zagan and Zerubavel. A little further down on nearby Dzielna Street there was the union of Jewish typesetters and printers, famous for their huge library, excellent string orchestra, and well-organized self-help institution which supported their unemployed members. Opposite them, on the even side, was the prestigious Karmelite Order hospital, in honour of which the street was named. On the corner of Novolipki Street was a kosher tavern where tradesmen, storekeepers and kibitzers used to come in after the traditional Friday night meal, ordering beer with peppered chick peas, roasted duck, and goose livers on credit. They would sing liturgical songs and folksongs — celebrating their hard earned day of rest and talking politics.

All of this was destroyed in the Ghetto uprising when the last forty thousand walled-in, isolated rebels raised the blue-and-white flag of mutiny against their Nazi oppressors. Here on the corner of Dzielna and Karmelicka, opposite the laundry and dry cleaning store of the Muhrmelsteins and facing the Beth Yakov religious girls school and Aguda local on Dzielona 20, a dogged battle took place in which Jewish kids — boys and girls from all walks of life — fought tooth and nail, proving themselves to be not simply Ghetto dwellers, wearing the badge of shame and not simply passive gas chamber assignees but intrepid, biblical descendants of King David, Samson, and Yehuda the Maccabee.

"Where did Herr Muhr fit into this scene of densely populated Jewish tenement buildings?" I asked myself.

And then it dawned on me with the force of a metaphysical revelation. I knew Herr Muhr from before the war! I had seen him in the Muhrmelstein's store behind the counter when I brought my clothes in for dry-cleaning. Like me, my boss was a modern Marrano, but of a truly unique calibre. I was flabbergasted by my discovery.

Overseeing the functional capacity of the telegraph and telephone lines around Apostolovo became my new responsibility. Every day, at eight o'clock in the morning, I and my four man team would assemble in front of the caboose. Herr Muhr would come out and firstly instruct me in German as to what to do and which railway section or Kolkhoz zone should get priority service. Afterwards, he would give me a written travel itinerary in numerical order with a little map of where the respective points of trouble might be, concluding with the single Russian word "poyechali," which meant "get going." On the sound of this signal eight healthy arms grabbed the hand car parked behind the caboose, put it on the proper track and, by manually propelling the pump handles, they rolled off in the assigned direction to check pole by pole, post after post until the broken connections were found and repaired.

There was no physical hardship or danger of electrocution on the job. The crew consisted of ex-post office supervisors in the telephone and telegraph department of Apostolovo, who had behind them many years of skill and qualification in their line of public communications. Although relegated to the lower rank of field workers, they were still a happy bunch, gratified by the privilege of remaining with their families in Apostolovo, in their own homes.

I treated them fairly and with respect, stopping every hour for a smoke break. I also permitted them on their own initiative and time to knock, once in a while, on a remote Kolkhoz cottage and in true proletarian fashion to invite themselves in for lunch on fresh buttered potatoes with milk. With disarming, populist simplicity they would approach the lady of the house and simply say to her, "Aunty, we are hungry." For her part, the lady of the house always welcomed the male company. Her men-folk were invariably off with the Red Army or forced to work in Nazi factories.

The only time I felt uncomfortable concerning my crew, was in a situation when we did some work in a Kolkhoz or other large farm where there was still a Nazi representative, usually a uniformed Wehrmacht officer. On such occasions, as one who spoke German, I was frequently asked to dine with the Hitlerite and my men were served separately, which gave me an uneasy feeling of anxiety and embarrassment. However, our basic rapport was not destroyed and my men still invited me over to their own homes on weekends and on special festive occasions.

I tried to establish a relationship with my boss, Herr Walter Muhr. Muhr's indication that he had taken me under his wing was not just perfunctory lip-service — there was something to it. On the second Sunday after my arrival, Muhr invited me to his house for supper.

I was delighted and hoped for some intimate conversation. But, when I entered the Muhr house and saw the other invited guests I knew immediately that a heart-to-heart chat was out of the question. There were a score of people, some of whom were in the uniforms of the military, the Reichsbahn, or the police; there were some medical personnel of delayed Red Cross trains waiting for clearance, and some important looking civilians, who came down all the way from Odessa to talk things over with Inspector Muhr concerning new emergency procedures.

Herr Muhr's housekeeper, Genia, had with extra help prepared a sumptuous meal — baked carp with rice and mushrooms, vegetable soup with sour cream, strudel, fruit desserts, cantaloupes and grapes and a punch which definitely contained more alcohol than tea and spices.

As I watched the continuous gluttony on the part of the Germans, I felt uneasy until I realised that there was another purpose behind this exquisite reception. The sober Herr Muhr was using the occasion to gather otherwise secret information. As the Talmudic Sages so eloquently say: "Wine loosens the tongue, you just have to be there to make the proper mental notes."

Within three weeks, Apostolovo began to lose its peaceful atmosphere. The station tracks and sidings all began to fill up with hundreds of box cars, creating a tempting target for Soviet pilots whose reconnaissance-planes also started to show up.

Herr Muhr was busy trying to keep two main track lines open for hospital trains with their wounded Wehrmacht casualties going west and ammunition shipments going directly to the battlegrounds.

I and my men also lost our easy-going work tempo and congenial travelling conditions. With the bottlenecks of train cars stretching for kilometers now, it was not feasible to use any kind of a four-wheeler on the blocked tracks. So, the repair team had to switch to an ordinary horse-drawn wagon, which slowed us down considerably. In addition, saboteurs were damaging the tracks in the middle of the night, and that increased our work-load as well.

I began to feel myself hedged in. The influx of thousands of front-line soldiers, the installation of artillery positions and rocket launching sites, and the permanent presence of military police checking stringently for deserters, runaways, fugitives, refugees, suspicious elements, and anyone who was not to their liking, disturbed me greatly.

The most worrisome aspect of the whole situation was the real possibility that, while working with my crew on line repair in forested areas, some partisan might classify me as a Nazi henchman and pick me up as a target on his sniper telescope without even knowing that he had killed an oppressed Jew on the verge of liberty. There were, indeed, continuous cases of German-clad Ukrainian, Russian, and Asian Wlasow guards — who were supposed to protect the railway tracks from saboteurs — suddenly switching their allegiance to the approaching Russians and joining the guerillas in the surrounding woods.

There was no time for idleness and well-mannered subtleties. I had to get through to my landsman Herr Muhr. I needed his counsel, his advice, and perhaps even his connections to help me survive.

I went to the caboose on a Tuesday morning, one hour earlier than the usual arrival of Herr Muhr. Soon enough, the station master appeared and, noticing me, greeted me as a friend and asked me into his office. We two men "who were not what we appeared to be" looked at each other for a while in complete silence. Both of us were blond Jews with Slavic noses and Aryan features. We could even have passed for father and son, being the same height and having the same light complexion, almond shaped eyes and symmetrical little ears. Herr Muhr was, of course, middle-aged, wore glasses, and smoked a pipe which added a certain paternal, dignified aura to his personality.

"Well, Mister Arendarski," the station master broke the silence. "It must be something of importance which brings you here, at the crack of morning."

I looked at the panel with the built-in semaphore switches, the telegraph paraphernalia with the Morse apparatus and other communication gadgetry, and wrote down on a piece of paper, "Can we talk here freely?" which I handed to Muhr, while officially saying, "I came to ask you, Herr Inspector, to give me an additional man to help carry the new equipment which is very heavy."

"I will see what I can do," Muhr responded, seeming to grasp the hint. "Why don't you come by around five o'clock and we'll walk home together and talk over the whole situation. I am too busy now."

As agreed, we met again after work and this time I received the full attention of my boss who took me along for a home-cooked meal. At the dining table, the conversation was just chit-chat, small-talk about trivial things like the weather conditions and the working performance of my men. But when we left the house and began to walk towards a section of Apostolovo that I had not seen before, we felt free to open up and talk, as the Russians say, "Po dusham," which means sincerely, "straight from the soul."

It was a street unlike any other in the rest of the town. Architecturally, the dwellings were alike, with the same size backyards, front gates, and entrances a few feet above ground level. Yet, in contrast to the other uninhabited dwellings in the rest of Apostolovo, these were not only empty but dilapidated, with their windows torn out of their frames, the doors missing, the front lawns overgrown with weeds.

Before I had time to say a word something unbelievable happened. A sudden evening wind surged through, depositing a prayer book page in Hebrew, right in front of us. I picked it up. It was a leaf from the Selicha part — the supplications said during the days preceding the High Holidays through Yom Kippur, the Day of Atonement.

"Can you read it?" Herr Muhr asked me.

"Yes," I quietly responded.

"So tell me what it says in the original."

"O.K." I agreed, pronouncing the quadrant-shaped letters with ease: "Avi yesoymim aneynu! Dayan almunos aneynu!"

"What does it mean?" my boss persisted.

"It means," I said sadly, "Father of the orphaned, answer me; Judge of the bereaved widows, answer me."

Muhr looked at me in disbelief. "Who are you really?" he whispered in awe and in an excited, vibrating voice.

"I am the Tzosmerer Rebbe's son, your neighbour from Warsaw's Zamenhofa Street number 27."

"My G-d! You are the young boy with the biblical name of Amnon? You are the ear-locked young man who used to play the violin Saturday night and entertain the Chassidim after the "Hamavdil" song in your father's house of worship?"

"Yes," I replied with a sigh.

Muhr suddenly stopped, grabbed me and embraced me as if he had just found a long lost brother. "I knew your father," he said. "He was a charismatic scholar and a great asset to the Chassidic movement. Before I left to study in Germany, I used to come to your place and listen to his intriguing interpretations of the Torah portions of the week. I was very impressed with his profound, psychological understanding of the human mind, and with what he said about the human drive for wealth and fame, and man's subconscious longing for something more than the ephemeral, illusory passion for material and personal success."

"Yes, your father's lengthy sabbatical discourses were a great spiritual experience. He managed to emulate the true spirit of the Baal Shem Tov's teachings in his ability to inspire ordinary people with his feelings of the beauty, sanctity, and real necessity of G-d's laws. You could see that they shared the feeling of purpose and of belonging to a true community. I also remember that your father was very kind to everyone, no matter what he did for a living or how much he knew of the Torah."

"What happened to him?" Muhr asked in a low, sympathetic voice.

"He was deported to Treblinka together with my mother," I said.

"And what happened to your sister? I believe her name was Tamar."

"She was shot by the Gestapo," I replied with a hollow voice.

We reached the end of Kaganovicza Street where most of Apostolovo's Jews had lived.

"Adam," Muhr said, "let's go back to my place. Let's get out of here! I have the feeling that we are treading on tombstones. You see the little grove," he pointed to a hilly field in the distance, "this is the mass grave of all the local Jews — men, women and children. They themselves had to dig the execution pit. And, according to people in the area, the earth still moved three days after the massacre."

"Come on my friend," he energetically pulled my arm. "Enough emotional stir for one time. We could both use a strong and relaxing nightcap and my housekeeper, Genia, knows how to fix one."

I stopped in my tracks with a big question mark on my face as if to ask, how can one trust a housemaid not to eavesdrop. "Truthfully, I might as well tell you," Muhr assured me, "Genia is my kosher wedded wife. In case I get into trouble my helpmate carries a separate identity as a Ukrainian Greek Orthodox lady from Tarnopol. In reality, though, she is the daughter of a well-known prewar cantor of Poland's capital."

"By the way, Adam," he turned to me, "did you know who I was when you walked into my office over a month ago?"

"Absolutely not! With your looks, uniform, bearing, impeccable German, and the warning of the local people that you were a staunch Hitlerite and that I was risking my life in approaching you, I rather thought of you as a rude, brutal Nazi who was going to give me a lot of grief. However, when you did not chew me up, did not severely reprimand me after seeing my doubtful papers, and told me to come back in two hours, I figured that I had a fifty-fifty chance. Yet the moment I heard you speak Russian, and then you handed me my legalization documents along with the extras of food and clothing, and even mentioned Karmelicka Street — something clicked in my brain. I started to search every nook and cranny of my memory. I simply sifted through my mind for everything that I could recollect about Karmelieka Street, the dwellings, the landmarks, the people, the corner vendors, but nothing concrete came out of it."

"I went to bed, fell asleep, and wound up walking in person on both sides of Karmelicka Street, visiting unions, organizations, institutions, stores, restaurants, until I got to the laundry and drycleaners that the Muhrmelsteins had on the corner of Dzielna — and suddenly everything became crystal clear, like a rainbow on a summer day. I knew with certainty who you were. It was a remarkably pleasant surprise which I had to keep to myself, not having the chance to talk to you face to face."

"Did you know that I was Jewish when I first came into the caboose looking for a job and an employment certificate?" I in turn asked my protector and benefactor.

"No! There was nothing in your posture, gait or talk to imply that you belonged to the seed of Abraham, Isaac, and Jacob," the station master said. "The only thing I could see and deduce from your clumsy papers, which were insufficient and looked like forgeries already tampered with, was that for the Nazis you were not kosher. So, to me, you were immediately extremely kosher, and I did my best to accommodate you about which I am very, very happy."

As can well be imagined, I spent a wonderful night with the Muhrmelsteins. Wolf Muhrmelstein, alias Walter Muhr, and Tova Muhrmelstein, alias Genia Shymko, were probably the most colourful and courageous of all the people I had met on my long odyssey to freedom. They listened with patience, sympathy and concern as I told them the story of my escape from Warsaw and my close shaves with the Nazis since that time. After commending me for my endurance and urging me at some future time to tell the true story of Jewish resistance to the Nazi horror and of Jewish infiltration of actual Nazi units, Wolf, alias Walter, reluctantly returned us to the present.

"I don't think that Apostolovo is the proper place for you," he said. "There is too much risk in being here. You went through much too much to gamble away your chances of liberation in a terrain which might soon become an inferno of death and destruction."

Deep inside, I agreed with him wholeheartedly, but after enjoying a five-week period of protected, relatively peaceful life, under the auspices of the station master and forming a deep attachment with him, I was reluctant to give all that up. Yet, I knew that I could not afford to fool myself and avoid planning for the future.

"What do you suggest I should do?" I asked my senior compatriot and benefactor.

Walter Muhr showed that he still remembered the Jerusalem Talmud's maxim by quoting in the original, "Hamatchil bemitzva omrim lo gemor." ("Whoever starts a good deed, to him I say: See that you finish it!") "Since I took you under my wing I would like to complete the job by sending you off to Odessa, which is, in my opinion, a much better place for you to be. With hospital trains going there twice a day on the way back to Germany, you should have no difficulty in sneaking along for the ride. Once you reach Odessa, you will have the address of an underground contact memorized by heart. He is an ex-student of mine, by nationality a Georgian. He lives on Babela Street Number 31 and his name is Vitya-Shynkeradze. Engrave this name and address into your mind and try to become his neighbour. For safety reasons don't divulge your Jewishness. Keep the "Arendarski Adam" cover. I am convinced that you will hit it off together and he will become your most dependable guide and smuggle you over to the Russian lines when the time is ripe."

I knew by now that when Walter Muhr said something, it was not just idle chatter, frivolous prattle, or lip service, but something on which one could depend and stake one's life. By now, I knew the entire biographical history of this remarkable, childless couple, a history which held another astounding surprise for me.

Mr. and Mrs. Muhrmelstein, both graduated in communication engineering at the Heidelberg University in Germany in 1932, where they fell in love and were married. In 1936, they were expelled to Poland, and Warsaw became their temporary home where they opened the laundry and dry cleaning business on Karmelicka Street.

In 1937, they succeeded in obtaining teaching jobs in a Jewish vocational high school in Lwow-Lemberg. With the outbreak of the Second World War, they were in the eastern part of Poland which came under Russian rule.

The Soviets, after discovering that they had engineering diplomas from a German polytechnic, removed them from the high school and mobilized them into the army intelligence units. People with their qualifications and flawless command of the German language were in short supply and too valuable to be left in the classroom.

The Muhrmelsteins were sent off to appropriate academies in Frundze and Kuibyshev, where they received special training and indoctrination. Wolf Muhrmelstein — after going through certain surgical procedures and physical adjustments — became an ethnic German from the Volga region, called Walter Muhr, outfitted with the proper identification papers and back-up registration files to corroborate his fake identity. Tova Muhrmelstein became Genia Shymko, a spinster from western Ukraine, working loyally as a servant for her Volksdeutsche boss and following him wherever his work assignment took him.

When the Hitlerite assault began in 1941, Walter Muhr was already thoroughly acquainted with the nature of his mission in the occupied Nazi territory. As a German-speaking inspector on the Soviet railway, he was considered a "precious find" because of his racial Volga origin and promoted to regional Reichsbahn director of the whole Krivoy-Rog district. His first job was the translation of all professional manuals into the German language, which elated his superiors.

As planned, it took him a while to win the complete and unreserved confidence of the Reichsbahn hierarchy to enable him to start the preliminary activities as information agent for General Kowpak, the chief commander of the Soviet guerrilla forces in the Ukrainian forests. The instructions of the top man in the Directoriat, though, were clearly formulated to them at graduation. "Don't get involved in minor initiatives on your own. Wait patiently until you are contacted by the General's man with the appropriate code."

After the Stalingrad debacle the scenario was ready for the partisans to come into play with their intensified attacks on the retreating, discouraged Nazis. By that time, Inspector Muhr was solidly entrenched in his prestigious capacity as the most trusted, most capable and competent Reichsbahn authority behind the Ukrainian front line in regulating the flood of choking railway traffic, and becoming the irreplaceable wizard of the tracks.

It was then that contact with General Kowpak's headquarters was established and Muhr began to fulfill his operational assignment, transmitting daily cryptic front position reports in Morse code as well as the number and kind of arriving munition trains and their exact destination.

After spending that extraordinary night with Wolf and Tova Muhrmelstein I knew how very privileged I was to have met such valiant and extraordinary freedom fighters, and how lucky I was to be receiving their help. I also knew beyond a shadow of a doubt that this encounter would be the decisive catalyst in the closing phase of my salvation.

CHAPTER 8

From Swastika to Hammer & Sickle

WITH THE help of Walter Muhr's contact in Odessa, exactly fifty-six months after the first Nazi air raid on the Jewish north section of Warsaw transformed it into a blazing gehenna, Amnon Ajzensztadt, alias Adam Arendarski, escaped from Nazi-occupied territory and made it through the front-lines to the advancing Red Army. I had finally made it from Hans Frank's hermetically-sealed General Government, as the Nazis referred to Poland, to the periphery of Odessa on the Black Sea.

A red-haired sergeant and three impatient Red Army conscripts were out on routine patrol when they encountered me and took me back to their lines. I was given a somewhat less than enthusiastic reception. Five meters from where I was ordered to wait, a Roumanian deserter was also awaiting his fate, smiling subserviently. He was in military uniform and wore many flame-coloured ribbons, as if to emphasize his solidarity with the victorious proletarian army.

From nowhere there suddenly appeared an officer, with an obvious dislike for the ex-rulers of Transnistria* and Nazi collaborators in general, who walked calmly over to him, pulled out his gun, and shot him point blank in the forehead. The Antonescu soldier fell wheezing with the last breath of a dying person. But the young lieutenant had not yet satisfied his lust for vengeance, and he stepped furiously with his heavy boots on the rattling face of the expiring man, smashing it to a pulp.

As if enticed by the smell of blood, one of my patrolmen pointed his submachine gun suggestively in my direction, and said heatedly, "Hey, Sarge! What are we going to do with him?"

"Yeah," the second one joined in more bluntly, "Finish him off. He's a liability, keeping us from moving ahead."

"That's right," the third one echoed. "How in the hell are we going to drag ourselves three kilometers back to deliver him to Headquarters?"

---

* Transnistria: A territory including Odessa proper, of about ten thousand square miles of land corresponding to old Podlia. It was located between the Rivers Dniestr and Bug, with an undisclosed frontier.

The tenth of April, 1944. The day I had long prayed for. The Red Army was in full offensive against the retreating, crumbling Nazi hordes. All the suffering, all the dreaming, all the risks in the final sequence of crawling through the mined and booby-trapped Odessan catacombs to reach Rozdielnaya and this moment of salvation! Once again my life was hanging in the balance. I had finally made it to the oasis — only to find it inhabited by cannibals!

"Wait a minute, I beg you!" A flurry of beseeching words came out of my constricted throat, in Russian and Polish. "Tovarischi! Koledzy! — I am not the enemy! I am an ally, a confederate and associate. I am a Polish underground fighter and partisan involved in the very same life and death struggle against the bloody German fascists for your and our freedom. I have extremely important things to tell about life and conspiratorial activities in the occupied territories. Pozhaluysta — Please, take me back to your commanding officer."

The red-haired sergeant kept his eyes riveted on me while I was talking and desperately gesticulating with my hands. Suddenly he barked out a command to his subordinates: "Ladno! O.K., you guys! Go ahead. I'll catch up with you at the city limits command post. I'll take this westerner back to the interrogation division of the NKGB, myself."

The journey back to the field office of the NKGB was an unforgettable experience. As far as the eye could see, there was nothing but the advancing Red Army. The turning point in the war had long since been reached and the Soviet forces were unstoppable in their thirst for retribution. They were like a deluge of enraged ant colonies forging ahead on foot, on horse-drawn two-wheelers, on armoured jeeps, on ordinary wagons and supply trucks, on motorcycles, on Red Cross ambulances, on bicycles, on fuel-carrying heavy military vehicles, and on plain Cossack horses mounted by Marshal Buddionny's cavalry men in their black, wide-shouldered capes, fur-trimmed round caps and slightly curved sabres at their left sides.

A mammoth procession of armed forces and equipment was incessantly moving westward to the accompaniment of zooming red-starred Ilyushin bombers and the background music of reverberating distant echoes of heavy artillery. There were infantry, motorized divisions, engineering and communication brigades, tanks, maxim machine guns, swivel guns, ten pounders, mortars, mine throwers, flame throwers, troop carriers, howitzers, bazookas, searchlights, pontoons, prefabricated bridge sections, short necked anti-air zenith Ak-Aks and stout long-necked, far-reaching 144 millimeter cannons. All guided by units of military field militia with semaphore type flags directing traffic, multitudes of wooden signs and huge, coloured arrows pointing the way to Berlin, displaying the number of actual kilometers yet to be covered in reaching the Third Reich's capital and Hitler's chancellery.

In the midst of this gargantuan armada I was led eastward, past all the red banners and even the limp human bodies hanging from the improvised gallows that dotted the recaptured territory. A single, surviving Chassidic Rebbe's son from Warsaw, I was now a prisoner-of-war. I was about to be introduced to proletarian justice in the Soviet Union.

For nineteen days I was entombed in a solitary cell beneath the ground with no one to talk to or ask a question about the kind of treatment I was receiving.

After the red-haired sergeant delivered me to the field office of the NKGB, they told me to sit down on a bench and wait. And so I waited until past midnight, sized up by every passing NKGB officer who said not a word.

Well past twelve, a lieutenant-colonel with golden epaulets, similar to those in the czarist imperial army appeared with a jailer and told me that since I claimed to be Jewish in a terrain where there were no more Jews, with the last 58,000 of them soaked with gasoline and incinerated to death at the Odessa airfield, and since I admitted possessing a second name besides Arendarski, things had to be investigated.

"In the meantime, this man," he pointed to the guard, "will put you into a secure place where you will be safe."

The secure and safe place was a hole in the ground which had once served as a potato storage depository and had now been rearranged with an earthen slanted roof, concrete stairs, a heavy door with a little round latch for the jailer to look in and the convenience of an elevated 4 by 8 bare piece of plywood, without even a straw mattress as a bed.

Still, when the massive door closed screeching behind me, emitting the click of an outside bolt being locked, I did not protest nor panic. I was sure that the miserable, paltry misunderstanding and ill-treatment would be temporary. Soon they would start talking to me, find out my true identity, and set me free.

My new abode was damp and warm, but had no electricity — just a primitive, old small ink-holder with an oil wick in it spreading shadowy contours in the tiny, shapeless cell. Near the entrance stood a pail of water and a paratrooper's round cannister used for dropping supplies from the air; obviously this was to be my toilet.

Exhausted physically and emotionally, I took off my coat, rolled it into a substitute pillow, and lay down to sleep. "I finally made it," I whispered, devotedly saying the blessing for very special occasions. "Blessed are Thou, Lord our G-d, King of the Universe, who hast granted us life and sustenance and permitted us to reach this season and this moment."

I started to fall asleep, somehow still sedated by the tranquil feeling that I was definitely better off incarcerated behind Soviet bars than masquerading as a "free and pure" Aryan in Gestapo territory.

Quite possibly because I myself was under lock and key and about to be questioned by the NKGB, the thought of the Gestapo triggered an association in my mind. I remembered in vivid detail the sad episode of a close friend who was caught and interrogated by the Gestapo on the sixth floor of the Korolenko Street office in Dniepropietrowsk.

Reuben Fuchs, or as his adopted Christian name was, Richard Lis, was a very special and remarkable man. Tall, broad-shouldered, with green eyes, dark blond hair and bushy moustache, he had the looks of a true Slav of the purest pedigree. But even more important and valuable than his "perfect" looks was his natural, carefree bearing, his good disposition, contagious optimism, incessant humour, and never-say-die attitude in the darkest, most threatening moments and situations.

Always polite, considerate, willing to help with word and deed, he was a beloved member of the Dniepropietrowsk Underground Marrano colony and one of its most energetic leaders. Everybody looked up to him and respected him for his wit, cheerfulness and daring, tempered though with reason, logic and profound understanding of reality.

He was the unofficial father figure of the whole bunch of Kashtans, that derogatory name applied to Jews on Aryan papers, and the only married man who managed to save his lovely wife, Clara, and bring her along to stick it out in the faraway Dniepr River city almost two thousand kilometers away from their hometown of Tarnopol, near Lwow, Lemberg.

Richard was also a man of moral principles and character, an ethical person who would never infringe upon the rights of others, but neither would he ever allow anyone to take undue advantage of him.

He was the senior Jewish-Aryan who originated the idea of a *quid pro quo* policy against the blackmailers consisting of retaliation against the informer each time a Jew was denounced. He also was an ardent believer in strict concealment, in keeping a low profile, and in avoiding frequent get-togethers, knowing that two is company and three is a crowd. He strongly advocated separate quarters for each Marrano and urged them all to avoid group living and the unwelcome attention of their neighbours. As a matter of practising what he was preaching, he and his spouse lived at two different addresses, for security reasons.

The whole colony was thus startled and in shock when they found out about his arrest by a Ukrainian gendarme. He was transferred to the Gestapo headquarters.

Fear came upon subterranean Jewish Dniepropietrowsk. Panic and confusion set in among all the members of the illegal community, because nobody knew what information they would discover on him, what they had already extracted from him, and what they would still be able to squeeze out of him with their diabolical "truth-serum" injections and their other inquisitorial torture methods.

Almost overnight, everyone deserted their permanent dwelling place, looking for one-night shelter among his Russian friends and acquaintances. They used different, improvised excuses. And then, early in the morning they hastily took to the streets, bazaars, or remote city parks and inconspicuous cemeteries, playing the role of bereaved people visiting their dear ones' graves. Many left town altogether, taking a chance without proper documentation and marching papers, fearing the worst.

However, true to his convictions, and determined not to cause harm to his wife and friends whom he loved dearly and for whose safety he felt responsible, he decided that the only solution under the circumstances was to make it thoroughly and totally impossible for his captors to extract any information from him. That, of course, meant the ultimate price of self-destruction for the sake of others — which he was unequivocally and resolutely willing to pay.

As they led him battered, bloodied and handcuffed from one of the interrogation sessions through the corridor of the infamous sixth floor where the torture chambers were located, he suddenly made a run to the large windowpane, hurled his 220-pound body through the glass, and fell to his death in unsung martyrdom as an uncrowned, unofficial, but intrepid leader of a small modern-day Marrano community, who chose suicide so that others might live.

"Get up, you sleeping beauty!" The guard was banging with the bottom end of his flashlight on the cell door, and then directing a beam of light straight into my face.

"You! Get ready for breakfast!"

The door opened with a creak, and I was handed a can filled with a steaming liquid.

"Enjoy your kipiatok (boiling hot water)," the guard grumbled, bolting the squeaking door behind him.

I took the can back with me to the wooden cot, looked at it in the dim light of the little oil-wick lamplet, then I put it down on the floor near the pail of water.

Though I had not had anything to eat or drink for the previous 24 hours, I did not feel hungry or thirsty.

I was still too busy with my psychological transition from "brown" to "red"; from a vast devastated planet where the Jews were absolutely eradicated to a world where there were still millions of Jews in towns and cities, in factories and offices, in the armed forces and in all the cultural, scientific, administrative and legislative institutions of the U.S.S.R. The U.S.S.R. was, relatively speaking, a Garden of Eden where there were still Jewish generals, Jewish scholars and professors, Jewish doctors and artists and writers, where there was still an Ilya Ehrenburg and a Jewish anti-fascist committee in Moscow, and even a Yiddish daily paper entitled *Emes* (Truth), read by thousands and thousands. What would life under the Soviets really be like?

I went back to my wooden bunk and resumed my day dreaming. I saw myself again in pre-war Warsaw on a Sabbath afternoon, walking briskly towards the prestigious downtown area — driven by the compulsion of a determined young man who resolutely knows where he is going and why. I was not taking the risk of walking to the non-Jewish sector of Warsaw just for the exercise. I was making a pilgrimage to a prominent side street near the majestic Aleje Jerozolinskie, Warsaw's Champs d'Elysée, where the bour-geois-looking edifice of the Soviet Embassy was adorned with the Red Flag, fluttering freely on the massive balcony, beckoning conspicuously liberty, equality and fraternity; promulgating openly: righteousness and justice and deliverance for all.

Anti-semitism was rife, from the bigoted snobbery of Marshall Ridz Smigly and the sanctimonious hate-mongering of Premier Skladkowski down to the man in the street. Anti-Jewish slogans were everywhere, mass parades against the Jews were commonplace, as were assaults on individual Jews.

And, although my heart and soul were affiliated to Jabotinsky and Hebrew statehood with an everlasting yearning and bond of eternal faithfulness; although my song of songs was Naftali Imber's "Hatikvah" and Yehuda Halevi's poetic oath never ever to forget the land of Israel, I stood spellbound at the Communist legation, muttering the lyrics of the Internationale, the hymn of all the oppressed, all the underdogs, all the salvation-anticipators.

It was an anticlimax. A rebbe's son, deeply religious and militantly nationalistic myself, holding the position of general secretary of Brith Hachashmonaim (a national-religious youth organization dedicated to the idea of armed struggle for the liberation of what was then Palestine, from the British) and actively involved as an official in the illegal immigration depart-ment of the New Zionist Organization (N.Z.O.),* I stood across from the Kremlin's outpost, infatuated by a G-dless redeemer, a red messiah who would, perhaps, one day redress all injustices, heal all rifts, and usher in a new kind of society.

Those visionary images were clashing with the eyewitness accounts of returnees to the German zone, who told of innumerable Polish communists to whom not only was the Red Carpet Treatment not extended, but who were, instead, dealt with contemptuously and sent to Siberia; of refugees arrested merely for saying something ambivalent which could be interpreted as criti-

---

* N.Z.O.: The New Zionist Organization founded in the second half of the thirties by Vladimir Jabotinsky, disenchanted with the sluggish and servile policies of the official Zionist establishment and devoted to a non-conventional rescue programme and evacuation of European Jewry to Pal-estine.

cism of the regime — being arbitrarily banished to remote districts of the Urals and Asia, forced to hard labour at mines and Kolkhoz farms.

I returned to the present and the memory of what I had just seen while being brought to my present place of confinement. I was perplexed and even alarmed by acts of brutality that I had witnessed on the way and by a speech given by a Soviet general in red-striped riding breeches. His speech was in complete discord with the image of the Red Army as a populist, emancipating force.

Halfway to the staff headquarters, off the highway, in a glade, a red-army battalion was assembled in a semi-circular formation, listening to the apparent pep-talk of their brigadier before being shipped off to the battlefield for combat.

The red-haired sergeant had stopped for a rest, and we all listened to the senior officer's pep talk.

He did not talk at all about such things as the human condition, the suffering of mankind, and the martyrdom of all the tormented victims of fascism and racism.

"Listen!" He told them, "You sons of bitches! You unfortunate side effects of five-seconds' pleasure! You poor bastards and fraudulent show-offs! This is the Red Army; the fighting force of peasants and workers; the strong arm of the Proletariat . . . I am not going to give you any intellectual bullshit about the sacredness of the fatherland; the nobility of heroism and the socialist future of humanity. I don't want to educate you into well-behaved intelligentsia. I don't want to turn you into delicate idealists feeling the pains and aches of the world. I don't need soft humanists. I need cut-throats without scruples; killers, murderers, destroyers, rapists. I am not looking for divine sparks in you. I don't want to promote your better nature. I want to incite and stir up your lowest instincts; the very animal in you which will go out with you to the frontlines and make you into vicious cannibals; throwing yourselves on the fascist imperialists and tearing them to pieces. Smashing them to bits! I am not going to use lofty words or promises or reward of eternal fame and inscribed names in the pantheon of charity and gentleness. But for one thing I can give you my word of honour: whoever will help me capture the next city and remain alive all the women and the whisky will be at your disposal for three whole days and three whole nights!"

"Hey, you, westerner! Get ready to pick up your bread!" Although the guard spoke rudely, at least someone from the outside world was speaking to me. The squeaking door opened to a 45 degree angle, and a two and a half by four inch lump of a dark, sticky mass was put into my hand. This was the most important item of the entire daily ration. Nothing else would be forthcoming until six o'clock in the evening when a litre of Balanda (prison jargon for soup), would be ladled out again to complete the day's ration of food.

I took out my handkerchief, rolled it around the brown, soapy slice of bread, and hid it in one of my coat pockets. I did this completely without thinking as for the next two days I still did not touch any food.

In seventeen days time I would be twenty-five years old. I knew that I had no real cause for complaint about my condition. After all, my time had been up two years previously, in 1942, when the mass deportations and exterminations had started. Two years later I was not only alive but relatively well besides. So what if I was not living in an elegant apartment with a panoramic view and a four-piece bathroom? So what if I was buried alive in a vermin-infested cell below the ground? As Colonel Niekrasow had affirmed while ordering me to be incarcerated, I was indeed secure and undisturbed. Despite all the odds against me, I had managed to evade Umschlag-Platz dragnets, ghetto walls, identification lines, border posts, Gestapo traps, and front-line positions to make it to freedom. Would I, the only survivor of a whole family, really be better off as a soldier in some Polish battalion participating in active combat against Hitler's hordes? Would I honestly rather be lying in a dugout, shooting and being shot at with real live ammunition, exploding grenades, blasting cannon shells, and detonating mortar shrapnel which kill and maim indiscriminately thousands of young people every day and ever hour?

For the first time in years I was able to engage in some peaceful thinking to myself. For the first time in years I did not sleep with a loaded revolver under my pillow. Nor did I have to wake at the slightest sound of something out of the ordinary. "G-d does everything for the best."

I spent several days sifting through bygone episodes of Israel's history. I thought of Rabbi Simon Bar Yochai, the luminous creator of the Zohar and his son Eliezer, who were forced to hide for thirteen years in a cavern to escape Roman persecution. I thought of the amazing life story of Joseph, who was thrown into a pit, sold into slavery, put in jail under false accusations by an immoral woman who, in a trumped-up libel, blamed him for indecently assaulting her.

They and others maintained their inexhaustible faith in G-d almighty, made it back not only to freedom and the regaining of their civil rights, but also achieved the highest ranks of royalty, personal righteousness, eternal fame, and holy authorship which enshrines them as beloved, exemplary, and legendary pillars of Judaism's spirit in the annals of the everlasting book of chronicles of the people of Israel.

I concluded that the supremacy of mind over body was crucial to my survival. I had to dwell on the spiritual aspect of my existence, and call on Chassidic pragmatism, faith and prayer in order to weather the low points of despair and doubt. Using my imagination, I started to pen allegorical verses in the manner of La Fontaine* on the smudged and earthen cell walls, which I converted into huge billboards for the occasion. Into the verses I poured my frustrations and hopes.

On the sixteenth day of my confinement, I was attacked by an onslaught of acute claustrophobia, which I tried to combat with psalm therapy, singing liturgical music, hallelujah hymns, and Hava-nagila songs — but not too successfully. The shadowy, dirty walls were closing in on me, like nightmarish spiders slowly crawling, nearer and nearer to their victim. I was convulsively trying to get out of the intricate sticky web before the blow of fortune came down.

Days seventeen, eighteen, nineteen — laryngitis germs apparently got through to my throat, inflaming it with hoarseness and severe discomfort in swallowing and talking. I soon noticed a darkish substance — probably some bloody discharge of an irritated tonsil or mucus membrane.

"My G-d," I thought to myself uneasily, "I am sitting here completely cut off from everyone and everything, like some unknown dog in the city pound." Is this what it had all come to, being buried alive by the Soviets? What if I were to get a fever, or to come down with typhus, pneumonia, or diarrhea? What if the blood that I had coughed up was from my lungs?

I began to experience a peculiar, painful pressure in the upper part of my head, like a volcano that was about to erupt. I felt awful, lacking oxygen to breathe, and utterly depressed in my predicament. I suddenly realised that if I continued to behave like an uncomplaining model prisoner I would simply die unnoticed.

With a heart-rending shriek of despair, I started to rap and kick at the door, screaming through the round judas-hole at the top of my congested lungs — recklessly, impulsively, without regard for the consequences. "I didn't go through all the Nazi-gehennas and torture, all the fascist hell and high water to die like a derelict non-person in an airless cellar! I didn't come through all the suffering and pain, all the dangers and perils, all the insults, hazards, and disdain just to die like a rodent in an unmarked pit. I came to Soviet Russia, to the land of the proletariat to live! To save myself from Hitler's murderous killings which annihilated my whole family and my people! I demand to be seen by a doctor! Daytie mnye Wracha!"

---

* La Fontaine, Jean de (1621-1695): French poet of the seventeenth century, whose works are considered to be masterpieces of his people's literature.

I kept up my uproarious one-man storm on the metal door, bombarding it with all my might, while lamenting incessantly. "This is the land of supreme justice and equity! This is the land of workers and peasants and other good people. Surely you cannot permit a refugee from the Warsaw Ghetto to expire without medical attention?"

"Help! Spassaayttye! Ratevet! I don't want to die a senseless death in anonymity, in solitary confinement like a thief and criminal!"

The guard came running down, cursing loudly. "What's all the commotion? Have you gone berserk? What kind of behaviour is this? You better shut up and lie down quietly before we plug up your disrespectful yapping mouth with rags!"

Nevertheless, the next morning after breakfast a doctor in the uniform of a high ranking railway official appeared with his satchel, stethoscope, and complete examination paraphernalia. Even before I saw him I felt intuitively that the doctor would be Jewish. When I was called out to the little corridor, I took my first look at him in the daylight streaming in from the unbolted, wide-open upper entrance, and I knew instantly that my premonition was correct.

The doctor was a man in his mid-thirties with a finely carved, delicate profile, dark hair, and velvety-sad eyes which told of lost relatives and dear ones, massacred in places like Babi-Yar and Transnistria. I knew instinctively that I had to speak to him in Yiddish and Hebrew. "Shema Yisrael," I intoned the Jewish credo, spoken only when seriously praying, or when facing supreme crisis and possible imminent death.

The doctor turned his head with a dumbfounded expression on his face, as if he had just seen a ghost. "I am not allowed to talk to you," he whispered softly.

But a torrent of fiery speech was already pouring forth from my lips. In a voice charged with excitement, the sentences came out with the heat and intensity of piercing bullets. It was a blizzard of desperate, chaotic words. I had to convey my whole life story in seconds.

"You have got to help me! I am an innocent ghetto survivor! I am suffocating in this terrible subterranean cage! I am bleeding and hurting all over! I will die here if you don't take me out of this miserable hole! Have pity on a lonely escapee from the Warsaw Ghetto! Rakhmones! Pomilujtye! I can take no more! Bauh maim ad nofesh, for the waters are come in even unto the soul!"

The doctor continued the check-up in silence. He looked into my throat, felt my neck glands, listened to my heart and lungs, took my pulse, and measured my temperature, without uttering a word.

But his eyes — the mirrors of the soul — betrayed his inner agitation, reflected in two continuous streams of tears dripping down from his cheeks to his navy blue jacket, forming large wet spots on his bemedalled chest.

The two descendants of the House of Jacob brought into contemporary focus a flashback to the story of Joseph's concealed identity as governor of Egypt. Only in this case, two brothers from Warsaw and Odessa, a Polish Jew and a Russian Jew, met and recognized each other not in the glorious surroundings of royal palaces, but in a smelly, gloomy subterranean NKGB prison cell.

"Arendarski, Adam, alias Amnon Ajzensztadt," wrote the doctor in his report (as I later found out) "suffers fromn reactivated secondary tuberculosis, and should be transferred into an above-ground cell where there is sufficient air circulation."

On my twenty-first day under Soviet authority I was elevated from subterranean anonymity to the full-feldged status of a regular prisoner in the interrogation network of the National Commisariat for State Security.

ENDURANCE: CHRONICLES OF JEWISH RESISTANCE

THE HUMAN CONDITION

The english translation of Rabbi Alexander Zisze Ajzensztadt's
(the Tzosmerer Rebbe) Torah discourse, dictated to his son--
the author of "Endurance"--while hiding in a bunker during a
Nazi pogrom in April 1942 in the ghetto of Ostrowiec.

The rush and the noise of our present daily life is great. Never
was human existence so hurreid as during our era. Never was human
ambition to acquire "the good things in life" so strong as during our
epoch.

Every one of us can, in his own circle of friends, notice
individuals of various mentalities and characteristics, who are chasing
and running, often even sacrificing their health, risking their lives,
in order to attain their ambition.

As if chased by the secret power of some mysterious stimulant,
most people strive for all sorts of aims which tempt their imagination.

Moved by a hidden driving force, these people are instinctively
and forcefully drawn like a bee to honey or a firefly to flame, in
order to satisfy their longing for fortune and wealth, honour and
popularity.

The question arises, therefore: Why?

What is, after all, the root, the basic factor, which causes in
all these people the undaunted will, the unwavering patience, the
tremendous initiative to attain their limitless wants?

Is it a factor which exists within the desired aims themselves?
Do these desires themselves contain some magnetic power, some potency
which is capable of overwhelming the chosen one of creation and propel
him forcibly towards itself?

Or is it an internal subjective tendency, which is hidden
within the being of man proper?

When you observe life and analyze the psychology of the never
ending. unsatiated desire for these objectives; when you try to
penetrate the psyche of despair, of disappointment, and the results in
suicide which take place more often among the supposedly "fortunate"
and "rich" than among the so-called "poor" and "destitute," you draw the
conclusion that the entire sound and fury, the whole searching, striving
and reaching for one's goals is not something which is created by external
experiences, but which comes solely from within. It lies within the
very being of man himself.

Let us, however, try to understand that creation is, according to
mysticism and metaphysics, a radiation of godliness that is--no more and
no less--something which was at its origin and in its genesis pure
spirit in the infinity, in the endlessness. At a certain moment, during
the creation of the universe, it was converted by the creator into
actual and tangible physical entities.

AMNON AJZENSZTADT

In the Kabalah it is expressed in a picturesque phrase [Benhadin Kamtza dilvusheh minaieh] concerning a snail whose garment is an organic part of his being.

And in philosophy the term is: "emanation."

Man, being the most intellectual, most sensitive and most imaginative creature of this creation, feels, therefore, subconsciously and intuitively like some lost soul, who actually was privileged to be of a godly sovereign descent, and thus had once the good fortune to find himself to be of a godly, majestic origin, thanks to which he could enjoy all the possible pleasures of the world in a condensed form.

The chosen of creation is therefore confused and desperate. He wishes to recapture for himself the most satisfying source of happiness in the previous "royal court" when he was still under the wing of the shekinah, or divine presence, and in blissful heavenly serenity.

However, he becomes, alas, lost in his hasty and erroneous, groping and scurrying. With a blurred consciousness and earthly materialistic conception, he grasps at every shimmering, shining, sparkling immitation object. He is like a thirsty desert-wanderer who falls upon an oasis of salt-water, which not only will never satisfy his thirst, but, will also increase his thirst many times and make it unbearable. It is only an exercise in futility.

The truly happy person, however, is he who raises himself above the low, merely earthly concepts, to the highest comprehension, to a clear and bright world-outlook and sees unmistakeably the necessary genuine attraction.

That comes, however, only when he can distinguish and see that the tempting illusions are, in the final analysis, no more than a fata-morgana, a mirage for shortsighted human earthlings.

Human lust does not originate from external sensible, observable sources, but is born from the inner spiritual longing for the secret and godly genesis-sources, which became concretized in the eyes of mortal homo sapiens as material and enthralling objects of his lust.

Fortunate is he who understands how to counteract these misleading illusions and blurrings of a banal, shallow world-conception, as we are cautioned to do by the first Chassidic declarations.

Endowed is the man who has open ears and is privileged to hear the echo of the heavenly call: "It is I who am the proprietor and illuminator of the world-mansion."

Then his eyes are opened and he sees how the entire material creation of minerals, plants, and all that lives seeks for the wings of the divine presence and strives to reach their original creator; continuously imploring for his mercy, so that he should again accept them into his godly arms--as of old--before the creation of the universe.

That is the height from which man must see the world. Those are the desires which should have been the final goal of our nervous, confused and rushing generation.

Only a return to the source of genuine happiness, to godliness in Jewish faith can revive and save the whole world, which is in great danger, and which longs unconsciously for the time when, as Isaiah said, "They shall beat their swords into ploughshares, and their spears into pruning forks."

Only a return to the principles of Judaism, to all the Torah values, can cure a world that had been blinded by materiralism, where one must have a more beautiful car than that of his neighbour, a better and swifter flying airplane, and a more deadly bomb.

That is the choice: to discern and select the true essence of life, and to extract it from its materialistic shell.

This is the way to recovery for an ailing humanity, the only road leading to recuperation for a morally-diseased mankind bent on homicidal and suicidal self-destruction.

Symbolic Memorial Stone commemorating the Jewish victims of the Nazis in Tzosmer (Sandomierz). Erected by the Tzosmerer Society in Toronto at the Roselawn Cemetery on Bathurst Street.

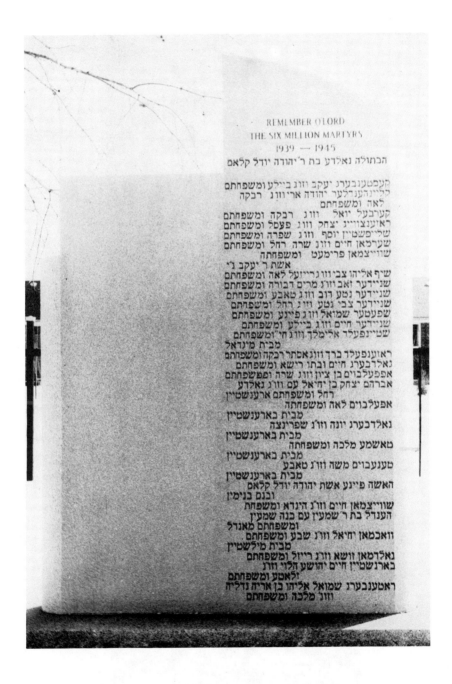

Rabbi Alexander Zisze Ajzensztadt, known as the Tzosmerer Rebbe, the author's father; deported from Ostrowiec to Treblinka in January, 1943.

Tamar Ajzensztadt, the author's sister, murdered by the Gestapo in 1942.

Amnon Ajzensztadt at the age of twelve, in his father's house of worship at Zanenhofa Street in Warsaw.

The Synagogue in Sandomierz, built in the twelfth century.

The Monument in the Jewish Cemetery of Sandomierz, assembled out of the pre-war tombstones to the memory of the annihilated community.

The author's finger printed yellow "Kenn-Karte" (Jewish Identification Card) of the Ostrowiec ghetto in April 1942.

Amnon Ajzensztadt with his "Aryan" mustache as Adam Arendarski at the end of 1942.

The National Religious Mizrachi Organization in Ostrowiec on a "Bon Voyage" party for their member, Moshe Morgenlender, who left for Palestine before the German occupation.

The marketplace in Ostrowiec.

Jewish youth of Ostrowiec. Among them are Pesele Grosman (nee Sztainbaum), Schlomo Rubinstein and Moshe Mayerczyk who survived the holocaust.

The Ostrowiecer Tzadik, Reb Mair Yechiel Halshtok (left) who, together with the author's father (right), the Tzosmerer Rebbe Reb Zisze conducted a "Shalosh-Seudoth" (third meal eaten on the termination of the sabbath) in 1930.

Rare specimen of Lodzer ghetto money; a 5 mark bill signed by Chaim Rumkowski, the Judenrat (Jewish Council) President, 1940. (Courtesy of Mr. I. Widawski, Tel Aviv)

One of Eastern Europe's great Cantors — Mr. Abraham Barkin — grandfather of Toronto lawyer Akiva Barkin — passed away in 1939 at the age of 57.

Reb Moshe Levi from Tzosmer — the author's tutor in music, mathematics and Chassidoth — deported from the Lodzer ghetto to Auschwitz in 1944 together with his wife Necha Levi (nee Nozic) who originated from Stopnice.

Marysia Ajzensztadt, a beloved young vocalist called the "Nightingale of
the Warsaw Ghetto" — daughter of the famous Choirmaster of the
Tlomackie Synagogue — murdered by the S.S. during the deportations
of 1943.

The heroic partisan of the Ostrowiec ghetto, Shlomo Zwaigman.

The Standard Bearers of the Revisionist Paramilitary Youth Organization, Brith Hachashmonaim in Warsaw. Reuven Dorn, Baruch Wagenstein and Nachman Klinger. All 3 died fighting the Nazis in the Ghetto Uprising.

Ostrowiec's ghetto orchestra in 1940-41 with its members wearing the "Juden-Bands" on their arms.

Jewish journalists and leaders of the Toronto Jewish community meet the former Commander of the Irgun and Herut Opposition leader, Menachem Begin.

Friends of the author from the Warsaw Brit Hachashmonaim. Centre, Mordechai Miodownik. All of them joined the Jewish Brigade in Italy.

Co-worker Moshe Poznerson from the Lodz Brit Hachashmonaim, resides at present in Ramat Pinkas near Or Yehuda-Israel.

Mr. Moshe Segal, Commander of Brit Hachashmonaim during the British occupation in Palestine.

Vladimir Jabotinsky, the President of the New Zionist Organization, who the author was privileged to work with in his Warsaw office, foretold the catastrophe of European Jewry. He tried desperately to organize a last-minute illegal rescue and immigration to Palestine and founded the national Jewish military organization of the Irgun Tzevai Leumi.

The author standing next to Menachem Begin, the Commander of the Irgun.

Musical compositions of the Tzosmerer Rebbe — Rabbi Alexander Zisze Ajzensztadt — taken from the manuscripts hidden at Sienienska 54 in Ostrowiec. Top: "Save Us O Lord" (Rativeh Unz, Got); Below: "Remember Us for Life" (Zochraynu Lechayim) and "We Pray Thee O Lord" (Ono Adonoy).

VEHOYO BAYOM HAHU

ITZU EITZU VESUFOR

More of the hidden liturgical compositions by Rabbi A.Z. Ajzensztadt.
Top: "Vehoyo Bayom Hahu"; Below: "Itzu Eitzu Vesufor."

Kad Ayil Shabatoh — Aramaic mystical Friday night prayer in Rabbi
A.Z. Ajzensztadt's musical interpretation.

AMNON AJZENSZTADT

PARTISANER LID

Partisan song composed by Amnon Ajzensztadt.

Burial of Tzosmerer Youth, Resistance Members and Ghetto dwellers murdered outside the city limits.

Honouring the fallen heroes of the Warsaw Ghetto Uprising.

The symbolic sewer-cover through which the last ghetto fighters escaped into the Aryan side of Warsaw.

A facsimile of Rabbi A.Z. Ajzensztadt's poem, "Answer Me O Lord" (Aneni Elokai) written in a bunker during the deportations in Ostrowiec, October 1942.

Chamele Glass (on far left of photograph), a Jewish policeman in Tzosmer (Sandomierz), rescued the author during the initial dragnet of deportations in the town. He allowed him to escape despite a Nazi policeman's order to take the author to the assembly point for a labour camp.

The author's relative, Luba Mala (third from left), from Tzosmer (Sandomierz) escaped in 1944 from an S.S. labour camp in Pionki. She returned home to her agrarian estate only to be murdered with blunt instruments by her neighbours.

Nazis, in implementing their program of Jewish eradication as propagated by Rosenberg's theory, were motivated by words — "We will never give up our struggle until the last Jew in Europe is rooted out and is truly dead."

Jewish paratroopers from Palestine were parachuted behind Nazi lines to help the resistance and the Jews of Eastern Europe.

In 1939, the author (on far left of photograph) led a course of instruction in Falenica, near Warsaw, on self defence for Brit Hachashmonaim.

The military prison of Warsaw on Zamenhofa Street # 21, was located a few buildings away from the author's residence. It became the main battleground during the Warsaw Ghetto Uprising.

The entrance to the famous Krasinski Park on Nalewki Street, located in the heart of Warsaw's Jewish district.

The hill in Krasinski Park called "Moshe Rabbenu Hill" was a popular site where neighbourhood Jews spent their leisure time.

משרד ראש הממשלה
PRIME MINISTER'S OFFICE

GOVERNMENT PRESS OFFICE   לשכת העתונות הממשלתית

Tel Aviv , 9.8.66
Mr.Amnon Aizenstadt,
רחוב פינסקר 68
תל-אביב

Dear Mr.Aizenstadt,

Your visit to an army unit has been arranged for

Monday,August 15.

Please, be at my office at 13.15 hours(1.15 p.m.),on

that day. An army officer will be waiting to escort

you on your visit.

Best wishes

A.Fyetan

The author, in 1966, as a member of the editorial staff of The Daily
Hebrew Journal in Toronto visiting the Israel Defence Forces training
camp in Sarafand.

The author's pre-war "Brith Hachashmonaim" comrades — whose illegal immigration to the shores of Palestine he arranged — reciprocated with a festive welcome on his first arrival to the state of Israel. Among the Participants were Mordechai Miodownik, Yehuda Patron, Yakov König, Moshe Poznerson, Aryeh Polosecki, and Menachem Engel and Eliyahu Laneil of blessed memory.

Aryeh Rozenson Z.L. with his wife, Sarah, underground members in the fight for a free Israel, arranged a hiding place for their "Lechi" Commander, the Honourable Itzhak Shamir, in the suburbs of Tel Aviv.

Author's cousin (second from left) — Musicologist, Rabbi and Cantor, Areh Leib Ajzensztadt of blessed memory managed to escape from Nazi-occupied Poland to the Soviet Russian side.

Active as educator in different American and Canadian Jewish communities, he passed away in May 1979 and was interred in the Mount of Olives Cemetery in Jerusalem.

Mendel Beilis in the company of his family after his release from 2 years of imprisonment. He was falsely accused by anti-semitic conspirators of committing a ritual murder.

CHAPTER 9

Life as an Inmate

THE NEW chamber, located on the main floor of the NKGB complex, was certainly a considerable improvement over the subterranean potato pit. A constant breeze brought fragrant smells and scents from the surrounding fields and orchards. Not only were there living, moving people to be seen through the barred windows, but there were also cellmates to talk to, play cards with, and even to roll and light up an aromatic Makhorka cigarette.

The most appreciated aspect of my new quarters was a surprise, a trip to the lice-killing station, located about a kilometer away from the main NKGB compound. Once every four weeks approximately forty prisoners from all the main floor cells were lined up in rows of four, and sternly warned that any suspicious stepping out of line would be considered an attempt to escape and would be rewarded with a bullet in the head. The prisoners were then marched off to the public cleansing institution. Luckily for me the day after my transfer was bathing day. Three weeks of darkness were assuaged by a walk through sunlit, local streets to inquisitive and compassionate gazes from the curious passersby.

What a pleasure it was to be caressed by a stream of hot water! There was no soap, but some sort of abrasive, suds-producing powder in a tin box was placed on the benches; it was utilized instead of soap or shampoo. The clothes and under-wear were handed to a special professional crew which put them into a huge vat, where they were heat-cleaned and disinfected in steam, leaving yellowish spots in the returned garments, as if overbaked. But they were absolutely free of vermin for the next twenty-four hours.

Within days my laryngitis was gone, as were the dark substances in my phlegm. The mental horrors of having to talk to myself all the time were also over. I now had four fellow inmates to talk to on all kinds of topics from battlefield stories to Nazi atrocities, Kolkhoz life, culture and theatre, and the miseries of convict life in Siberia.

Before long, however, a far less enjoyable kind of conversation began. Colonel Nyekrasow began to call me after midnight for nocturnal "chats," to be written down word-for-word in a special investigation file.

"This is your case history, your dossier, and ticket to the future," he said jovially, pointing to the cardboard portfolio on his desk, talking amiably like a social worker and not like a uniformed NKGB interrogator.

Nonetheless, at dawn, when I was led back to my chamber after hours of exhausting "chat" with Nyekrasow, I knew that despite his pretense of friendliness, the Colonel was weaving something evil against me. I had also noticed something very familiar on the Colonel's outstretched hand — my own expensive, brick-shaped Omega watch. I had been formally relieved of it when I was booked, together with my leather belt, shoe laces, pocket knife, pen, and money. This was before being ushered into my first, subterranean cell. I felt as if my possessions were being inherited while I still lived.

Colonel Nyekrasow's smooth talk and politeness were neither genuine nor sincere. Like the nineteen days of "secure and safe" solitary confinement, they were just a camouflage for bad intentions. As the days passed, however, my mental worries about Nyekrasow were eclipsed by a new and painful affliction: hunger.

While in subterranean solitary confinement I had experienced neither hunger nor thirst, but now that I was in a roomy, airy cell on the ground floor I felt incredible pangs of hunger all the time. I even tried to skip lunch a few times in order to make my daily portion of bread stretch to the evening, when I could eat it with the watery concoction that was called soup. The trouble was that I then had to subsist on absolutely nothing but water for the next twenty-four hours, and that was almost unbearable.

It was clearly an established NKGB policy to slowly starve the prisoners. Along with prolonged solitude this was intended to break the prisoners' spirits. The Nazis had done the same thing to the Jews in the Ghettos, so much so, in fact, that some Ghetto-dwellers, weary from continued hunger, caved in to the Gestapo offer of receiving a whole loaf of bread and a pound of margarine for volunteering to go on a transport to "The East," a euphemism for the slave labour camps and gas ovens.

What I needed was the near-miracle of finding someone within the very walls of the NKGB prison who would take an interest in me to the point of getting involved, spending money, doing shopping for me, or maybe just sending me a one-time gift in a food parcel. I was sure that it was simply wishful thinking to expect anything like that but, miraculously enough, through the mysterious ways of the Lord, that is exactly what happened.

It all started on a summery Monday morning, when a swivel chair and a little table were placed in the very centre of the prison courtyard. A woman clad in white walked over and from a paper bag fished out clippers, scissors, a brush and a straight razor. She placed everything on the improvised stand. It was obviously time for the customary hair-cutting service, periodically made available to prisoners. Only one style was offered, the shaved head look.

Glued to the window, I kept my eyes focussed on the whole monotony-breaking procedure. A guard opened the last chamber on the end of the main floor cell wing, took out a prisoner, led him over to the swivel chair, told him to sit down and entrusted him to a second guard standing next to the lady barber. The hair-cutting and shaving process, also using clippers, lasted about eight to ten minutes. A new prisoner was then brought over and the man was escorted back to his cell.

The lady barber was positioned with her back to my vantage point, so I could see only the movements of her arms and legs, not her face. But when she abruptly turned around to light up a cigarette, her full countenance became visible, and it was the visage of a Jewish woman in her forties, with an aquiline nose, high cheek bones, hazel eyes, and curly hair. I felt a surge of adrenalin and the beat of my heart quickening.

"She is my only chance," I muttered feverishly to myself.

I have at least a couple of hours until my turn comes up — and I have got to let her know my predicament and ask for her help! But how can you convey a plea when you are not allowed to talk? When you haven't even got a pen or notebook to write a message and you are forbidden to have contact with anyone — period! So I have to use some other form of communication, I told myself.

But what sort of communication could it be? The sentry would be watching everything with suspicion. "Telepathic impulses!" I chided myself with a bitter smile.

Vexed, I put my hand on the barred window sill, as if instinctively trying to remove it and free myself from the whole nightmare. I touched something metallic and movable, a little triangle-fastener which a glazier must have left while putting in the window pane.

I wiped it off, looking at it intensely. Its pointed sharp edge gave me an idea. From my cap I peeled off a piece of brown paper. Next, I made an incision in my forearm with the newly found tin fastener. Then, breaking off a sliver from the wooden cot plank, I dipped it in blood, and wrote in a calligraphic Yiddish, with small red letters: "Dear Lady! I am a fellow Jew, 25 years old, an escapee from the Warsaw Ghetto who by some miracle or act of G-d managed to make it to the Soviet lines. I am utterly alone. My parents and my whole family were murdered by the Nazis in Poland. They are keeping me here to check my identity which will surely end in my release and freedom. But in the meantime, I am suffering greatly from lack of food and need your help badly! Please! I beg you! Do whatever you can to alleviate my terrible, terrible hunger. Your brother in distress. Adam from cell #3."

"Hey you, Zapadnik! Let's go! Your hair mop needs attention and grooming. You're beginning to look like a hermit." I was led to the swivel-chair. As I sat down and looked at the lady barber, our eyes met. She must have wondered about me in my strange, western European fancy shirt, crumpled neck-tie, and casual wool suit, so different from all the other inmates in their Rubashka clothes. I knew instinctively and deeply that she saw in me a fellow Jew. There was something in the way our eyes met that convinced me to make the effort at passing my note to her.

The clipper started to cut into my blond hair. I felt the matriarchal, tender fingers of a "Yiddishe mama" and it reminded me of my own mother's personal touch who was almost of the same age when she put her arms around me to say farewell before my departure from the Ostrowtzer ghetto.

Instinctively, I clutched my petition, written in blood, determined to deliver it to the lady barber despite all risks. The sentry, however, was also very interested in the "showy" looks of the strange foreigner who was so elegantly clothed in jail with a monogrammed handkerchief in the breast-pocket of his soiled jacket.

There were only a few minutes left and then, it would be too late. My whole effort would go down the drain. Slowly I pulled out my hand from my pocket with the brown paper folded, inserted between my fingers, and covered by the palm of my hand. As if intuitively cooperating, the lady barber bent over me to remove a few hair-patches remaining near my ears and neck, blocking for a moment the guard's view. Swiftly I deposited my letter into her apron-pocket without being detected.

Back in my cell I lay down on the plank-cot, closed my eyes and elaborated on the different possibilities that could now arise. I was no longer a completely unknown speck in the vast NKGB system. I had made contact with a fellow Jew. I knew, however, that the lady barber might be unable to read Yiddish and might be afraid to look for someone to decipher the letter for her. On the other hand, this was the Ukraine, heartland of Yiddish traditions, where for centuries Jews kept special Heder teachers in every little village and hamlet to imbue their children with Jewish knowledge, instructing them in ancestral stylized translations of sacred texts in the native tongues of their forefathers.

Here, Jewish Magidim preachers in the olden days travelled from community to community and with their sing-song fables told the simple folks inspiring stories about great Tsadikim, saintly men and learned scholars, and about the Kabbalistic Lamedvo'vniks, the thirty-six hidden good men on whose merit the whole world depends at any one time.

More recently, after the revolution, in the '20s and '30s, Yiddish theatres, Yiddish vocalists, writers and poets gave concerts in their mother tongue. Many of the Kolkhoz collective farms bore Yiddish names like Stalin-Dorf and Sholom-Aleichem Dorf and Zeydi Mendele-Dorf.

The chances were about even, I concluded. The next few days would tell. At least I had tried and, under the circumstances, I had done my best. However, it did not take even a few days to find out that Jews were indeed merciful sons and merciful fathers. The lady barber might not have appeared to be so — being a part-time employee of the NKGB — but she really was a tender-hearted, compassionate Yiddishe tochter, a genuine Jewish woman, swift and brave in her desire to help.

The very next morning she appeared carrying a pillowcase filled with food-stuffs — 2 large 3-kilogram loaves of bread, a sizable bundle of zwieback, some garlic, a bunch of onions, fresh cucumbers, two dozen small reddish apples, a stalk of black grapes, 6 hard boiled eggs, a package of Makhorka tobacco, a few pages of Moscow's daily *Pravda* as substitute cigarette paper to roll it in, and even some precooked butter in a little box of the kind that shoe polish comes in.

How she managed to move all this through the gates and formalities remained a complete mystery. The fact was that the turnkey opened the cell-door and with a magnanimous smile called out, "Come here, Zapadnik! An anonymous donor sends you all these goodies! You were born under a lucky star. So, take it easy. Don't overeat, because you'll kick the bucket."

I was dumbfounded. I handled the box with caution and some awe, as if it were a rare and fragile Stradivarius violin. Again and again I examined the pre-cious commodities with the joy of a cashier who has discovered an extra and substantial surplus in the cash-box which legally and legitimately belongs to no one but himself. Then I washed my hands, said the proper benediction, and sat down to eat an oversize, luxurious meal of bread and butter with onion and garlic. "Thou preparest a table before me in the presence of mine enemies," I recited a verse of Psalm 23, so apt in these circumstances.

As I fortified myself with a wonderful dessert of fresh apples, I remembered the mysterious blond girl in Warsaw whom I had saved from a group of Poles who were threatening to denounce her as a Jewess. That was just before the Warsaw Ghetto uprising when I had gone to Warsaw in my role as a supposed S.S. man. And I never even found out who she was. Now I in turn had been saved from malnutrition and hunger by an unknown NKGB functionary whose name I would probably never know either. As Jews we had each per-formed a secret almsgiving at a very special time.

The food parcel arrived just in time because the very next day Colonel Nyekrasow sent for me again. This time there was no pretense of cordiality. "Adam Janovich Arendarski, Amnon Alexandrovich Ajzensztadt," he told me point-blank to my face, "I am preparing an indictment against you as a perpetrator of serious crimes against the Soviet Union."

I looked at the colonel with shocked disbelief and a silence which I hoped was more articulate than the roar of a wounded lion.

"Don't look at me with those Talmudic, Rabbinic, innocent eyes,"

Nyekrasow thundered. "The congenial social get-togethers led nowhere and are over and out. I must speedily finish your case for the higher authorities, so socialist justice can be meted out."

"But how can you do such preposterous things without a shred of evidence that an offence has even been committed?" I asked.

"Well," Nyekrasow smiled, devilishly benign again. "Don't worry about that. In your personal belongings we already found enough tangible proof which any writing expert, any professional graphologist will attest to as your own handwriting."

"Here!" he pulled out from his top desk drawer a few sheets of paper on which smaller notebook sized pages were immaculately fastened down with tape. "Do you recognize these?" He handed them to me with a triumphant and ironic look in his piercing, beady, bear-brown eyes with the bushy brows.

"Yes! They are mine," I replied without hesitation.

"Oh! What touching sincerity!" The colonel did not relinquish his sarcasm. "You agree then that they are yours."

"Of course I agree," I could not yet grasp where the next trap was being set for me.

"So, maybe we will get somewhere with you after all, and you will, on your own, confess the whole sordid affair of your covert disguises and mysterious clandestine hieroglyphics?"

"I'll be very glad to do it," I responded with a steadfastness and self-assurance that surprised and simultaneously disappointed the NKGB's persistent interrogator.

"O.K., then, let's hear the hidden code meaning of all this anti-Soviet scribble-scrabble! Go ahead, decipher it!" Nyekrasow leaned back in his chair as if in pleasurable anticipation.

"They require no deciphering and it is not a secret code. These scripts are simply written in Hebrew and Yiddish."

"Well! What are you waiting for? Read them! Let me hear your lofty words of inspiration."

"This," I began, "is a portrayal of the Nazi attack on Warsaw in 1939. In the midst of overwhelming turmoil I tried to retain a sense of order by finding words that rhymed:

Ta ra ta ta ra ta ta ra ta ta tam
Roar of gunfire, mortar's thunder
Seem to tear the Heavens asunder
Bombs are falling all around
Through the fury, through the sound
Soldiers rush in to attack
Grenades flying, rifles crack.

Szi, szi, szi, szi, szi, szi, szi, szi, closely listen
Sunlight on their wings aglisten
Planes swoop in — machine guns rattle
Joining in the hellish battle.

Track, track, tra, ta, ta, ta,
People rush for bunker's shelter
Parents, children, helter-skelter
Fear and panic on their face
Pushing, screaming, how they race
From the horror
Of the place.

Sounds of salvos mixed with weeping
From the planes machine-guns sweeping
Mama! Papa! children cry!
Bloody murder from the sky!!!

Now a curious wailing sound
Seems to come from all around
Flames are leaping fierce and tall
Buildings crumble, house walls fall
The barracks burn, and everywhere
Stench of sulphur fills the air . . .

But . . . Life goes on, and people wait
in patient lines for bread to eat.

Look up! Oh dreadful scene —
Arms and legs blown off — obscene
Hanging from wires overhead,
Warsaw's city squares are piled with dead.

The German eagle flaunts its might
Over the carnage, the terrible sight,
Of mayhem, murder — how I despise
This century of the Nazi-rise!

I pray that G-d will, in his wrath,
Sweep this filth from off the earth . . ."

"And this I call: The Remembrance of a Ghetto Escapee," I announced introducing the second poem to a visibly unmoved Nyekrasow.

"I'm all ears," the NKGB sleuth grumbled. "Cut the introductions and read."

I began: "I was there, when they shipped us off in cattle trains, to the concentration camps, for the final solution; when they initiated the most gigantic killing industry in mankind's history; where nothing goes to waste; when they manufactured mattresses stuffed with human hair.

I was there when they took the chosen of creation, molded in the image of the Lord, and turned them into dung-like fertilizer; when they marched in a million and a half children through the hermetically sealed doors of the gas-chambers, and processed them into pure, innocent smoke, coming out of the crematoria chimney; when a camp-guard told a silver-haired grandma to "kneel down, you old bitch" and with a single blow of a two-by-four smashed her head; when two-legged beasts tore apart infants in their mother's presence; when they branded tender young girls with the sign of field-whore.

I was there when they inflicted diabolical pain, forcing sons to rape their own mothers in a public show of sodomy; when veterinarians emasculated men like capons and spayed women like cats, by cutting out testicles and removing ovaries without anaesthetics; when sucklings were choked to death by their own parents in panicky fear of their hideout's discovery.

I was there when the last remnants of engineers and chemists organized clandestine laboratories and subterranean bunkers, where they put together hand grenades, dynamite bombs and electrical mines to greet the Nazi destroyers when they came to destroy them.

I was there when the hellish finale took place, and the last Ghetto fighters jumped from collapsing buildings and rooftops, into the flames, accompanied by some bystanders' remarks about the beautiful aroma of frying Jews.

I heard the outcry of the degraded, the shriek of the violated, the sob of the flogged, the howl of the maimed, the moan of the emaciated, the weeping of the swollen, the lament of those selected to die, the whine of the crowd led to the gallows, the scream of the tortured, the hooray of the barricade defenders.

All this accumulated into such a wail of woe that my eardrums were bursting as if hit by a tremendous boom.

But even more devastating was the shock of the peace and quiet on the Aryan side, when I managed to get there! To me it was the serenity of a spiritual cemetery! It was a society sterilized of humanity, devoid of pity, spontaneously doing nothing while millions perished gruesomely.

It was a community satiated with the mental calmness of people without a conscience, indifferent to the suffering of others.

It was the deafening silence of an uncaring establishment which shook off all the biblical teachings and which stood idly by while fellow humans bled in peril.

It was a merciless league which did not give a damn about what happened to the Jews . . ."

"Wow!" Nyekrasow mockingly commented. "Bravo! Adam — Janovich — You're a very accomplished vocal fellow, and your ingenuity is admirable. I really should applaud your bosses — the German Krautheads who improvised such a brilliant camouflage! Espionage through lamentation poetry. This is excellent, impressive and wonderful! But not enough to outwit the NKGB."

"My dear fellow we here are not merely dilettantes but are thoroughly skilled and state-trained professionals. We are knowledgeable and informed in the most complicated, international code-systems."

"What didn't the enemies of the Soviet Union do in their subversive attempts? Liturgical music, bibles, coded shortwave radio messages, priests with concealed pockets, industrialists using hollow machine parts to smuggle across classified documents and now, finally, you, a young punk!"

"Do you really believe that through your melodramatics about Jewish suffering you will lead us down the garden path? You think that your torrent of verbiage will make us grow soft and spread out the red carpet for you? You think we will grant you your freedom?"

"No brother! We in the Soviet Union have a unique sense when it comes to detecting our enemies."

"Your recitation about the overhanging electrical wires adorned with human limbs immediately suggests the relevance of associating hands with wires . . . in prosaic terms it links the hand of the enemy to the conspiratorial clicks of the Morse code apparatus, relaying information for purposes of espionage."

"Your reminiscence of a Ghetto escapee causes me to immediately sense your desire to don the cloak of the socialist appreciation of justice."

"Amnon Alexandrovich! As the English say: Nice try! But, it is useless for you to try to confuse me and to catch me off balance. You will only cause yourself enormous trouble and inconvenience. Let us change course. Better begin with straight talk. Relate in detail your functions on Soviet territory. Who are your accomplices? What targets are marked for sabotage? What do you possess in technological devices and paraphernalia? Who are your messages intended for?

"I caution you, till now I have displayed patience and courtesy. But that's it. No more can I procrastinate over your case. If you don't open up on your own and tell the whole story, the true story of how you succeeded in arriving here and what is honestly in the very inner recesses of your mind — then you force us to employ more extreme and drastic methods of breaking you down until you'll spill out everything to the last iota."

I was aghast! I felt instinctively that the Colonel's menacing words were more than mere empty threats. I had already seen and heard enough to know that I was in real danger. I had to do something to appease the investugator's anger. Silence or taciturnity would no longer do. I had to tell him a lot more about what happened to Amnon Ajzensztadt from the moment he became Adam Arendarski and hope that he would believe me.

"Citizen-Interrogator!" I formally addressed the Colonel. "I am willing to tell you everything about myself, my activities, and how and why I got here. Please give me a chance to tell it in totality, to avoid misunderstandings and misinterpretations."

"All right!" Nyekrasow said. "But before you start your guilt-monologue, I want again to point out to you that the Soviet Union does not execute even its worst enemies. The death penalty is part of the judicial system of the bourgeois, capitalistic countries. Communists are humanitarian, and here, as a rule, we never execute anyone. There is ample employment in Siberia, and convicts of every kind, including reactionary traitors are provided with an opportunity to redeem their sins by helping to build the socialist future."

"As you yourself admit, in any case, we rescued you from the Nazis, so you will therefore reciprocate by working on one of our development projects. We will provide you with a quilted jacket and trousers, underwear and socks, and boots manufactured out of pressed felt. We will feed you well, commensurate, of course, with your production quota."

"Now listen attentively, and do not regard me as your personal enemy. As for me, I bear no grudge against you. On the contrary, to tell the truth, there are times when I feel sympathy for you. But you must realize that the Fatherland and its security take precedence over any other considerations. We can't afford to be soft-hearted and sentimental. Accordingly, it is necessary, as a defensive measure, to apply the drastic surgical method. This means that if anyone, for example, on Kirov Street, if anyone commits a crime against the state, and we are not able to determine who the criminal is, we round up all the residents, as well as those of the surrounding streets to the north, south, east and west. We deport all of them to Siberia. Of course, 99.9 percent of them are innocent, but the chief point is that the one who is guilty is included among them."

"The justification for this treatment should be apparent to all, for, if they are patriots, they readily realize that Siberia represents Soviet soil as well. The sooner they adjust to the new conditions, the more rapid will be their acclimatization."

"The same considerations apply to you. The sooner you resign yourself to your situation, the easier will be the task of managing your life. I wish to give you some more personal advice before you start your potpourri of inequities."

"When you finally arrive at some camp in Siberia, do not stand still, gaping with admiration at the beauty of nature, and the snow-covered trees glistening like crystals — reserve your poetic leanings for better days."

"At the labour camp, immediately take the tools, the saw, and the axe, and produce your alloted quota, so as to receive the full food portion. If you can keep your energy, you won't lose your last chance for longevity."

I felt completely sickened by the Colonel's voluble remarks, and his pretence of caring about me. The whole thing was obviously a set-up; I was quite sure that either way I would lose. Even were I to tell the truth down to the minutest detail the NKGB was sure to dispatch me to a labour camp in Siberia.

The Colonel noticed the change in my expression and the flatness in my voice at once. "Hey! What is the matter with you Zapadnik? I can hardly hear you!" Nyekrasow complained. "Come on! Put some life into your confession! or perhaps you're having a change of heart and want to crawl back into your uncommunicative shell?"

In a half-hearted tone of voice, feeling low-spirited and bitter, I proceeded to tell my story which the Colonel wrote down for inclusion in my interrogation file. I could hardly tell the Colonel everything that had happened since leaving Warsaw at the end of 1941. And I was concerned to protect the identities of at least some of the people who had helped me.

"My crime consists of having successfully escaped from the Ghetto. All I did was to save my own life. My sister, Tamar, and her one year old child, Naomi, were killed by the Nazi beasts. My brother-in-law, Eliezer, was tortured to death in a concentration camp. My parents were carted away in cattle cars to Treblinka, where they died in the gas chambers. Of the whole family, only I got over the Ghetto-wall. It helped to have blond hair and a Gentile-looking face. I was only 21 then, and I powerfully wanted to live. So I wrestled with my lot as a Jew and tried to surmount the problem. Who wants to bite the dust at such a young age?"

"Now, after three years, I'm not sure if everything I've been through was worth it. It all began with my trip to Poland's second largest city, Cracow. I hoped to become assimilated among the Hungarian Jews there, who were still considered to be privileged foreign citizens. They did not have to wear the yellow star of David."

"During my trip, I met a group of Poles who were travelling to Winitza. They were working for the German organization, Todt, building highways and bridges. My sense of self-preservation told me to take this only chance to escape from Poland. I therefore joined the ranks of the Polish peasants and arrived with them in the Ukraine. However, I didn't realize that I was moving from the frying pan into the fire. Some Polish extortionists told the Gestapo that there were Jews pretending to be Christians among the volunteer labourers. So, the Nazis staged a pogrom, and many of my friends (also Jews on forged Aryan papers) were captured, tormented atrociously, and later their bodies were displayed, hanging from trees on the main streets."

"Panic-stricken, I began to run through cities and towns like Novy Archangelsk, Uman, Kiev, Kirovograd, Charkow — until I reached Dniepropietrowsk, where there was a fairly large community of secret Jews. In spite of the immense risks, they were involved in carrying out anti-Nazi activities. They supplied deserting Italian soldiers with gasoline, set fire to Wehrmacht warehouses, and sabotaged military installations. Still, it was no picnic to be a so called Arytan who wasn't what he seemed to be. It was no easy task to play the role of a full-fledged Nordic in a city swarming with Shutz-Polizei, S.S., and multitudes of local collaborators, agents, fascist blood-hounds, provocateurs, and informers — greedy to collect the reward for delivering a disguised Jew."

"There were continuous problems with shelter and places where one could find refuge in a time of need. Police bulletins kept on warning landlords to watch out to whom they were renting out their premises and furnished rooms — threatening them with harsh consequences if it was found that their tenant or lodger was indeed a Yid."

"Every day was fraught with uncertainty and one had the feeling of moving about as if he were in quicksand."

"I remember one wintery day, in 1942, when I came home to my temporary abode on Pushkinskaya 38. Before I even had a chance to take off my coat and drink a cup of tea, I was confronted by a uniformed Luftwaffe Sergeant who suddenly appeared out of nowhere. He simply pointed his pistol at me and said, irritably, in the presence of the landlady whose 10 year old boy solicited him on the street as a one night guest, 'Listen, you guy! Tonight you have no room in this apartment. I am taking over your place! I just got back from the front-line and I need some peace and quiet in a non-military environment.' "

"When I tried to explain that I would not be in his way and that I was willing to sleep on the living-room sofa he became real nasty and gave me only 3 minutes to pick up a couple of blankets and leave. 'Listen you Polnishes Schwein!' he seethed. 'I don't know why you are dressed in a Wehrmacht's uniform and live privately as a subtenant with a Russian family. Something here is fishy! To me, you don't look like a bona fide member of the auxiliary forces. But I don't give a shit! Get out before I drop you right here on the spot!' "

"I walked out of the warm flat at once, in no position to start an argument. A bitter Ukrainian winter chill with a gusty snowstorm greeted me in the backyard. It was dark and past 10 p.m. when very few pedestrians were to be seen on the slippery city streets. In addition, having no alternative accommodation I had nowhere to go."

"Without much of a choice, I quietly climbed a staircase to the very top where there was only the entrance to the attic. I sat down on one blanket, covered my feet with the other blanket and lit up a cigarette. It did not take very long for the biting frost to creep into all my limbs."

"The most sensitive to the miserable cold were my fingernails and my toes which began to sting as if stabbed with a thousand pins and needles. I took off my boots and massaged and rubbed my soles and toes fighting the numbness which was beginning to set in. But, as time went on, I knew that I would not be able to continue doing this right through the night. Nor was the sitting position on the tenement attic platform enhancing my chances of surviving the awful cold."

"I got up and decided that if I wanted to stay alive I must keep walking all the time. It was close to midnight when I started my escapade through the empty streets of Dniepropietrowsk. Not a single soul was to be seen. With the blankets under my arm and my shawl improvised as ear muffs I kept on striding towards the bazaar near the train station. There, around the depot section, I knew a local, liberal Pole but did not remember his exact address. I also hoped that the city's military cafe and restaurant, would still be open. It was only minutes away from the station and it was open to all men in uniform. Perhaps I would be able to spend the rest of the night there. Unfortunately, both places were closed for the night, and there was nobody around at all."

"The only doors open and the only place where I could warm my stiff and aching body was the waiting room inside the station. To go there would have been really stupid as the military police were always there, checking people's travel documents and papers and always on the lookout for loafers, deserters, and other suspicious characters."

"I was certainly in a tight spot, caught between the bitter cold outside and the alluring heat of the station waiting-room, which it would have been nearly suicidal to enter. Although I was only twenty-three years old, I felt something like an old man, in fairly good physical shape but in desperate need of somewhere to rest my tired and aching bones."

"I began to think that I should have stayed in the building on Pushinskaya. At half past one in the morning my frustration and fatigue peaked. I could not go on any longer. I had to sit down no matter what, at least for a little while. From afar, I noticed a bombed-out streetcar standing lopsidedly, some way down Sheroka Volitza, the former Karl Marx Avenue. Instinctively I started out towards this only available spot. The immobilized tram with its doors wide open was like a miniature Tower of Pisa — leaning on one side with its rusting rear wheels grotesquely hanging in the air. It looked like a derailed train coach after a collision. But the wooden seats and benches were, for the most part, still there, tempting me to use them and let my exhausted body take a rest. I picked up a broken piece of plywood and cleared a bench in the center of the desolate electric carriage and noticed frozen filth — mostly excrement of some characters who had utilized the place as an improvised privy. I tried again the next row and was luckier, managing to remove the accumulated snow and ice. It was not a moment too soon. My eye lids were so heavy, as if they had been weighed down with lead and my legs were at the brink of physically refusing to carry me any further. I let myself down on the cleaned up bench, arranged both blankets to cover my head, shoulders and back and experienced the sublime joy of an ill-treated, persecuted animal who found itself a temporary home. My eyes closed and I succumbed to a strange, sweet tiredness which began to take over my mind and body."

"What a lovely way to depart from this cursed world, it flashed through my dizzying brain. Nebulously and haphazardly I began to switch from one vision to another. Somehow a quotation from Isaiah appeared before me with huge ruby-like italics: 'Saith the Lord; though your sins be as scarlet, they shall be as white as snow!' Then I was quickly fading away into the dreamland of sleep, perhaps eternal sleep — no more did I feel the pestering cold, the sharp-edged prickliness of frost-bite and the discomfort of numbness. No more did I feel worry, or fear, or pain, or panic. Everything seemed to change and slide into a sphere of everlasting serenity where there were no problems, no questions, and no enigmas."

"However, to my dismay and confusion, I suddenly felt a tremendous thump, a brutal whack. Someone had hit me very hard in the face and kept on hitting and slapping my cheeks, not allowing me the final peaceful transition to the hereafter. Obviously my time on the planet Earth was not yet up. As it turned out the impudent harrassment and physical manhandling was done by an angelic, elderly female street-cleaner who most probably came in to relieve herself and noticed the odd sight of a young man in a German uniform bundled up in blankets, lingering in the last stages of life and death, almost frozen stiff. Moved by simple pity which makes all flesh kin, her determination and persistence to awaken me from my semi-clogged condition finally paid off. When I opened my eyes I saw tears of joy and compassion on the wrinkled face of a kind grandmother."

" 'Lord in Heaven!' she cried with sympathy and softheartedness, once she succeeded in getting me off the streetcar seat and made me stand again on my own two stilt-like feet. 'Look down from above merciful father and see what's happening to our young people in this accursed war.' With the tenderness of a natural mother she then took me by the arm and led me to a nearby backstreet cellar apartment which was her home. Within minutes she quickly heated up some water, pulled off my boots and made me soak my feet in the warm fluid while simultaneously feeding me with nutritious soup and corn bread. Finished with carefully thawing out my body, she pointed to the only bed in the house and said in a strict maternal voice: 'Now son! I have to go back to my job. You get undressed, lie down and warm up the congealed blood in your veins. I will wake you up later when I return from work!' "

"About 10 a.m. she was back with her primitive twig-broom in hand like a mythical good genie. She woke me from my life-saving, balmy sleep, turned discreetly around when I put on my clothes, and then fed me again with sweet tea and home-made flat onion crackers after which she made it explicitly clear that I had to leave her quarters immediately. 'Don't be angry, son,' she said apologetically. 'I know that although you wear a Nazi uniform, you are not a bloody German. A Hitlerite soldier would not hide or try to spend the night in a broken down tram carriage. There is something very wrong here. The truth is that I don't even want to know who you really are. I, myself, have a son in the Soviet army and in all probability he is also exposed to all kinds of perilous situations trying to stay alive. Here son! Have a shot of this.' She put before me a glass of home-distilled, smelly, potato whisky. 'And may G-d almighty guide and watch you wherever you go,' she said, tearfully wiping her eyes with the corner of her apron."

"Compelled by an inner gratitude to say something appreciative I blurted out with an emotional voice, "Thank you so much! It is written in the good books that whoever saves a single human being, it is as if he has created a whole new world. And you, dear lady, did quite a job with me today. Thank you! I will always keep your righteous image in my memory. Wsiyekhda forever. Stay well, Boodtye Zdorovi! Dosvidanya! Goodbye!' "

"Again I was striding on the streets of Dniepropietrowsk with my two folded blankets. However, my woollen scarf was this time wrapped around my throat in the regular fashion of a winter shawl. The sidewalks were now brimming with people despite the freezing temperature, and slippery roads and crosswalks. Relaxed and regenerated I was heading back to my furnished room on Puszkina Street from which I had been evicted and where I still had all my belongings. I knew that after the set-to with the Luftwaffe sergeant my prestige with my landlord would be down to zero and that he would have many questions about my real identity, questions which might make it too risky for me to go on living there.

"So I decided to handle the matter cautiously. First, I would have to obtain my possessions and announce that I would be leaving town. And then I would start again the tedious wandering Jew's search for shelter and refuge, avoiding

midtown or downtown locations where a repetition of the previous day's perilous confrontation was a distinct possibility."

"Only individuals who have been on forged underground papers and passed for ethnic Germans, Catholic Poles, and Aryans of genuine Nordic pedigree can know the nerve-shattering agony and anxiety of always being in the
process of moving and inquiring about secluded living space in some dead-
end ravine, tree-lined court or side street, in labyrinthine basements or unnoticed lofts with reserve entrances and, most importantly, with double exits for
an abrupt get-away."

"Food and apparel were not so much a problem for the Jew masquerading
as Gentile as was a secure place to come home to and, in case of trouble, to be
able to stay hidden in, possibly in a prepared and camouflaged bunker, hollow, old-fashioned ceramic oven, or hidden double wall. Asking around by
word of mouth about a good dependable landlord became a permanent feature and a compulsion in every modern Marrano's life, and everybody was
forever restless. As the Old Testament says, 'In the morning thou shalt say,
would G-d it were even! And at even thou shalt say, would G-d it were morning!"

"The Jew on forged Christian documents became, in time, an oversensitive
person whose worry about strict anonymity often made him suspect and see
peril in situations which were only a coincidental merging of circumstances."

"If someone, for example, looked at him penetratingly, or if an unknown
man or woman happened to walk behind him on the street for a while; or if an
unfamiliar character happened to indulge in reading the tenant list displayed
in the entrance to the lobby — he immediately saw this as a warning and a new
odyssey of hunting for living quarters began. He continued until the whole
city became repulsive and loathsome, and there was in it no more air to
breathe, no more parks to stroll in, no more friends to confide in, and no more
perspective to keep one's own sanity in a society where everybody — from
superintendents in apartment buildings to babushkas in the bed-renting business, to small scale innkeepers, knew that a Polachok or Zapadnik was perhaps
a clandestine Israelite trying to save himself from the Gestapo roundups by
posing as a non-Jew."

"In such an insufferable atmosphere of fears and fiascos, blackmail and
arrests all over occupied Ukraine, I took a chance and sneaked into a German
Red Cross hospital-train which was transporting wounded Nazis from the
Eastern front back to the Third Reich. I did it because I had discovered from a
Russian station master that the ininerary of the Red Cross wagons led through
Odessa which was under Roumanian administrative control. Odessa was a
much larger metropolis than Dniepropietrowsk; there would be considerably
more opportunities for someone who was *persona non grata* to maintain a low

profile and thus immerse himself more easily in unsuspected anonymity among the millions of her inhabitants."

"And the rest you already well know! As the Red Army went on the offensive I befriended my next door neighbour's son, Vitya Shynkeradze, a tempermental, proud Georgian and fiery disciple of his countryman, Joseph Wisarionowiez Stalin. The young man, after weeks of heart-to-heart talks, became my liaison with a group of Komsomol members, party functionaries, Czechoslovakian guerilas, and other underdogs of unfavourable status in order to make it through the allegedly mined Odessan catacombs to Rozdielnaya where I was detained and delivered to you by the red-haired sergeant."

"Adam Yanovich Arendarski! You are an audacious, impertinent, but very prodigious yarn-spinner; a fabulous story teller!" Nyerkrasow said in a mysterious way which was nondescript and elusive; impossible to identify as threat or flattery, criticism or recognition. "You know, you really have got a nerve, keeping me here most of the night in the belief that you are going honestly to acknowledge your outrageous wrongdoings, unburden your conscience of all your misdeeds, and in good faith show trust in the socialist system's policy of reform, reeducation and rehabilitation for truly repentant criminals and sinners! However, like a shrewd, sly con-artist you take me instead on a journey down memory lane, and all that I hear is a repetitious saga of your personal bellyaching of hardships, sleepless nights, and mistreatment as a displaced, persecuted Jew who is tragically assaulted from all sides and circumstances by a combination and a multitude of evil forces out to get him. Even according to your own chatterbox version of past days a few characteristic things become absolutely clear. They attest quite tangibly to the fact that you are a fanatical cleric who always superstitiously refers to biblical quotations and allusions to divinity and G-d almighty. It is, thus, not at all hard to figure out by inference and deduction that you are an extreme nationalist with a narrow-minded view of the future of all humanity, remembering and keeping in mind only the tortuous annals of your own Jewish tribe. From what I have heard so far it becomes utterly clear that you are infected with Zionist leanings and, therefore, automatically and without doubt are an enemy of the October Revolution and all the concepts of Leninism and Stalinism committed to the liberation of all mankind and cessation of all suffering and exploitation of the family of all nations. In your lengthy oration there was, in essence, nothing new at all! The same continuous harping away on your personal martyrdom and the suffering of your Jewish people. Only one additional aspect of criminality surfaced and that is your collaborative activities with Mussolini's fascists, which in your perverted way of thinking you are trying to pass off as an act of daring and heroism, as you so smoothly and cleverly describe it, as a tangible patriotic deed of supplying Italian deserters with gasoline."

"Adam Yanovich! I am afraid I can't see eye-to-eye with you at all on this serious matter. Of course, in your recollected narrative, you lump together the Italian episode with a general one-paragraph statement about sabotaging Wehrmacht installations and putting to the torch military warehouses. But all of this is just unproven gossip, rumours and hearsay. There are no specific facts, no photographed evidence, no witnesses. All that we could do is just take your word for it. And this, my dear fellow, is entirely unacceptable. Furthermore, until now, we knew only of your involvement with the Nazi organization, the Todt-Detachment, which is pretty heavy stuff in itself. Now we suddenly discover, according to your own undeniable testimony, that you also had dealings with the bloody Carabinerie and followers of the Duche who came to help Adolph Hitler in the ruination and plundering of our country. And you, instead of letting the macaronis ensnare themselves into conflict with their diabolical Axis partners and kill each other, you insinuate yourself voluntarily into the picture and facilitate their way home with illegal fuel for their military vehicles making it possible for them securely and in style to drive on towards Italy. Adam Yanovich, I suggest that for your own good you had better go back to the shadowy Italian episode and tell the whole story in all its details, including the rotten business of fraternizing with and supplying war materiel to a bloody enemy of the U.S.S.R."

"Alright," I said with mounting displeasure, annoyed with the investigator's method of continuous torture. "You want the whole story! I shall tell you the whole story, with all its particulars."

"It happened in 1943 after Marshal von Paulus' defeat at Stalingrad. The *Volkischer Beobachter* published all kinds of face-saving communiques and high-spirited reports of victorious, strategic withdrawals, but everyone knew that the fiasco on the Eastern front meant that the Nazis were going to lose the war. All those who were so quick to climb on the victorious Nazi bandwagon were now just as quick to pronounce themselves in favour of the hitherto beaten Red Army. Even the Nazi soldiers were far less cocky than they used to be. They made up some defeatist lyrics that aptly expressed their mood: 'The Russians may run in May but we run in December as well!' "

"The first ones to break the Axis solidarity and to leave the front lines, giving up the idea of conquering the U.S.S.R. were the Italians. They showed conspicuous defiance towards their snobbish and racist Nazi partners."

"That's when I met Signor Rafaelo! He was forlornly standing on the Chechelovka Bazaar trying to communicate with Russians who did not, alas, understand his tempermental gestures and Italian language. I walked over and asked him in German what the problem was and if I could help."

"Are you German?" was his first question.

"G-d forbid!" was my spiteful reply. A satisfactory smile appeared on his handsome face.

"Then to what nationality do you belong?" he inquired further.

"I am Polish," I answered.

"Oh! Viva la Polonia!" he shouted excitedly explaining that there was no declaration of war between Poland and Italy and therefore we were not foes but friends.

"Viva la Italia!" I replied, wholeheartedly agreeing that we were not adversaries, but free citizens of countries fond of one another.

"This calls for a drink!" he said joyfully.

"That's fine with me," I replied gladly. As we emptied a bottle of vodka he told me in a low, hushed voice about his dilemma. He was stationed not far away with a battalion of other Italian soldiers and a captain. They had all decided to leave Russia on their own, no longer willing to participate in the crazy ambitions of the Third Reich."

"So what precisely is the problem?" I asked him.

"You see, we ran away from the front line, abandoned our positions and we are — to call a spade a spade — deserters in the fullest sense of the word. However, we are fed up with the bloodletting and cannibalism of the Nazis; our urge to get out of this execrable mess and go home is so powerful that we undertook the voyage on our own, buying the necessary fuel for our 28 trucks on the black market. Our predicament is such that we fear to approach the Germans who might get wise and perhaps arrest us or, even worse, declare us traitors, bringing in the killing squads of the S.S. to finish us off."

"Humph," I mused. I had found myself a brother in distress from faraway Milan. "So how much gasoline do you need?" I asked him.

"Ten thousand litres," he answered, without batting an eye.

"And in what kind of currency will you pay for them?" I asked again.

"Oh, there is no problem with money," Signor Rafaelo said jovially. "We have a whole truckload of first class leather ski shoes worth a fortune and I am sure that you, Adam, would help us to change some of our merchandise into cash."

"Of course I will!" I assured him thinking that it was about time to find out his views on the Jewish question. Signor Rafaelo was a middle-aged man of distinguished looks and tall stature with horn-rimmed glasses and an elegant officer's uniform. He made no secret of his contempt towards the butchers of the Third Reich. "Those bastards from Berlin started a conflagration that has already annihilated millions and millions of people, leaving millions and millions of widows and orphans and invalids and refugees."

"I agree with you wholeheartedly," I said, as we began a new round of toasts, "that Hitler, Goebbels and company are a bunch of psychotic madmen intent on enslaving the whole of the civilized world. Don't you think, however, that the Jews have been incredibly greedy and have helped to provoke the Nazis in all of this? After all, didn't they pretty well control the business and industrial corporations, the cultural and scientific institutions, as well as the press in pre-war Germany? I wonder if the Jews aren't just a cabal of conspirators intent on gaining financial control over the whole world!" I concluded, looking him straight in the eye.

Signor Rafaelo almost choked on his drink, spasmatically coughing as if something were stuck in his throat.

"Adam!" he looked at me in surprise and disbelief. "How can you say such terribly bigoted things? Listen!" He x-rayed me with piercing, fatherly brown eyes. "I have a very strong instinct and my intuition tells me that you are also a staunch opponent of the Nazi-barbarians. I can also tell that you are basically a fine and kindhearted young man. So how can you collectively accuse a whole nation like the Israelites of wanting to do something as preposterous as rule the whole world financially or otherwise? They are an old, old nation which has contributed an awful lot to human civilization and it would really be just and appropriate for us to help them build up their own homeland in Palestine."

"It was the summer of 1943 after the Warsaw Ghetto uprising; after most of Europe's cities were already Judenrein, with their Jewish inhabitants extinct. And here, in front of me, sat a Milanese gentleman with a vociferous and passionate aversion for Nazis and a genuine sympathy for the most maligned victims of Hitler's plan for a new Europe."

This time it was my idea to refill our glasses and have another toast to the success of our undertaking. While sipping the vodka, my brain began to work feverishly on how to find a way of influencing this decent, unique man to take me along on the forthcoming flight to freedom in sunny Italy. Yet, the first priority was to see to it that the acquisition of gasoline went smoothly for the monumental and clandestine exodus under the noses of the Gestapo, the military police and the transportation authorities in four transit countries."

"When we left the little tavern we were both quite high on vodka but still in full command of all our senses. My Italian acquaintance, Signor Bruno Rafaelo, was now a dear friend who shared my disgust for Hitlerism, the whole Germanic pure-race theory of superhumans and subhumans, and all the other National Socialist inventions such as the Final Solution, concentration camps and gas chambers and goose stepping and Wagnerian bombast!"

"You know," he suddenly told me straight to my face, "As soon as the war ends there will be no sovereign state of Germany for a long, long time, as the country will be carved up into military zones, administered by the victorious allies. This bastard Adolf Hitler is soon going to lose the war, if only for what he has done in destroying Europe's Jewish communities."

"I needed no more proof that Signor Rafaelo was completely trustworthy and a truly humanitarian man. I told him then and there that my earlier anti-Semitic remarks had been intended merely to sound him out and that I was, in fact, a Polish Jew, a survivor of the Warsaw Ghetto massacre, and the only living member of my whole family. At that point Signor Rafaelo burst into tears and wept unashamedly."

"Die verfluchten teufel!" he said wrathfully, then he stopped for a moment in the entrance to an apartment building and, putting his hands on my shoulders, declared with great determination, "Adam, don't worry anymore! I will save you from those murderous Nazi-beasts. Let's make the arrangements with your business contacts and then we will go immediately to see our commander who is a prince of a man, my personal friend and fellow townsman."

"I agreed at once, feeling a surge of admiration for this Milanese pharmacist who so compassionately sided with the victims of the Nazi killers. We hailed a passing horse-drawn cab and I told the coachman to take us to 71 Gogola Street, the address of my wheeling-and-dealing friend Gospodin Piwowarow."

"Mr. Piwowarow was the most prominent black marketeer of the main bazaar in Dnipropietrowsk proper. He was the king of all speculators and had at his disposal a well-organized staff of underlings and lieutenants who, according to his instructions, bought and sold any type of merchandise for which a deal could be made.

"Gospodin Piwowarow was interested in almost anything. He was willing to purchase everything from razor blades to telephone poles, rubber tires, leather, linen and yardgoods, foodstuffs of all descriptions, cigarettes and tobacco, hardware and household goods, kitchenware and china, silver, gold, watches and cutlery, lingerie and underwear. He also paid top prices for cosmetics, drugs and especially for sulphur, solvarsau and other medications used in treating venereal diseases for which there was a tremendous demand. Even out of circulation Soviet rubles, officially worthless, were diligently bought up by his representatives and astutely accepted by himself as part-payment for goods, since he obviously believed in the return of a victorious Red Army. Special attention and priority were, of course, given to wholesale negotiations where large sums of money and truckloads of materials were involved. In such cases, Piwowarow wisely took into partnership the smaller Bazaar businessmen, sharing with them in percentage the acquired commodities as well as the eventual profit.

"To shield his operations from unwanted eyes and to give himself a credible aura of respectability, his official job title was as owner and manager of a large machine shop and smithy, well-established in a huge barn-like hall which was once a sports club auditorium. Yet, people who did large scale business with him knew about the 'magic' back doors hinging on hydraulic chains. By pressing a hidden button, the back doors could be electrically opened to let a loaded five ton truck straight through to the backyard. Once a running track, the yard was now converted into an alleged scrap yard with a myriad of little chambers, compartments, cells, magazines, and pigeonholes that discreetly and conspiratorially stored his multifarious wares."

"One thing, however, that Mr. Piwowarow did not have was an office, a secretary, a bookkeeper, records, or written financial statements. His grey-haired bull-sized head set atop a wide reddish neck on muscular shoulders, was his office. Incredibly competent in mathematics, all his deals were figured in his head within minutes. If interested, he usually arrived at an immediate and final offer. No dickering or horse-trading, no bargaining in a cheap penny-pinching manner. There was a certain statesmanship and dignity in his way of doing business."

"As soon as he saw us inside the shop he was all smiles. He remembered well that a couple of months before I had brought him a corrupt German Hauptman and sold him the fantastic, beautiful amount of twenty tons of pure white flour on which he had probably made a fortune."

"Adamchyk-dorogoy," he put out his large hand and greeted us warmly. While we exchanged cordialities about our health, and the way life was treating us, he sized up Signor Rafaelo as well as he could. Obviously, he was interested in intuitively determining if he was a seller or a buyer. Piwowarow was able to read a man's face as someone reads a book. He could unfailingly classify a person as trustworthy and honest or treacherous and deceitful."

"Evidently, Bruno Rafaelo made a good impression on him with his mildness and musical baritone voice. A bottle of pre-war Moskovskaya vodka appeared in Piwowarow's hand as if he were a sorcerer. From a cupboard above his head, he fetched clean glasses and poured us each a hefty drink."

"When the toasts were over, I told him the reason for our visit and that we desired 10,000 litres of gasoline. Without blinking an eye, Piwowarow asked matter-of-factly, 'In what currency will it be paid? German marks, Italian lira or Ukrainian karbovantzy?' 'None of them,' I said. 'My associates are willing to pay with a finished product very much in demand and better and much more appreciated than any kind of money.' "

" 'And what would that be?' the stocky host asked."

" 'A hundred percent, triple-soled, Italian leather ski shoes — and perhaps some French brandy.' "

" 'Can we see a sample?' Piwowarow asked. Signor Rafaelo took out of his field-bag a beautiful tan-coloured pair of ski boots and handed them to him."

"Piwowarow smiled approvingly while admiring the fine craftsmanship of the Italian shoemakers. Like a judge and connoisseur, he smelled the aroma of the shiny leather, untied the shoelaces and checked the lining of the footwear, simultaneously establishing the exchange value of fifty litres of gasoline per pair."

" 'You want 10,000 litres of gasoline? Bring me another 199 pairs of different sizes and a case of French booze for my own private use and you've got yourself a deal!"

" 'I translated the offer to Signor Rafaelo and he instantly accepted Piwowarow's conditions. They shook hands again and Piwowarow instructed a couple of his assistants to make the necessary preparations so that the first load of 1000 litres of gasoline could leave with us back to the Chechelovkas, then we would pick up 20 pairs of shoes and return for another load — until the full quota was in piecemeal fashion fulfilled."

"When we rode back in the panel truck I felt euphoric. I was helping to wean more than 200 Axis soldiers away from the Russian front, and perhaps, I thought, I had also found a way to freedom by going along with them as their translator, since I spoke German, Polish and Ukrainian, plus I could make myself understood in Czech as well."

"As the gasoline was being unloaded in the backyard, Signor Rafaelo introduced me to the senior officer of the battalion, Captain Minnelli. 'This is the young man whom providence sent to me this morning and without whom it would have been far more difficult to find the gasoline that we so urgently need. His name is Adam Arendarski.' The captain nodded his head in a friendly manner and remained seated behind his desk, obviously waiting to be filled in with the details of the transaction."

"When Signor Rafaelo had finished, the captain exclaimed, 'Molto Bene! Grazia Bruno! Like always I knew I could depend on you.' "

" 'Captain, there is something else,' Signor Rafaelo said, while he walked over to the office door, shut and locked it so that no one could come in unexpectedly."

" 'What is it?' the captain didn't hide his curiosity."

" 'It is about our friend Arendarski. I promised him that I would talk to you on his behalf. He is the only survivor of all his family, which was deported to an extermination camp where they all perished. He is the son of a prominent Rabbi but because of his blue eyes, blond hair, and knowledge of the German language, managed to elude torture and death. However, the continuous, incessant posing as someone he is not has drained him mentally and physically. Besides, the Gestapo have gotten wind of this gallant fight to stay alive and intensified their search for any remaining Jews who have so far succeeded in slipping out from under their murderous hands.' "

" 'Captain! As a deeply religious clergyman's son, Adam sees in us a symbolic G-dsend and his only chance to get out of this miserable, life-threatening mess — I beseech you to grant him his wish and allow him to come along with us as a good omen and as a constant reminder of our own yearning to be free and to get safely back home.' "

" 'For the first time, Captain Minelli got out of his chair and started agitatedly to pace the room, apparently while pondering the issue of my future. He stopped in front of me as if viewing me in an altogether new perspective. He was a distinguished looking man with an intellectual face, aquiline nose, and greying hair around his temples. His bearing was somewhat non-militaristic, with none of the snobbish rigidity and stiffness of a professional career officer."

"When he started to talk to Signor Rafaelo I did not understand very much of what he was saying. I felt, though, in the benign sounding words, good, favourable tidings. I was now completely depending on Signor Rafaelo who was reciprocating as my translator, mentor, and guardian."

" 'Captain Minelli tells me firstly to let you know that he himself is also a profound believer in G-d almighty and in divine providence. He wants me to convey to you that it is his earnest faith that your appearance on our horizon today is not just a mere coincidence but, indeed, a heavenly sign for him personally as a childless family man to fulfil a long standing dream, namely, to adopt a son of his own."

"I could not believe my ears. My heart was pounding and I most probably also began to blush, which the captain might have interpreted as a consequence of his coming on too strong."

" 'Please tell Adam," Signor Rafaelo translated, "that he should not misunderstand me. He still has a lot of time to make up his mind whether or not he wants to become a member of my family. I am financially well off as proprietor of a factory which manufactures auto parts. My wife and myself will be very glad to look after his well being and education. Should it happen, however, that for some unforseen reason he does not like it in Milano, then, I give my word of honour that I will personally accompany him to Switzerland where he will again become a free man, with no strings attached."

"Bruno Rafaelo! Your representation on behalf of Adam Arendarski is hereby officially sanctioned. From now on I bestow on him the authoritative rank of battalion translator and his name should be Adamo Arendi. Perhaps in time he will himself decide to become Adamo Arendi Minelli. Take him down to our supply magazine, dress him in a nice uniform befitting his vocation. Tomorrow at 6:00 a.m., when we leave Dniepropietrowsk, Adamo Arendi is going to be sitting together with me and you in the command jeep spearheading our drive to liberty."

"When we left the captain's office, a new gasoline shipment had just arrived.

Piwowarows's organization and his men functioned like clockwork. We passed through a big recreation room and school gym requisitioned by the battalion. Soldiers were simply lying on the concrete floor, on top of their green military blankets. Some were writing letters, others were playing chess and table tennis. A larger group of them sentimentally sang the Italian version of the famous war hit, Lili Marlene.

"Signor Rafaelo took his time in finding me a proper uniform. I had to try on quite a few of them until he approved one that looked as if it were made to measure. 'Now,' he said, looking at me fondly, you are under Italian jurisdiction and the hell with all Hitler's barbarians.'"

"Adamo! This really calls for a drink! We both have good reasons to celebrate and toast one another."

"It must have been the most unique drinking round in the whole city of Dniepropietrowsk. A brown-haired, semitic-looking Italian Gentile and a blond Aryan-looking Rabbi's son from Warsaw were drinking to the downfall of a commonly abhorred enemy — the Nazis."

"As we rose, having imbibed a whole bottle of Tre Stella brandy, I wanted to go home, pick up my belongings and return to the Chechelovkas to be on time for the early morning departure. However, Signor Rafaelo was definitely against it."

" 'Listen Adamo!' his persuasive baritone went into action. 'It is utterly ridiculous! Why should you come back right away and slumber on the cement floor, when you can sleep like a human being in a regular bed with a mattress and in the privacy of your own place. It is perfectly alright so long as you come back before 6 o'clock in the morning. The hour is still early. Go home, pack up your things, sleep off today's excitement, dream good dreams, and I'll see you tomorrow!' " We shook hands and each of us went our separate directions."

And that was the last time I saw that lovable Milanese pharmacist or his superior, Captain Minelli. I had consumed too much alcohol and my emotions were too worked up. I overslept! When I opened my eyes the next morning it was already nine a.m. I was three hours late already! Like a madman I got into my uniform, grabbed my knapsack and ran out of the house. I stopped a passing motorcyclist and gave him 200 karbovantzy and pleaded with him to take me speedily to Chechelovkas high school. The young man, a building engineer, did his best and at about a quarter past 9 we were already there."

"When we approached the picket fence of the schoolyard, the bulldog-shaped structures of the Italian military vehicles and heavy trucks were nowhere to be seen. I was shattered, as if hit by a thunderbolt. The yard was empty and so was I. With a palpitating heart, I entered the building and I knew immediately that something irreparable and indescribably terrible had happened. My one and only chance to break out from under the Nazi yoke had gone up in smoke. I was marooned. Adamo Arendi, the only Italian in the whole city of Dniepropietrowsk! In bewilderment I ran through to the captain's office — but there was nobody there. I walked through the corridors and down the round circular staircase to the gym. There was no one there either, just empty cans of military rations, morsels of dried up food, cigarette butts, and garbage remained on the huge concrete floor."

"I felt a fainting spell coming over me. With superhuman effort I dragged myself out to the yard and leaned on a basketball post. 'My G-d,' I wept bitterly. 'Why did you do this to me? Why did I not awaken in time? Why did I have to miss my last chance of getting away from the accursed swastika rule?'"

"My smart Italian uniform was no longer an asset. It was now a liability, the clothes of a deserter giving himself away by wearing it. I was like a painted bird belonging nowhere. My hopes for the future were brutally and mercilessly amputated."

"The janitor, an elderly white-haired grandpa, came into the schoolyard with a broom and trash sack and began to sweep the leftover rubbish. I wiped my face and walked over to him."

"When did they leave?" I asked him with a hollow voice.

"Just over an hour ago," he replied. They were actually supposed to leave much earlier, but," he looked at my uniform, "I believe they waited for you! As a matter of fact they searched for you all over the neighbourhood. They kept asking 'Where is the translator, Adamo Arendi?' But nobody knew where you lived. Not Mr. Rafaelo, not Gospodin Piwowarow or any of his men. Nobody knew where or how to find you. So around 8 o'clock they got into their machines and left very disappointed and very upset, unable to figure out what had happened and why you had not shown up."

"The old janitor must have noticed my red eyes and mental turmoil, because he offered me his Makhorka tobacco and paper while suggesting that I should calm myself with a smoke."

"Grandpa," I said to him, "What you have witnessed today is something of an intense human drama." He understandingly nodded his head. "Please, like a Russian man keep it to yourself. Dosvidanya!" And I began to leave slowly, all the while looking back at the fading tire marks of Captain Minelli's battalion trucks."

"I walked back to my old abode, my euphoric illusion of freedom shattered. I knew explicitly now that I was not Adamo Arendi or Adam Arendarski, but Amnon Alexandrovich Ajzensztadt — a Polish born Jew who tried to run away from himself and his fate and did not succeed."

"You did not succeed then," Nyekrasow said icily, "and you will not succeed now, because you are a born loser. The problem with you and all of your people is that you have to complicate things; reach out with the left hand to the right ear. You take simplicity itself and turn it into unbelievable complication. The poor luckless boy from the ghetto with Jetro's names: Adamo Arendi, Adam Arendarski, and Amnon Ajzensztadt who lives with the glory of the past, hovering in a world of fantasy, super delusion, and self-deception. So now we have a brand new identity to deal with, Adamo Arendi!"

"Let me tell you something! You and your people have a frightful timeless gift for inviting your own misery and trouble. When you started your recollections of the Italian episode, I could feel resentment in your inflection. However, as you proceeded and got into the trance of reminiscing — which started arbitrarily on my order — you apparently began to enjoy it more and more. You ignited your own imagination. You liked the cloak and dagger element in it; the alleged daring and intrepidity; the cat and mouse play with the Gestapo; the forged papers and travel documents; the larger than life characterization of your own self. You elevated yourself to the highest plateau of martyrdom. The eternal victim; Adam Arendarski, alias Amnon Ajzensztadt, a Jewish martyr persecuted by the Inquisition, lynched in the crusades, pogromed by the Czar's Cossacks, poisoned by the Nazis, abandoned by the Italians, and now incarcerated even by the NKGB. A classic sufferer, a permanently shorn lamb, everyone's victim."

"To give it yet more ideological clout you started to cover everything with the chosen people idea and quoted the sages, the Talmud, the Pentateuch, making it almost into a universal tragedy when, in fact, you are as much to blame for all of this as are all the bigots and villains right through the centuries."

"You think that you are smart and noble by insisting that you are Jewish, taking pride in your outmoded, archaic heritage and in your precious Mosaic ten commandments. Well, I am utterly convinced that all of your contributions to mankind's endeavours and progress were not altogether motivated by pure altruism. You had your gratifications and ulterior reasons. Money, fame, intellectual superiority, and especially the international spotlights focussed on your inborn attribute to always be number one, tops! Number one in theology, number one in poetry, number one in astronomy and physics. Number one in theoretical hair-splitting. Number one in nuclear fission, in genetical and biological engineering, number one in reconnaisance with your first biblical aggressor, Joshua, sending spies to Canaan. Number one in finances, economics and banking. Number one even in upheavals and revolutionary movements."

"Compulsively, obsessively, you kept on cultivating the chosen people idea from generation to generation. You were put on the stake, led to the gallows, made to dig your own graves. Yet, ostentatiously, you still demonstrated the number one doctrine, sticking to your obsolete, mildewed, timeworn religion and all the other old fashioned accumulated rabbinical dogmas and teachings."

"Did it really do you any good? Of course not! Your obstinacy and refusal to assimilate made you *de facto* into the most unhappy and victimized ethnic group in humanity, always plagued with sighing and grief."

If you had fully assimilated yourselves into the nations of the countries in which you lived, you would surely have done the whole world as well as yourselves a great favour. Let me give you my specific case in point, my final summary with you yourself, young man, as an example."

"Five months ago I had my first conversation with you. I explained to you sincerely the lousy predicament you were in. I told you that your line of defence was absurd and that the bravado of playing the unfortunate Jew caught in a web of unfavourable circumstances would do you no good. I advised you for your own sake to sign an admission of guilt based on paragraph 58 which would have given you a chance for a speedy trial and the opportunity to exchange the confinement of jail for a decent job and productive life in a labour camp. But you, being imbued with the *numero uno* concepts and inherited stiffneckedness of your ancestors, decided to fight the Soviet judicial system and do it in your own way by claiming absolute and complete innocence."

"If there was any deviation or breach of the criminal code, you said it was unintentional, done out of ignorance and committed by someone on the run for his life. Basically, you claimed to be pure in heart and untainted in soul with positively nothing to dread."

"Well, open my washroom door and have a good look at the mirror hanging on the wall. Okay. What do you see? I will tell you what you see: a stubborn, pigheaded biped cursed with a mind that cannot yield to reason; a pinheaded brain without a sense of reality; a haughty individual with the *idée fixe* of prophetic righteousness and heavenly justice, mumbling prayers to a higher celestial force which does not exist, and hoping that this will enable him to prove his innocence and be set free."

"Have you ever heard of the adage, 'the operation was a success but the patient died?' Do you have any idea of how long it is going to take to check and verify all your mirages, hallucinations, and doings according to the letter and spirit of the law in all those cities and towns and villages and regional centres you gypsied around in? Well, almost forever! And, in the meantime, you will go on living, or rather existing, under the rigorous, disciplining restrictions of being under investigation which means no work, no reading material, no letter writing, no visitors, no recreation; just sitting, waiting, and vegetating. You unlucky metaphysical cripple! You idiotic vagabond! Why in the hell did you have to start up this whole triple personality thing of a badge wearing ghetto-dweller, a uniformed Nazi-collaborator, and an Italian fuel-supplier? Why couldn't you simply remain Arendarski, Adam, the Pole? We would then have treated you as a regular Polish citizen who became a prisoner of war and would most probably have you transferred to the Polish army. By now you would already be a free man participating in the liberation of your country. But no! You could not overcome the chosen people complex, holding onto something visibly instilled in you with your mother's milk — which is, in essence, a moronic *fata morgana*, a big blown up bluff, a precipice by which you are going to be victimized for good!"

"That's all!" Nyekrasow closed my file and put it back into the pink coloured folder. "Now you are out of my hands! Tomorrow you are going to be sent to the Odessa Regional Headquarters of the NKGB. They are taking over your case. And if it takes a lifetime they will get to the bottom of it all and finalize it in the proper manner! O.K., march back to your cell. It's already nearing dawn."

CHAPTER 10

Sympathizers & Accusers

HER INHABITANTS affectionately called her Odessa Mama! She had the reputation of being good to all her inhabitants. Her climate was warm for she lay near the Crimean Peninsula and was, therefore, abundant in gorgeous flowers, fruits and vegetables. She had a beautiful architecture and was world-famous for her tree-lined boulevards and for her shopping districts, restaurants, theaters, movie houses, and nightclubs. Odessans were especially proud of their artistically ornamented opera house, officially recognized as second only to La Scala in Milano.

What Warsaw was to Polish Jewry, Odessa was to Ukrainian Jews. It was a prominent center with dynamic Jewish activities, Yiddish theater and Yiddish newspapers. Yiddish literature blossomed here with all the charm and graceful folklore of Sholom Aleichem, Peretz, and Dinenzon. Other Odessan Jews still enjoyed the mystical tales of Rabbi Nachman of Bratzlaw (Uman), the wonder stories of the Maharal (Rabbi Yehuda Low of Prague), the Dubner Magid fables, the good old Perek (Ethics of the Fathers), and the Mishle (the proverbs from King Solomon's classical work of wisdom and life experience).

The metropolis of Odessa was a mother-city to her Jewish residents who constituted a high percentage of her citizenry. Here, great Zionist leaders emerged who contributed immensely to the first and second aliya, the pioneer immigration to Palestine. Here, the illustrious Vladimir Jabotinsky was born and started his journalistic career as a fiery publicist in the paper *Rasviet*. From here, he went to Kishinyev after the pogrom and wrote stirring articles about Jewish sorrows and suffering. From then on he began his life-long mission to awaken Jewish people around the globe from their national languor, inspiring them to fight for liberation and kindling their souls with unfading patriotism and sacrifice for a resurrected Hebrew statehood. Here in Odessa, the passionate poet and great linguist probably conceived his prophetic visions of Jewish sovereignty achieved by a Jewish legion ready to do battle and die for the deliverance of the Jewish homeland. Here, in all likelihood, he formulated the idea which became the first paragraph in his New Zionist Organization's constitution, proclaiming the importance of instilling and imbuing the sanctity of Torah into the life of a freed Am-Yisrael, a free people of Israel.

From here, only around a thousand sea miles to Palestine via Turkey, modern Marranos of the Nazi-auxiliary forces viewed the foaming waves and dreamt of organizing an illegal escape by motor boat to Haifa or Tel-Aviv. Here, daring local Jewish girls on Christian identification papers, their hair bleached platinum blond, opened a commercial venture on the French Bazaar, selling safflower oil to German soldiers for deutsche marks and gathering from them data and information for the underground.

What Dzika Street and its surrounding side streets were to Warsaw's Jews, Babela Street and the surrounding neighbourhood were to the Jews of Odessa. Jewish people were concentrated there in almost every house. Nicknamed in Czarist times, The Jew Street, Babela Street now housed the regional headquarters of the NKGB, at Number Eleven.

From the outside, the building did not differ from all the others around it. Erected most likely in the 19th century the whole street consisted of prestigious four and five storey tenement houses with large gates open at daytime but locked before midnight by the building superintendent.

Into this enclave of free Odessan Jewish life, with many Jewish families already repatriated from their temporary war-evacuation centers deep inside Russia, Amnon Ajzensztadt alias Adam Arendarski was delivered in handcuffs to the acting duty officer of the Regional National Commissariat for state security. A young lieutenant signed the papers, took over Nyekrasow's file, unlocked me from my restraining device and proceeded to take my fingerprints for the purpose of a better and more effective identification. All of this was done with the complete indifference and detachment of a routine job, with few words spoken. Obviously, silence was an important component of the disciplinarian regime in the new place.

The youthful officer in the green khaki uniform with the gaudy red ribbon around his military cap handled me without any curiosity, with a blank stare as if I were an inanimate object, not a human being. It was a very discouraging indication of potentially harder times to come than those I had already endured. Even when the silent receptionist did look at me, it was as if I were simply an 'item,' something to be entered in a book and then forgotten about.

"Get undressed!" the reticent NKGB official barked out an abrupt, staccato order to me while pressing an electric button installed on the top of his semi-circular reception desk.

A husky man in a civilian Stalin-tunic came in and was told by the lieutenant to check over and examine my clothes. This was also part of the regular procedure for every new arrival at 11 Babela Street. The tall fellow's name was Tolia and he executed his assignment methodically, examining every single seam in my pants, jacket, and overcoat as well as every piece of lining, every cuff and every double layer of material. Tolia inspected the garments with the scrutiny of a scientist behind a microscope paying special attention to the padded jacket shoulders, the coat's collar and hem, and the interlining of the trousers' belt area where conceivably some contraband of foreign currency, precious stones, or gold coins could perhaps be concealed. First, he turned everything inside out feeling the textile with his professional, sensitive fingers inch by inch. Then he took out from the desk drawer a large sack needle and pierced through certain points which seemed to be suspicious.

Having finished inspecting my clothes he double-checked my shoes — examining meticulously the heels for possible hidden compartments. Then he bundled everything up into the coat and placed it all on a nearby unpainted stool, before proceeding to the hygienic-prophylactic aspect of the prisoner's cleanliness. From the very same drawer where he put back the sack needle he took out a large clipper which looked more like a veterinarian's tool to trim canine and feline hides than human hair. Making me sag my head he gave me a quick, standing haircut which was the most demeaning and miserable experience of my whole life.

He was not quite finished, however. After winding up his barbering performance, Tolia ordered me, with an obscenity, to bend forward with my forehead touching the desk. He pulled my thighs apart with both his hands to check that I was not trying to smuggle any forbidden objects into the prison in the most intimate part of my body.

When I was finally led to my new cell, I felt humiliated and degraded. It troubled me that the forced, indecent exposure scene was a part of the formalities in screening incoming prisoners for further investigation. I felt that I had just been through a miniature Auschwitz-type selection in NKGB style, albeit minus the gas chambers and crematoria. The contemptuous rudeness to the incarcerated was the same! The disgrace of standing bare naked like on a concentration camp appell was the same! The searching spectacle was the same! The sloppy haircutting was the same! The bedless lodging on the empty floor and the starvation rations were the same! The sanitary conditions were the same, or perhaps even worse!

What kind of judicial system was this! In the sixth month of my confinement they began to look on my person for contraband and kept a Ghetto survivor's case in limbo, failing after all this time to verify my true identity despite being given the addresses of witnesses who could, with their testimony, clarify the entire matter.

I was soon to learn that not only the state's judicial system was heartlessly peculiar, but so were my new cell-mates when they discovered that I was really not a genuine Christian Catholic but a Polish Jew who had managed to stay alive by infiltrating the allegedly pure German Army.

Twelve prisoners were cooped up in Babela's Wing One, Basement Cell Number Three. Four of them wore military uniforms without their epaulets. Three were locals from Odessa proper. One was a yellow bearded engineer from Nikolayev (also a port-city on the Black Sea about 200 miles north of Odessa). One was a Yiddish-speaking Ukrainian from the Moldavanka sector (a special quarter of the city where fishermen, stevedores, truck drivers and port-labourers lived). One was a Kolkhoz secretary. One was a one-legged footware cutter, and one was the administrator of a factory cafeteria.

In a way they represented a fair cross-section of Soviet citizens from all basic walks of life, from the lowest ranks of manual labour to the highest strata of university alumni and military academy graduates. All of them had in common the political blemish of being charged with counter-revolutionary activities under Paragraph #58, Sections I and II. All of them carried the stigma of anti-Sovietism, of being one with the enemies of the proletarian regime. And all of them, as it turned out, except one of the Red Army men, a broad-shouldered Cossack called Matway, were also infected with chronic symptoms of anti-Semitism.

When Tolia first brought me to Cell Number Three, the yellow bearded engineer and Diadia, Unlce Ignatyeyev, the Kolkhoz secretary, ran across the room to meet me at the door. They greeted me with friendly handshakes and gave me some bread and buttered corn in a military utensil, while the rest of the prisoners continued without interruption with their regular daily pursuit of energetic lice-killing. There was a congenial and festive atmosphere in their welcome. I was like a breath of fresh air, bringing news of life in the newly liberated society outside, as well as news concerning the progress of the war itself. Some of them might even have been wishing for a reversal on the battlefield and a return of the German overlords, whom they preferred to their communist jailers.

At six a.m. the guards unlocked all the cells and made everybody move upstairs to the first yard where Tolia, with an automatic rifle cast over his shoulder, took command. "Line up in fours," he ordered, "and remember! one step to the right or one step to the left out of the column and you get a bullet in the head! Now! Forward march!"

Sixty wrong-doers, transgressors in all shapes and sizes, traitors and felons, arsonists and larcenists of government property. Big-mouthed prattlers and maligners of the Soviet regime. Deserters from the army. Murderers of Communist party members. Malevolent syphilitics who had infected masses of citizens with their venereal disease. Embezzlers of state funds. Wlasow legionnaires. Ethnic Germans who joined the Nazi invaders.

Three score of outcasts and cutthroats striding — with the disciplined pace and the dark sinister faces of straight-jacketed bipeds — under an improvised canopy of thick barbed-wire nets, installed all over the place, rendering null and void any notion of a possible escape from this walled compound.

There were no towels, no soap, no toothbrushes, no toothpaste, not even a flat-river stone to rub the accumulated filth off one's hands, which came from constant contact with the unswept cellar floor and the dirty, undusted cell walls.

Sixty derelicts, ex-people, born as human beings, as the chosen of creation, stood pathetically one behind the other like animals, like dumb cattle before a manger waiting for the cue from their overseer to get their sixty seconds at the flowing water faucet. And then, having enjoyed the refreshing coolness of the life-sustaining susbtance for a single minute, they returned to their place in the column, ready to march clockwise back through the other end of the complex, which had an extra arched gate, leading past the two-storey grey interrogation offices, past the large garbage bin erected right in the center of the middle yard. The heap of rubbish in the center of the whole layout was a grotesque, mocking but poignant monument to the cancelled ephemeral ambitions of the incarcerated "have-been citizens."

Exactly an hour later, at seven on the dot, everyone was back in his assigned place, on the floor of cell number three. According to the NKGB's health regulations, the prisoners had had sufficient exercise, an adequate wash-up and ample chance for silent fraternization and recreation with their fellow inmates.

It was feeding time now.

There was not much difference between the cuisine on Babela Street and the menu of Razdielnaya. Both served the same ladle of plain, hot boiled water as the complete morning sustenance until noon, when a small portion of black bread was handed out to all the inmates as official lunch.

Positioned between the pock-marked Cossack Matway and the Yiddish speaking Ukrainian Kowalenko, I sipped the colourless tea, observed by the veteran dwellers of the cell. I had no snack to go along with the flavourless drink and my stomach and intestines mercilessly craved for something solid. The yellow-bearded engineer got up and handed me a delicious canape spread with a cheese-like mixture. Matway took out from his sack a blueberry bun, broke it in two halves, and handed one part of it to his new neighbour.

"Bon appetit," he said jovially, exposing a full mouth of neglected, tobacco-stained teeth.

Of the thirteen cell-dwellers, seven had supplementary reserves of food supplied by their families to munch on with the hot water. Four just drank along with bread handed out by the parcel owners. One of the Odessans, complaining of stomach pains and claiming to have dysentry, did not even drink the heated water. Not to inconvenience his cell-mates, he moved his belongings to the center of the chamber and laid down in self-isolation, away from the others. Every little while though, he got up, walked shakily over to the corner near the door, and sat down on the chamber pot moaning and pleading for a doctor. His name was Yermoleyev. He was a simple, heavily-built night watchman in a wholesale food warehouse into which burglars had broken. They had emptied it to its bare walls while he had, unfortunately, fallen asleep. Since it involved state property and since Yermoleyev had not managed in the past to evacuate himself with the retreating Red Army, remaining in the occupied territory taken over by the Nazis, it was automatically a Paragraph 58 indictment.

"I pity this poor man," Matway said to me. "He is no big-shot entrepreneur, or black marketeer, or fast money speculator. It is his plain, honest tiredness and probably long, overworked hours of strenuous labour that did him in. It's like victimizing an innocent man."

Cossack Matway wore a soiled military rubashka with a coat that had no finishing seam underneath it, so that a shabby tuft of material hung down from it. Despite his rough looks and unaesthetic appearance, he was a tender man with surprising compassion for others and not a whit of self-pity for his own lousy predicament.

According to Matway, his own downfall was also a spinoff of insane circumstances, a side-effect of the terrible phenomenon called war, introduced and promoted by Satan and international fascism.

"You mean by England's Jewish war minister, Hore Belisha, and his cousins, the international, financial octopuses of the Rothschild family," Ignatyeyev remarked sarcastically.

Matway was now in a complete trance-like mood and I had to listen to his whole life story. The Cossack rolled up two Makhorka cigarettes, one for himself and one for me, and commenced with his verbal memoirs: "I am here for 'political crimes,' yet I was never engaged, actually, in politics. I operated a tractor in a communal farm. When war broke out I became a Cossack infantryman, stationed at the Polish border. I was captured, and that's when everything began to go downhill. The Germans rounded up several thousand of our men into an open field, surrounded by barbed wire and watch towers. The only nutrition we had was the grass and the rain water. After a few days, one third of our men had died and the rest were starving. After another week another third were still alive, or to put it more accurately, they were sort of breathing. Suddenly, a Russian officer, who had defected to the Germans, appeared with his secretary. He asked us simply 'Do you want to die here, or would you rather live to fight communism?' My bitchy soul lusts for life. I therefore put my signature to anything they put before me, just to get out of that foul-smelling cemetery.

"Several weeks later, dressed in a German uniform, I was sent to an encamped area assigned for grain silos, in a village near Perwomynsk. The Gerrys told me to keep watch on the confiscated corn, to guard it against thieves. However, I wish myself as many good years as the number of sacks I distributed among the poor, starving people. As for me, I wasn't neglected either. Food and vodka were available — loads of it — and there wasn't any lack of entertainment. We all had a delirious time. Every Sunday I would go dancing, and I enjoyed myself, just as if there wasn't a war. But if one is destined to have troubles, they arrive unsolicited. At one of these dances, I got pretty drunk, and went to the club house, where I started to dance with the bride of the former secretary of the Komsomol. When her fiancé disapproved, I, being drunk, drove a few solid punches to his face. I forgot about it, though, and then returned home to sleep, without paying a bit of attention to the matter. Meanwhile, things were moving very quickly. The Germans were receiving severe beatings, and they began to retreat. At the same time, they ordered us, the underlings of General Wlasow, to guard the rail communications and to fight the partisans in the woods. But when the front-line of combat moved closer, we turned our rifles on the Germans and knocked the hell out of them. When the Red Army moved in they forgave us all our sins, in recognition of our exploits, and they dispatched us to the front line to reinforce the struggle against the fascists. In this way, I lost several fingers of my left hand. But that was a small price to pay in exchange for my restoration to the status of a Red Army regular."

"Now comes the final part of my career as a lusting and bitchy soul. My commander shipped me to a camp in the Urals, with a trainload of German prisoners. Unfortunately, the train passed through Perwomynsk, where it was delayed overnight. As soon as I saw where we were, my unholy Cossack curiosity reacted within me, and I rushed to visit my friend where I used to lodge. The next day, I kissed my landlords goodbye, thanking them for their hospitality, and marched out the door, only to meet the waiting NKVD (police regulars) which was headed by the secretary of the Komsomol. He pointed me out as the one who had viciously attacked him because of his party affiliations. I argued that his version of the charge wasn't true, and that our fight was a private matter which took place while I was drunk. I told the NKVD that I had fought on the front lines, and that I had been wounded. But they didn't give a damn about any of this. Consequently, Paragraph 58, cell #3, and much time to think and meditate about the bitchy cossack soul! And all this because of an overdose of vodka and an intoxicated, mad caper."

Before I had a chance to comment on Matway's story with a word of consolation or sympathy Ignatyeyev shouted over from his opposite corner, "Well, Cossack, have you talked out your troubles? Are you finished displaying your self-pity and female emotionalism? Your behaviour is as typical of a Cossack as mine is of a Pope! You more closely resemble a moaning emaciated Jew pleading for mercy."

"Hey, Maxim Ivanovich!" the yellow-bearded engineer got into the picture, addressing Ignatyeyev, his neighbour to the left. "You are wrong to belittle Matway's compulsion to tell his war experiences. There is nothing wrong with wanting to share one's personal traumas with his comrades in misfortune. After all, everyone of us is in the same boat, and reminiscing about the past can do no harm. Besides, we are totally cut off from everything with no library, no recreation, no occupational therapy. It is a marvelous way to break the monotony, exchange ideas with one another, get things off our chest and perhaps do some soul searching together. We can learn from each other's mistakes."

"Very well and very intelligently put!" Matway cried in delight, without responding to Ignatyeyev's sarcasm. "Engineer! Tell us your own story, which I remember is most interesting. We might all learn something from it."

"That's right! Good idea," other voices joined in.

"O.K.," the yellow-bearded one agreed. "But let's see if we can't make this a psychiatric session of sorts, so that we can all discharge some of our repressed emotions and all get to feel better from it." And without further ado, Nikita Pawlowicz, the yellow-bearded engineer, plunged into his own history.

"I was a child of a proletarian family. My father, a participant in the October Revolution, worked in a foundry all his life. As a little boy I used to bring lunch to him at the foundry and began to sniff the aroma of different molten alloys and metals. The fragrances of steel, cast iron, copper, brass and nickel dug into my nostrils with the intoxicating charm of perfume. I admired the giant machinery in the foundry, the huge electric drills, the tool and die making department, the automatic perforators, the design stampers, the carving chisels, the punching presses, and the cast forms. Right there and then, I knew that my destiny was to become a metallurgist, involved in the science of extracting metals from all kinds of ores. As I became older, however, my aspirations crystallized more concretely and I decided that my best bet was to become a mechanical engineer. This would give me a chance to be involved with all kinds of metal and at the same time enjoy the creativity of building giant machinery for all the ports of Soviet Russia."

"And so I graduated from the ten-year school, immersed myself in studies in the polytechnical institute, and after four years of challenging and intensive studies passed the examination and received my degree as a crane engineer. Within a week I was a proud job holder in the repair docks of the port in Nikolayev."

"The well paid job did not simply enhance my social status and sense of personal fulfillment, but also escalated my economic well-being. I and my fiancé were now able to put away substantial savings for decent furniture and other household amenities. We began to plan to build a home and a family."

"Five years after our marriage, my life-companion overcame a gynecological condition and finally conceived her first child. Then, all hell broke loose. Everything was unexpectedly disrupted by a sudden earthquake of violence and war. Our supposedly invincible Red Army was pulling back in disarray and confusion. I and others like me were ordered by hastily affixed notices to evacuate with the retreating military. Yet, I could not leave my wife in the hands of a strange midwife in a city polyclinic with her baby about to be born, with which she was having extreme difficulties in labour, perhaps needing a caesarian. Torn by the dilemma of choosing between country and family, loyalty to my own flesh and blood took precedence and I remained behind holding my spouse's hand until my first born son came into the world. By then, the Germans were already on the outskirts of the city and I missed the last chance of escaping the occupation."

"What followed was the natural consequence of living under Nazi rule. I had to go back to work to a newly assigned job in Odessa and I had to keep on building cranes — not for the Soviets any more, but for the new bosses of Bucharest and Berlin."

"Down deep I knew I was doing something wrong. Yet I couldn't help myself. We were now a family with an infant and I had to make a living to support them."

"When the Soviet authorities returned, I was arrested and accused of building industrial equipment for an enemy in wartime. I bloody well know that I am guilty and will probably get from five to seven years in a labour camp. However, looking back on the whole affair, in some mysterious, intuitive way, I feel it was worth it. My wife and I are still in love with one another, as always. Like clockwork she still shows up — despite my Paragraph 58 charge — every two weeks with food parcels and a change of underwear. She has certainly not let me down in my moment of distress."

"Not like my Jezebel," Yermoleyev sighed with a deep audible breath of grief. "The moment the NKGB came for me she walked out of my life. Since then I have never again heard from my official church-wedded wife of 25 years. It's as if I did not exist anymore."

"Nikita Pawowocz! You are indeed a *raconteur par excellence*," Gugarin, the shortest, frailest but most articulate of the four military personnel, jumped in right after the engineer had finished. "The only thing though that's a bit tart in your otherwise most interesting story is the charade of trying to idolize family-life, feminine loyalty, and the undying love and mutual dedication of your wife and yourself. Well! The hard facts of life don't bear out your beautifully concocted narrative of the idyllic devotion of one Soviet spouse for another. I myself am also a member of the pre-war generation and thus your contemporary, perhaps only a few years your junior. Yet as someone who did heed the notices calling for evacuation and mobilization, as someone who participated in active combat on the battlefields — until I went astray — I can tell you from my own keen observations that the war turned all of our ladies into a promiscuous breed of treacherous bitches and none of them is to be trusted anymore as a dependable, faithful life companion. It is no more as in the olden days, when couples married for better or for worse until death separated them from one another. I don't want to spoil the illusion you are holding on to, that your wife is angelically trustworthy and waiting for you with the patience of a saint, feeding you in the meantime with regular parcels every second week. It is undeniable that she has not yet given up on you and still shows interest in you; but not for altruistic reasons or because of fiery love. It's most probably intact because she does not want to become a single parent. And that is why she is still in contact with the father of her three children."

"From my experience up to the day I was apprehended and put in the slammer, I know that the majority of them are like Yermoleyev's Mrs. Maleficent. They are egocentric and selfish."

On the mentioning of his name, Yermoleyev opened his feverish eyes, lifted his dissheveled head with obvious effort and pleaded again for someone to get him a doctor. Matway went over and put a cold water compress on his forehead, while Gugarin continued his discourse without interruption.

"To me the idealism of the pioneer and Komsomol times fell apart the moment the shooting and killing started. The whole mental and moral fabric of Soviet society was, in my opinion, in very great peril, and almost on the brink of collapse when the Nazis reached the highways to Moscow and Leningrad. Let's not therefore give the Zapadnik newcomer to our cell the misleading impression that we are a perfect society, winning the war because of the proletarian Marxist beliefs and a deep-rooted wish to redeem all mankind from its woes and troubles."

"The party hierarchy in the Kremlin made the most eloquent decision in declaring our fight with the Nazis not as a battle for Communism's sake, but as a life and death struggle for Mother Russia. Nothing else would as profoundly have stirred the Russian soul and the Russian peasant out of the demoralization and apathy of resignation and defeatism as the consciousness that the Russian homeland was in danger of being defiled and that Russian earth was to be occupied by Germanic vandals."

"However, your biography, dear Nikita Pavlovich, has as its main defect the flaw that it breathes with too much normal life and serenity which we really never had. You are nostalgically reminiscing about your childhood and school years as a relatively tranquil epoch of peace and quiet. I am just a bit younger than you and I don't recollect such a period of uninterrupted peace and quiet. Somehow, I always remember our life being intertwined with blooodshed and misery. After the Revolution and the overthrow of the Czar, we had to fight Pilsudski, the Polish Marshal and his hordes who had expansionist, territorial ambitions and who came from Poland as far as Kiev. Then we had the foreign financed and armed brigades of Denikin, Machno, Petlura, and other Western-supported counterrevolutionaries. Then came the convulsions of the Thirties, the collectivization of the peasants into Kholkoz-farms and the regimentation of the working class into governmental factories, followed by the purges of the Kulaks, the tight-fisted wealthy peasants who employed labour and opposed the Soviet collectivization of farms, the sabotage and spy trials and shortages. The international bourgeoisie didn't give us a chance to build our future based on the five year plans, without intriguing against us and endlessly conspiring to do us harm."

"We prevailed and began to mature although with the disquieting knowledge that one day, perhaps sooner than we knew, the final confrontation for our existence would take place. And sure enough, in contrast to your straight forward, almost pastoral boys meets girl story ending without any personal casualties, I am going to acquaint our newcomer with the other side of the coin. I am going to introduce him to the shadowy side of Soviet life examplified by such a rotten apple and cynic as myself, the degraded captain of a tank command unit."

"You see, good people! I, too, was once a decent, idealistic young man singing patriotic Dunayevsky marches that urged us all to prepare against the enemy, if he should ever dare to raise his evil hands in attacking our homeland. I, too, was a post-Revolution child growing up with the dream of becoming an inventor and making my contribution to humanity. I was ecstatic when I was accepted into Moscow's prestigious engineering institute. But instead of doing post-graduate work in applied sciences, in electronics, in electro-magnetic laboratories, and in experimental precision construction of man-made push button systems, I was rerouted to a military academy for a speedy training course as a tank commander. Before official graduation I was already in the field facing Panzer units. In the beginning, I was quite heroic and scored a few direct hits on their supposedly impregnable steel tigers. However, when my own turret and tank were hit, my crew torn to smithereens and myself blinded in my left eye as a result of the hellish flash, I instantly became a different man. The Nazi-missile did not only rearrange my physical appearance but also injured me psychically. Damaged mentally and physically, I was no longer an engineer-inventor but a scarred, one-eyed invalid, a second rate male, disfigured and emotionally disturbed. The elevation to the rank of captain and the red star medal on my chest didn't ameliorate my hurt and anger. Something awful happened inside me, something cruel and brutish. When I was released from hospital I was not the same playful romantic Nikolai Gugarin who recited poetry, sang ballads, and hoped to surprise mankind with the brilliance of his ingenious mind."

"In desperation I lost all restraint and became like a wild beast. I murdered people. I raped women and left them with a blood disease for life. Later, I produced a counterfeit army stamp, and deserted my unit. I falsified travel permits and travelled across Russia, gracing people with my dazzling personality. Until one day my little friends in the NKGB finally trapped me and threw me into this cage."

"Well, dear Nikita Pawlowicz! I want to tell you that you are a genuine Russian and probably a terrific engineer with a golden heart and a generous soul, sharing your food with all of us. But despite all your erudition and goodness of character you are still exceptionally naive and your understanding of crime and punishment is primitive, ancient, and archaic! With you, justice is simply a two-times-two affair. A fellow citizen does something wrong and he is punished, imprisoned. He pays his debt to society and, presto! he is reinstated into the community with a clean slate, ready to start life anew. So, you didn't manage to follow the instructions to leave the territories that were about to be occupied by the enemy and you are willing to give seven years of your life to straighten your account with the establishment. However, my dear, it is not so simple at all. One has to understand the political make-up of our Soviet jurisprudence and its built-in pitfalls. A Paragraph 58 indictment attached to the top of your dossier is like a disease one can't get rid of so easily. It persecutes you all the time like leprosy and isolates you automatically from the rest of the community wherever you happen to be."

"I look at you and the Zapadnik newcomer to our little republic in cell #3, and I detect in both of you a common denominator of basic innocence and decency. Both of you have clear, straight forward looking eyes that reflect the purity of not having someone else's death on your conscience. Both of you are victims of bureaucratic semantics in the totalitarian interpretation of law and order. Still, I am sorry to shock both of you with my unpleasant premonition that after another few months of vegetating in this stinking, vermin-infested basement you, harmless puritans who know no evil, will be shown no leniency and sentenced to many years of hard labour in the Siberian forests. But I, a vagabond and scoundrel — no! let me like a true Russian treat myself with the proper epithet — I the goddamn pervert and monster will go out a free man, to live it up again. And here is the true-to-life little scenario of how all this is going to take place!"

"In reality, I deserve the death penalty on three counts. First, for deserting the army. Second, for infecting certain members of the Soviet population. And, third, for plundering and what not. Yet, I make this statement in advance!"

"Because the war is still being fought, I will not be shot, but will be placed in a separate battalion for criminals. We'll be a suicide unit, sent out to the front lines to capture and clean out the toughest and most stubborn resistance points of the enemy. Ninety percent of us will be killed. But, while the rest of the suckers will rush into the battle, hoping to be forgiven for their crimes, I instead will at the first opportunity jump into a trench and lie there to weather the storm. Afterwards, I will be one of the heroes who returned after having scored a glorious victory against the Fascist hyenas."

"For their undeniably intrepid courage, I will be restored to my former rank as an officer and I'll even get a new medal for extraordinary bravery under the most adverse combat conditions."

When my turn came to tell my life's story it was certainly the main attraction, a special event. I was entirely different from the others. First, I was a Zapadnik, a westerner, a foreigner, born in a far away capitalist land where life was completely different. Besides, there was a mysterious aura around my identity coupled with a strange Polish accent when I did converse with my fellow-inmates. I must have come across as a fellow who had been around — a globetrotter who had ventured well beyond his home territory into the outside world, crossing borders and living under diverse political regimes.

They obviously expected me to share with them the magic of all my wanderings through the thousands of kilometres between my birthplace in the picturesque little Polish town of Sandomierz to the Ukraine and Byelorussia until I reached the Roumanian controlled terrain of Transnistria, of which Odessa was the most prominent metropolis.

I looked at them and felt their eager anticipation. In no way was I in a position to let them down and destroy the fraternal warmth and attention they had showed me so far. In order to to procrastinate and thus even increase the suspense, I started to depict my childhood years when my parents moved from the small town to Poland's capital, Warsaw. I described to them the abundance of beautiful show-windows all over the metropolis, which was divided by the Vistula River into two parts, Warszawa and Warszawa-Praga. The whole city was surrounded with a gorgeous green belt of botanical gardens, parks, zoos, and amusement places.

Being an agrarian country foodstuffs were pretty cheap and plentiful. For ten Polish groszy one could buy seven fresh bagels and for fifteen groszy one could go to a delicatessen shop and buy a quarter pound of salami which was simply mouth-watering when put on fresh rye bread with mustard thrown in free by the store owner. However, not only was there ample nourishment for the Polish citizens' body but also plenty of spiritual food for his mind. It was a city of libraries and literary clubs, poetry societies and experimental theatre and artistic workshops and pantomime and ballet studios.

Warszawa was like a gigantic pomegranate filled with cultural institutions, universities, colleges, high schools, music conservatories and higher academies of learning. Ciechocinek, Zakopane, Sopoty, Krynica, Busko, Szczawnica and Otwock were famous recuperation and leisure spots with a natural beauty drawing throngs of tourists from all over the world. They all enjoyed Polish hospitality and reasonable prices as a consequence of the good foreign exchange rate.

Warszawa was of course the nerve centre of commerce and banking and international relations. Here all Polish ministries had their main edifices. Here all foreign embassies and consulates had their offices and any Polish citizen could, unhampered and undisturbed, apply for a visa to emigrate to any country he was interested in.

On the prestigious Marszhalkowska Street, the Square of the Three Crosses, Ujazdowskie and Zerozolimskie Aleje and the main railway terminal there were specially trained Polish policemen with little foreign flags sewn onto their left sleeve emphasizing the kind of language they could speak for the convenience of multitudes of tourists and sightseers strolling around freely in the city.

Only later, of course, did we find out that the fun loving tourists from the Third Reich were not just innocent, benign visitors having a good time, but Nazi fifth columnists preparing the ground for covert operations in collusion with the local ethnic Germans in Lodz, Poznan, Katowice, Gdansk, and Gdynia. Polish intelligence organs subsequently discovered a perfidious scheme of Nazi-intrigue in smuggling all kinds of weapons from the Third Reich to Poland in funeral caskets which were buried, allegedly as deceased people, in special private cemeteries. There were caches of machine guns, grenades, and mortars being readied for the late summer days of 1939 when the Führer would give the signal to start his war against Poland.

On the first of September, 1939, all the pent-up, dark forces of Teutonic evil were let loose on our country. The Nazis with their heavy tanks broke through the Polish border-line as their fifth columnist, clandestine S.S. men in Gdansk, Sileasia, Lodz, and the Pomorze and Poznan Districts opened fire on the Polish army from behind, stabbing us in the back.

In less than two weeks the Polish military machine was overwhelmed by the awesome technological superiority of the Nazi hordes. Only a few pockets of resistance fought on valiantly refusing to surrender. By the third week it was all over, only the capital stubbornly and heroically stuck to its decision not to allow the Hitlerites to enter Poland's capital and officially win the war, thus ending Polish sovereignty. The city president, Starzynski, inspired the military defenders and his civilian residents to go on fighting the Swastika demons for Poland's honour and freedom.

Polish cavalrymen on horseback showed amazing courage in attacking German motorized steel troop carriers and tank units with their bare sabres. In the meantime the Luftwaffe continuously and indiscriminately bombarded the civilian population, setting Warsaw's houses ablaze with incendiary bombs. The billowing smoke of burning buildings, the strench of fallen victims lying exposed in the streets, the rotting horses and cattle posed the real threat of dangerous fumes, forcing people to wear primitive, self-improvised linen masks. Hungry, without clean air to breathe, without water to drink, with all the canals and waterworks in ruins, people had to risk their lives and go under a fusilade of bullets to the shores of the Vistula to fetch some untreated river water to quench their thirst.

For four weeks Warsaw's beseiged and courageous dwellers delayed the entrance of Hitler's army, hoping that Poland's allies, France and England, would show up in the sky with their planes and rescue them from both starvation and the Nazi bondage. All the capital's residents became like one united family in the communal task of building barricades, laying tank traps, digging huge pits, and putting up barbed wire. All the rivalries and antagonisms among the different ethnic groups and minorities were temporarily shelved in a spontaneous moratorium. Bearded, orthodox Jews marched together with bigoted, ultraradical Polish nationalists; university professors strode in the same row with garbage collectors; business tycoons walked with street vendors and gypsies; ear-locked Yeshiva boys with uniformed high school students. All carried spades and shovels; all were volunteers offering to excavate the ground, to hollow out the anti-aircraft defence entrenchments for the civilian population.

But when twenty eight days of heroic resistance passed by with no sign of foreign help, no allied war planes showing up on the horizon, and the beautiful streets and boulevards turning into heaps of smoldering rubble, with every backyard becoming a cemetery for the multitudes of victims and all the ammunition used up to the last cartridge, Mayor Starzynski and the commanders of the military garrison decided to lay down their weapons. They had no choice but to stop the pointless self-sacrifice of the citizens.

Warsaw was taken over by the Third Reich and goose-stepping S.S. and Wehrmacht divisions triumphantly marched through Marszalkowska Avenue with fanfare and military bands, celebrating their first big victory of the Second World War. Warsaw was like a bereaved widow in mourning, watching in anxiety and painful disbelief the incoming forces of the Schwabs, her historic foe who had once again inundated her territory. And there was good reason to be concerned. Behind the front-line forces a whole armada of Nazi bureaucrats, District Chiefs, security officials and Gestapo were following. It did not take very long before people of intellect, fame, knowledge, and social prominence — writers, politicians, doctors, and lawyers — began to disappear in the middle of the night, picked up by the Gestapo.

Warsaw's city emblem of the mermaid was removed and replaced by the death-head skull and cross-bones of the S.S. insignia. Poland, the country of hospitality and friendliness, was being transformed into one gigantic prison. A horror-charged message of genocide was in the air. Poland, the land of politeness and hospitality became a network of killing factories and concentration camps: Belzec, Chelmno, Sobibor, Maidanek, Auschwitz, Treblinka.

Operation Barbarosa, a Nazi code name for the sudden attack on Russia of the 22nd of June 1941, also signalled the official and conspicuous final phase in the enormous crime of mass annihilation. Jews, Karaites, Gypsies, Socialists, Communists, mischlinge (offspring from mixed marriages of Jews and Aryans up to the fourth generation), Soviet prisoners of war, undesirables, 'subhumans', and anti-socials were blazing *en masse* on a never extinguished pyre. Whoever's lineage was not from hereditary German or pure Aryan stock, whoever belonged, therefore, to an irrelevant, superfluous, and unnecessary tribe with no importance in the construction of Hitler's new world order, was automatically, one way or another, sooner or later, sentenced to perish.

The Dark Ages had returned to the European heartlands with even more inquisitorial bestiality than ever recorded in the annals of human civilization. The death factories were going at full-speed ahead. The realization of *Mein Kampf* took on its most satanic shape.

I told them how with immense risks I finally succeeded in going through the Odessan catacombs and on April 10th, 1944 reached the Russian lines in Rozdyelnaya. "And here I am," I said, "arrested and accused of being a German spy of all things. The escapee from the Ghetto and only surviving member of a whole family — accused of being a secret agent of the Nazis!"

"Perhaps you are a spy and informer," Ignatyeyev commented caustically, as soon as I finished my story. "You fooled me alright with your talent for impersonation and your Slavic nose, into thinking you were a Polachok, while in reality, despite your blond hair and blue eyes, you are nothing but a Zid, a kike!"

"Yea!" the one-legged footwear cutter, Boris Nasimov, agreed. "Historically, since biblical times when your leader Joshua sent his spies to Rahab the harlot, you people developed through the ages a tremendous skill for covert operations in corrupting others to help you in your schemes of profiteering, cheating, acquiring high positions in the top echelon of society, and usurping power and control."

"Even during the October Revolution," Ignatyeyev hammered further, "there was a loud-mouthed guy from your cabal by the name of Leon Davidovich Bronstein, who changed his name to Lev Trotsky and worked his way up to the very leadership of the Red Army, destroying the Czar and the established true Russian way of life."

On the mention of the Czar, a delirious Yermoleyev crossed himself, mumbling semi-consciously, "G-d save the Czar!"

The Yiddish speaking Ukrainian also joined the choir of maligners, showing off his "profound" knowledge of history. "Even at the inception of Christianity a Jew by the name of Judas infiltrated the Nazarene hierarchy only to betray Jesus."

"Come to think of it," the yellow-bearded engineer mused, "Jews did indeed play a major role in the Soviet Army. I remember my father mentioning the names of Yagoda, Gamarik, Bucharin, and others as general staff members of the new revolutionary armed forces. It must be admitted, as a matter of fact, that Jews have not only shown superior intelligence in military strategy; they were also the most devoted and most dynamic nucleus of the Bolshevik power. Zinoviev (Hirsch Radomilski), Kamieniev (Rozenfeld), Karl Radek (Sobelson), and Maxim Litvinov were all Jews. Kaganovich and Venyamin Dimshitz are also Jews."

"The whole Marxist ideology is a Jewish creation," Ignatyeyev took over again, "authored by Karl Marx, a German Jew!"

"And this wretched ideology was brutally forced upon the heads of the poor, unfortunate Russian masses," concluded the hitherto taciturn cafeteria administrator. "Our people lived and laughed under the Czarist regime! We were well dressed, we ate heartily, and we made merry! Then the Jewish communists came. They brought the Revolution and they blessed Mother Russia with a regime of corruption and torn trousers."

I sat there, too stunned to say anything. Here I was, right back in the lion's den. When I started to tell my story the atmosphere was full of sympathy and keen suspense, but now the cell was filled with hate and malice, directed at me personally. I unburdened my soul to these people and all I received in return was poisonous bigotry. As the Yiddish proverb says, "The kinsman came to collect his inheritance and instead he was presented with a bill for the funeral expenses!"

Of the twelve fellow-inmates in the cell, the only ones to refrain from the vitriolic anti-semitic slanders were two elderly Odessans in military dress, Gugarin the tank commander, the sick Yermolyeyev, and of course Matway the Cossack. Matway could see how frustrated and upset I felt so he walked over to me and handed me Makhorka tobacco and a piece of paper to roll a cigarette.

"Adam," he said, as he almost physically lifted me from my place near the Yiddish-speaking Ukrainian. "After today's run-in you don't want to be sleeping next to an anti-Semite like that Ukrainian. Come on, Adamchyk," he said, tugging at my sleeve. "I want to sleep by you. You move over and take your place between me and Gugarin. And listen!" he pointed a finger at me. "Don't take any of that perverted racist garbage to heart. Those people are speaking only for themselves. The Soviet people aren't like that. Those people are quislings, scum, German boot-lickers. They're all contaminated with the gangrene of Hitler's ideas. They're irreparable counter-revolutionaries whose brains are so smitten with the sickness of hate and prejudice that there's no way that they can think straight any more."

"Exactly!" said Gugarin loudly accentuating every single syllable in his ironic, misanthropic manner. "They are indeed apparent vestiges of the olden days, ardent devotees of Nikolai Romanov's reign of serfdom and exploitation and affectionate chain-hugging, and they long for the good times when peasants were flogged and Jews blood-libeled and pogromed."

"Here Adamchyk, have a piece of butterbrot! My sister will probably come again tomorrow with a new food supply for another month," Mayway said, as he handed me a buttered slice of bread.

"Don't let them get to you, Adamchyk! Come on, loosen up! I assure you that you will outlive them city-slickers trying to become experts on scriptures, history, and the Jewish nationality. Even I, a Kolkhoz-Cossack of the Don Basin, know that they are nothing but a bunch of dark, ignorant burpers. Cheer up and listen to my enlightening anecdote."

"Two Soviet citizens were travelling together on the city trolley car. One of them was Russian and the other was Jewish. As you know, the women of Russia are unlike those of the Western countries. They are not mere prattlers who only discuss clothes, jewellery and sex. Our women are on a much higher cultural level. When they converse, they do not discuss trivialities, but matters of substance such as art, music, and literature. The Russian woman asks the Jewish woman, 'Do you know that Tolstoy is a magnificent Russian writer, a literary giant who has no equal throughout the whole world?' "

"Then the Jewish woman replies scornfully, 'Tolstoy, Schmolstoy, his real name is Tolstoyevitch! He was a Jew who lived on Babela Street in Odessa.' "

"The Russian woman found herself momentarily in a predicament but she recovered quickly and declared, 'Here in the Soviet Union everyone is really equal, and one's relation to a race, or people, is meaningless and of no consequence to us. As far as Tolstoy is concerned, despite his origins, he is nevertheless a giant in Russian literature.' "

"After a few minutes, she attempts once again. She turns to the Jewish woman and remarks, 'And do you know about Lermontov? What a magnificent classical writer he was — his characters, galleries of human types, sheer art!' "

" 'Lermontov, Schmermontov! Lermontovich was his real name,' she replies scornfully. 'Who doesn't know of him? He was a Jew from the city of Dniepropietrowsk. His father was a rabbi.' "

"The Russian woman becomes speechless and excited. Now she realizes for certain that matters are not in order. But for the purpose of verifying this, she decides to test her fellow-passenger with the name of a famous Ukrainian Cossack writer, Gogol. With a smile she turns to the Jewish woman and remarks, 'Do you know that in literature, on a world-wide scale, there is no one as colourful and artistic as the author of Taras Bulba, Gogol?' "

"The Jewish woman replies with her usual nonchalance, 'Gogol, Shmogol, his real name is Gogolevich, a Jew from Kiev. His father ran a food store near the train depot!' "

"The Russian woman is unable to contain herself and she cries out 'Jesus Christ!' whereupon the Jewish woman rejoins as casually as ever, 'Who do you think he was? Also a Jew by nationality!' "

Ignatyeyev neither laughed nor giggled nor even grinned. He was not a very gracious loser. With fiery, bloodshot eyes he mockingly referred to the Cossack and Gugarin as the two military Gruzenbergs defending the Polish Little Beilis.* By now, however, Matway was really angry. He went over to Ignatyeyev and threatened to squash him like a bed bug if he didn't shut up at once. That was enough to make Ignatyeyev finally simmer down and stop his abusive remarks.

Later in the night, Yermolyeyev died and the guard ordered me, Gugarin, Matway, and the Yiddish-speaking Ukrainian to carry the diseased, limp remains of the foresaken watchman to the second yard near the garbage bin. After returning to the cell, we all washed our hands with the only available cold water and went back to sleep. Before dawn, I was again awakened by the turnkey and taken to the office of Captain Woronow, my new interrogator.

"Adam Yanovich Arendarski, alias Amnon Alexandrovich Ajzensztadt. Quite an impressive dossier that you have. I just finished reading it and I must tell you it is almost like a suspense story. Very interesting with some definite cinematographic potential. A Rabbi's son who, in my understanding, is sup-

---

* Beilis Mendel was a Russian Jew charged in Kiev in 1911, with committing a ritual murder. The accusation was accompanied by violent anti-Semitic propaganda and by a wave of protest in liberal circles throughout the world. The trial lasted for 34 days after a preparatory investigation of 2 years.

There was a tangible conspiracy to convict the Jews of blood ritual practices. However, the renowned lawyer, Gruzenberg, managed to prove Mendel Beilis' innocence and he was acquitted in 1913. He then emigrated to the U.S. where he died 21 years later.

posed to be an introverted and shy individual, passively accepting everything as heavenly providence, kicks up such a storm to stay alive? It really makes no sense. A religious youngster of the Ghetto gets out from behind the barbed wire walls guarded day and night by the Nazis. He instantly changes his manners and traits from those of a passively suffering Ghetto dweller into the self-assured posture of a genuine, pure-blooded, Christian Pole. He cleverly adopts the fictitious name of Adam Arendarski to match the initials of his name in the past. Makes contact with a group of the Todt organization's auxiliary forces, successfully improvising a story about being an ex-Polish officer and a refugee from Poznan, speaking German fluently, and thus a potential asset while traveling from Poland to the Ukraine. Arrives in Winitza, which becomes his spring-board for further penetration into ex-Soviet territory to reach as far as Dniepropietrowsk. There he gets involved with his disguised co-religionists in German regalia working in the industrial city in subterranean activities against their bosses and overlords, committing acts of arson and sabotage while this time wearing a Luftwaffe uniform. Then he teams up with an Italian officer in a carefully organized scheme to syphon off 10,000 litres of gasoline, obviously from Nazi sources, through the entrepreneuring connivance of a Russian black-marketeer. Talks his new 'maccaroni' pals into taking him along as their translator, confessing in the secrecy of the captain's office to being the only survivor of a murdered Jewish clergyman's family. Gets drunk in a premature vodka celebration to mark his collusion with the Fascist alleged deserters who accepted him into their midst on the adventurous journey to freedom. Remains marooned in his brand new *Duce* uniform because of his imbibing of too much alcohol. Nevertheless, he shakes off despondency and makes it to Odessa in a Nazi Red Cross train after which he wins the confidence of a patriotic neighbour and manages to talk a Georgian partisan into taking him along on a daring escape attempt through dynamited catacombs to the Red Army lines. Surfaces in liberated Rozdielnaya with the prestigious record of having worn three different kinds of enemy uniforms and carrying a bundle of Yiddish poetry and chronicles about German atrocities, mass destruction and emotional longing for Zion!"

"It makes no sense to me, I'm afraid. A Chassidic young man without any training and involvement in intelligence work pulls off such a feat, accomplishes such exploits completely on his own, without any of the contacts and support of a major international intelligence organization? Eh, eh! Impossible!"

"I have in your file a bunch of names and places of your alleged comrades-in-arms and co-workers in the underground activities against the Nazis. They include the village of Dolgintzevo near Krivoy-Rog where you supposedly, with a local fellow by the name of Ivan Bebchuk, set ablaze in the fall of 1943

an ammunition train, destroying a large shipment of artillery shells desig-
nated to hold back the Red Army advance. I have also a family name,
Hruboshapka, in the Kolkhoz of Novoye Zhitye in the Uman district who participated with you in the destruction of a grain transport assigned for the Third
Reich. There are also other names from Nishni-Dnyeprovsk, Sasha Dulcin,
Vanka Kamburakes, Misha Dunk, and Petya Slavko — bricklayers, carpenters,
and electricians — who may have helped you as their foreman to sabotage a
Luftwaffe office building by intentionally using the wrong, non-fireproof
materials, chimney bricks, and wires, so that a month later a conflagration
burned down a large part of the Nazis' regional airforce headquarter. Then I
have the names of your Jewish Kashtan friends — as you call them — who,
according to your statements, are now for sure serving in Wanda Wasilewska's
army on the way to liberate Poland. Wladek Starozynski, Jacek Polanski,
Stefan Wrobel, Michael Papier, Walek Czuj, Wojtek Szymanski, Zdislaw
Kogut, and Mieczyslaw Sokolowski."

"Do you know how long it is going to take to get written declarations from
all those individuals to corroborate your chain of activities during a year and a
half? Do you really know, with the war still going on how long it is going to take
to unravel your Thousand And One Nights' stories of resistance, of being a
Jew, and of having a clean personal record?"

"You should not have refused Colonel Nyekrasow's proposition to sign a
confession on a lesser political charge and get it over with. In your condition,
with no one around to support you morally and physically with family warmth
and food parcels, you will, unfortunately, very soon be in a pitiful and
wretched shape."

"But every word is true," I burst out, with pent-up, choked anger. "I am a
Ghetto escapee, anti-Nazi fighter and a Jew!"

Captain Woronow kept his grey eyes riveted on me, studying my every
move and gesture, and listening to the very tone of my voice as I excitedly went
on with my deluge of desperate and bitter words.

"So," he calmly asked after I fell silent, "you are still determined to go on
with your claim that you are Jewish?"

"Of course I am! And if you would let me or rather allow me I could prove it
to you."

"How so?" Woronow moved in his chair, and sat up straight, obviously
curious to know how I proposed to do that.

"Very simply," I replied. "Call in a doctor and he will tell you that I went
through ritual circumcision!"

"Oh that! Big deal!" Woronow forced himself to laugh. "Circumcision,
shmircumcision. You think that I was born yesterday. I could call in one of our
NKGB operatives working in the Far East, a genuine Russian, on whom was

performed a bit of plastic surgery. And now, with his slanted, almond-shaped eyes and rearranged jaw he has the complete and perfect look of a full-blooded Asian. So what kind of proof is that? What do you think that I am, a dummy? Do not insult my intelligence! From everybody's penis a piece of foreskin can be cut off!"

I returned from Woronow's office exhausted and emotionally drained. To add insult to injury, Matway and Gugarin, my self-appointed protectors and defenders, were gone. I found out that after I was led off for the investigation, another guard came and led the Cossack and the ex-captain to the second floor where a military tribunal of higher NKGB officers sat behind a large desk covered with a green flannel tablecloth. The procedures and jurisdictional formalities were short and swift. Gugarin and Matway were both found to be guilty as charged. Both were convicted and sentenced to death, with an automatic commutation to serve in a suicide battalion. Socialist justice had given them the final chance to redeem their sins on the battlefield against the fascist enemy; and they were promptly sent off to the front lines under armed military escort.

Once again I found myself lying next to the Yiddish-speaking Ukrainian who this time was all sweetness. With a benign lovable smile he tried to cheer me up by talking to me in my native tongue. "Listen attentively," he told me, "to what I tell you, and don't lose your courage. The main thing here is to survive and stay alive. And where there is life, there is always a chance for improvement!"

I looked at him in silence, comprehending that his sudden goodness was probably a prelude to a proposition sure to follow. And sure enough, Kowalenko did not hesitate very long to formulate his idea. "You see," he told me, "the main thing in our predicament is to endure and tide over the investigation period, which is the toughest bit. Nourishment is the name of the game. If you have enough to eat, you will overcome this critical, drastic stage without being devoured by hunger and sickness and you will make it to a labour-camp where the disciplinary rigor is much easier and the living conditions much better, sometimes to the point that one gets a whole kilo of bread per day, besides soup and additional extras. But truthfully speaking, after yesterday's confrontation with the cell 'big shots,' I don't think you can expect any handouts from them anymore. I therefore want to suggest to you a logical solution to ward off the torments of miserable hunger, suffering, and perhaps in the long run, malnutrition and emaciation."

"You, Adam, have a good pair of European woollen trousers, which you wear on top of your long johns. Well, let me have them! I will then send them out with my dirty laundry to my wife. She will figure out the purpose of it, because I have done it before. She will then simply go to the bazaar, sell the pants and buy enough groceries to ensure that for the next couple of months we will live like kings, getting from her fresh vegetables, sour pickles, cheese, and plenty of home-baked cookies and white bread!"

I looked at the glistening, round, lustful eyes of my neighbour and they seemed like those of a vulture in anticipation of an upcoming kill. It made me feel indescribably powerless. That phrase, "let me have your trousers" reverberated in my ears with a ring of bygone, tragic days. It reminded me of a beastly scene in the Vinitza forest where another Ukrainian, a policeman, participated with an S.S. annihilation-squad in the liquidatioon of local families. It was deep in the woods where I came with a truck for timber and walked in on the macabre scenario of people digging their own graves before they were shot. A little boy of perhaps 3 or 4 years kept undressing like everybody else. But, when it came to his trousers he stopped, unwilling to remove them. The Wlasow-quisling walked over and yelled at the little toddler, "Let me have your pants!" "No! they are a present from my mommy," the child innocently refused. Minutes later he was machine-gunned into the excavated pit with all the others.

"Let me have your trousers," Kowalenko repeated.

"No," I replied, suppressing an increasing wave of contempt. "I don't think it is such a good idea to walk around in my underwear like a dehumanized clown, entertaining your compatriots with the look of a half-naked Jew!"

As we all went to sleep I lay there feeling all the events of the past forty-eight hours. I was nauseated by Ignatyeyev and the group's vitriolic anti-Semitism; by Woronow's smooth allegations and inferences concerning my future; and I was sick to my stomach with Kowalenko's solution on how to survive.

In the middle of the night I began to perspire and felt a piercing discomfort in the lower abdomen, with a terrible urge to drink. The cold, unboiled cell-water was not very soothing for the enraged intestines, or thirst-quenching for the dry, inflamed throat. As the hours dragged on, discomfort turned into a painful sensation in the whole stomach area, forcing me to evacuate my bowels every so often. At first I thought that it was only a passing inconvenience which was induced by too much fluid in an empty digestive system, with little fibrous, solid food and a lot of beverage. But as the pain did not subside and the bouts of diarrhoea repeated themselves continuously, I started to worry seriously about my condition.

The image of the diseased Yermoleyev suddenly appeared before me; the way he lay on the floor turning from one side to another, moving back and forth and moaning in agony. Then followed the systematic loss of consciousness and inability to look after his physiological needs, resulting in foul odours of urine and feces around him. Then came the silence and the expiration of life and the final pathetic procession carrying the lifeless remains to the obscurity of the garbage bin.

"Oh G-d," I thought in panic, "I probably got infected by Yermoleyev while taking his contagious body out from the cell to the middle yard. Merciful Father in Heaven," I whispered imploringly, "please don't degrade me to the wretched condition of wallowing in my own slime, to the vengeful, triumphant gaze of my enemies." Gnashing my teeth, I forced myself to walk straight on the morning march to the wash-faucet. It took superhuman effort to stop my rebellious guts from exploding and besmirching the only pair of underwear in my possession.

When they brought kipiatok for breakfast, Tolia was ladling out the hot water. I walked over to him and said in a desperate voice, "Citizen-Guard, I am sick with dysentery. I probably got it two nights ago when you picked me to help remove Yermoleyev from the cell. Please help me!"

Tolia lifted his steel-grey eyes onto me and gave me two portions of hot water without saying a word. Before leaving the cell he looked at me again as if making a mental note. But hours went by in drudgery. The cell was busy with its usual routines and nothing happened.

My condition was no longer any secret. The constant sorties to the pot blatantly told the whole story of my acquired plight, visibly producing perverse delight in Ignatyeyev's smiling face.

"You don't feel so good, eh?" he said as he walked over towards me. "Well, you can't win 'em all! You succeeded in imitating the Pollacks and the Germans. And now I see that you are doing a great job of imitating the late Yermoleyev. That is exactly the way it started with him! Running to the pot every half hour. Then the overpowering feeling of helplessness and inferiority which made him separate himself from all of us. Then followed the psychological succumbing to his illness. Then the physical deterioration started to set in. The bouts of deliriousness, the incoherent talking to himself, mumbling distracted prayers to almight G-d — just like you, Abrashka!"

While Ignatyeyev was taunting me, the yellow-bearded engineer and his chums nodded approvingly at this low spectacle of venomous double-talk. They apparently got a kick out of his comparison of my predicament to Yermoleyev's fatal condition and unhappy end. So they sat there leaning on the cell-wall like front row viewers in a circus watching the ongoing live show, enjoying how the Kolkhoz secretary teased the Ghetto escapee, dismantling him to bits.

Only Boris Nasimov, the one-legged footwear cutter, did not entirely appreciate the subtleties of Ignatyeyev's fancy double-talk. He believed in the straight forward, full fledged, lethal sting which immobilizes instantly, on the spot, and for good. So he grabbed his crutches, hobbled over to the corner near the door where I was now lying and took over the initiative from the Kolchoznik, who returned to his place.

"Abrashka!" he addressed me with the solemnity of a supreme court justice pronouncing a final precedent making decision.

I lifted my head to meet the two hate-filled eyes of an incorrigible anti-semite.

"Abrashka!" he spat out the words with the hiss of a rattlesnake. "Doomed, you are doomed! It's no use! You are finished! Kaput! You are going to kick the bucket and join the watchman six feet under the ground! Your Yiddish shtick won't help you any more. That's it! No medicine, no doctor. You will soon be carried out like Yermoleyev."

Although annoyed and disgusted with the repulsive anti-semitic harassment, I maintained my composure, suppressing a mounting impulse to kick the invalid in his only shinbone and then spit in the faces of the sanctimonious Yiddish expert and the beastly Kolkhoz secretary. I suppressed my compulsion to hit back into a superhuman effort to get up and walk around, pacing the long cell floor as if driven by an inner instinct, thinking that this was the only thing to do in order not to let the sickness or the angel of death get a hold of me.

This was no ordinary, regular walk. It involved moving through a gauntlet of cat-calls, mocking remarks, denigrating name-calling and accusations about deicide. A repetitious, ancient scenario in miniature took place; an Israelite among the nations, getting what is historically a consequence of Diaspora, of living on Esau's soil, and depending on the mercy of a potential predator.

The cell door suddenly opened and Tolia appeared behind the glittering, elegantly uniformed figure of Major Pushkin, the administrative commander of the whole Babela compound.

"Listen , you counter-revolutionary scum! What is going on around here?" The major's voice carried a distinct roar of displeasure. "What are you trying to do in this institution, create an epidemic? Who is sick?" he thundered at the top of his voice.

"I am," I lifted my right hand.

"Oh! The Zapadnik! Anybody else?" his booming baritone voice repeated the question.

"No!" came a chorus of voices.

"Okay. Zapadnik, pick up your belongings! You are being taken to the hospital."

As I left in front of the Major and Tolia, the cheerful looks of my tormentors turned into unhappy gazes of disappointment.

CHAPTER 11

The Legacy of Maimonides

Foxes have holes, birds of the air have nests and inmates of the NKGB have a hospital to go to for treatment and recuperation. Of course, the hospital for the incarcerated is hardly luxurious. It is a mini-medical institution within the prison walls where the wards are painted white, the bars on the windows are white, the beds are white, and the most important staple, the daily bread portion handed out to the patients is, in contrast to the regular cell-dwellers' payok, also white.

There were thirty-six patients in the Odessa prison infirmary when I was taken there. There were, however, only four beds which were allotted on a first-come, first-served basis. The beds came without linen, sheets, blankets, or pillows; there was only a spring mattress with metal headboard at one end and a wooden board at the other. In the large sick bay there were no night-tables, no cupboards, no clothes-hangers, no rub-downs at bed-time, and little by way of medicine other than a mild sedative and perhaps a spoonful of greenish mixture that was supposed to pacify one's stomach.

Nevertheless, it was enough for a patient to know that he was going to be seen by a doctor. That alone was therapeutic, as was the knowledge that he had got out from a foul-smelling basement cell and was now in a roomy area with walls that reeked of carbolic acid and with large, sunlit windows through which could be seen the prison yard.

The fact that there were thirty-six sick offenders in the infirmary reminded me of the thirty-six 'just men' on whom, in Jewish folklore, the fate of the world depends at any one time. The thirty-six of us ranged in age from teenage to octogenarian. As anonymous residents of the jail bolnitza we were entitled to preferential medical attention. The kipiatok breakfast was the same — colourless, boiled, clear water, but the soup at lunch-time was much better than the ordinary,. murky, and watery stuff that was handed out in the regular cells. Furthermore, there were major hygienic advantages to being in the hospital ward. There were regular toilets and sinks and much more space in the ward itself. Each prisoner had about seventeen square feet to himself in the six hundred square feet room. He could lie down, stretch, exercise, play cards, or even play hopscotch in all that space.

No one actually had the energy to indulge in any kind of exercise because everyone in the room was sick. Asthma sufferers sat lugubriously on the floor, leaning on the ceramic wall tile and labouring heavily to catch their breath. The malaria-stricken shuddered convulsively in alternating spells of hot and cold, covering themselves with whatever they could lay a hand on. The angina pectoris and heart condition sufferers, with congested, water-filled lungs, clogged veins and vapid, pale faces with baggy, sad eyes sat and lay right near the entrance, knowing very well what to expect in a place where there was no intensive care unit, no cathartic equipment, nor even an ordinary intravenous contrivance and oxygen mask. And the largest group of all, patients smitten with intestinal and digestive diseases from excessive looseness of the bowels to the more serious dysentery inflammations, scurried back and forth from the washroom, busy with cleaning themselves from the after-effects of involuntary bouts of diarrhea.

Fortunately, I belonged to the lighter cases with my fever subsiding and no discharges of blood or mucus. Forty-eight hours after my arrival from Babela, I was so much better that I began to feel slight pangs of hunger. The acute colic pain and abdominal spasms stopped. My body temperature went back to normal. The hot and cold flashes ceased. The weakness in the legs was gone.

I believed with complete faith that G-d almighty had heard my prayers and that divine intervention had saved me from a miserable death. In humility and gratitude I recited another of the Psalms of David that seemed to me to suit the occasion:

> Lord, how are they increased that trouble me! Many are they that rise up against me. Many there be which say of my soul, there is no help for him in G-d. Se'lah. But thou, O Lord, art a shield for me; my glory, and the lifter up of mine head. I cried unto the Lord with my voice, and he heard me out of his holy hill. Se'lah. I laid me down and slept; I awakened; for the Lord sustained me. I will not be afraid of ten thousands of people, that have set themselves against me round about. Arise, O Lord; save me, O my G-d: For thou hast smitten all mine enemies upon the cheek bone; thou hast broken the teeth of the ung-dly. Salvation belongeth unto the Lord: Thy blessing is upon thy people. Se'lah.

I was certainly recovering in more ways than one. Physically, I was feeling better and my appetite had returned. Mentally and spiritually, the traumatic feelings aroused in me by the anti-semitic outbursts of my cell-mates had given way to a renewed faith in the promise made to me by my father, that I would survive. From the depths of my Chassidic soul I began to experience a feeling of real hope. If, despite all the odds, a lady barber had saved me from the ravages of hunger in Rozdielnaya, then there was no reason why someone might not be able to help me in my present situation, for I was once again very, very hungry.

As if staged by some magic choreographer, a red-headed lady came in and authoritatively ordered everyone to line up to receive a tablespoon of brown sugar, as a supplement to the daily diet. I looked at her piercingly, observing for a while her every gesture, her every movement — the way she spoke to the inmates, the way she dug the spoon into the sugar, the way she carried the bowl carefully pressing it to her bosom. It began to dawn on me that she was perhaps a Jewish woman employed in the penal institution's supply department, which included the duty of handing out the sweet stuff to the prison hospital's patients.

When my turn came to receive the extra nourishing glucose, I simply told her: "I am a Jew, a survivor of the Warsaw Ghetto. Perhaps you can help me?"

Instantaneously, without lifting her eyes from the dish, as if she had not seen or heard anything, she replied like a ventriloquist in a soft Lithuanian Yiddish, "Get into the line again and I will give you another spoon of sugar!"

The "second" spoon of sugar became my most precious and most potent medication. Rimsky, my asthmatic neighbour, gladly gave me his bread portion for the remaining sugar whenever I was willing to make the exchange. With two rations of bread, the better quality soup, and the sugar supplement, I began to recuperate and make definite progress.

Five days later, another Jewish lady came into the picture, joining my gallery of good Samaritans as dentist and medical supervisor over the Babela arrivals. Doctor Miriam Moiseyevna Maimun, was not the sort of physician who aspired to a high position in Soviet society and the chance of making a lot of money. Her clientele consisted of a social stratum that did not have a Russian penny to their soul, and could not pay even if they wanted to. Monetary reward was not the reason for her professional vocation as a mender of the human body, under the most frustrating conditions. From the look of her sunken face with the projecting cheek bones, she seemed to be an undernourished female inmate permitted, for some reason, to walk from cell to cell on errands of the administration. She did not look like the chief medical practitioner with hundreds of incarcerated patients to look after.

However, the white coat with the stethoscope in the lower pocket and thermometer in the upper breast pocket — always sticking out like a special medical insignia — identified her right away as the medical woman who could help at least with a pain-killer, or a placebo tablet, or in cases of emaciation, by assigning one to the special cell for weak, enfeebled prisoners where an extra tablespoon of mashed potatoes was handed out in addition to the regular food ration.

And so, despite her not looking the least bit like the Mona Lisa, the prison doctor was the most popular and respected individual in the gigantic, concrete enclosure with grated windows that was Odessa's main jail. The inmates were like subdued beasts in cages, and they had an intensified instinct to sound out and appreciate who was a true and genuine friend in this cesspool of misery, indifference, and dejection. To them, the medicine woman was the only reminder that besides the penal functionaries of guards, prison officials, turn-keys, investigators, watch tower sentries and NKGB men — to whom they were all just cell numbers, files, cases, and counter-revolutionary garbage — there was someone who still thought of who they really were: human beings in trouble, starved for an encouraging word of hope, longing for consolation for their wounded psyches as well as decent care and treatment for their diseased and sick bodies. To them, she was psychologist, psychiatrist, healer, surgeon, dentist, and ombudsman, albeit with little authority to radically improve their life in a permanent way. She tenderly opened their abscesses, squeezed the puss out of their infected wounds and scabies, pulled their aching, decayed teeth from the inflamed gums, bandaged their hurt, ulcerated limbs and defused their anger and desperation with a quiet word of assurance for the future.

The doctor worked in a most peculiar kind of examination room. Located underneath the fourth floor stairway, in the corner of the huge, round prison balcony with the attached net in the center as a preventive measure against potential suicides. It had the nondescript look of a bohemian artist's atelier, with an enameled white, padded barber chair right in the middle as a centrepiece. It could also have been a small chemical or pharmaceutical labor-atory where one manufactured home-made drugs with all the different sizes of fluid-filled bottles standing on shelves in the glass cabinet and on the window sill and floor. The only decorous pieces of furniture in this cramped one hundred square foot area were a brown leather sofa and a little metal table with an electric two-burner plate on it. Right next to it was the water faucet, the sink, and an aquarium-like transparent box which was fastened to the wall and which was covered with a piece of white plywood containing such medical par-aphernalia as scalpels, scissors, syringes, different sizes of needles, pincers, clamps, and rubberized bandages. In emergencies, this small, crowded cham-ber served also as a resting place and private kitchen for the doctor to prepare some food for herself. There were no artifacts or medical diplomas hanging on the walls. The only thing, probably insignificant to anyone else but astounding to me, was a pencil drawing of Maimonides, carefully glued down on a piece of cardboard and hung on the inside of the parchment-coloured door.

I almost fell off the barber chair when I noticed the familiar face of the Rambam, with the majestic, handsome beard, beautiful eyes, and turban headdress, so well known to me from my youth as the venerable author of the *Guide for the Perplexed* and the prodigious compiler of *Mishne Torah*, the Halachic summary of Judaism in all its varied aspects.

Dr. Maimun had summoned me to her office for a check-up after the dysentery bouts. Noticing my astonished surprise she confronted me with her deep set, dark eyes: "Do you know who this is?"

"Of course I know who it is!"

"Well, why don't you tell me?"

"This is a portrait of the eminent and revered doctor and scholar from the 13th century, the Rambam, otherwise known as Rabbenu Moshe Ben Maimun."

"Doctor Moshe Maimun is the founder of my family," she said. "I must admit that I am very proud to be his descendant and to serve as a doctor myself. Our family has always worked as doctors, going back many centuries. It is a family tradition to undertake the work of healing the sick, and it was bequeathed to us by my illustrious grandfather in the 13th century."

I was really and truly astonished! Here I was, the son of the Tzosmerer Rebbe from Sandomierz, Poland, and a descendant of the Maharal of Prague, and I had met a descendant of the Rambam in Odessa, but emanating from Cairo. Despite the difference between her Sephardic, Spanish, and North African roots and my Ashkenazic, East European roots, there was an immediate and obvious affinity between us, as fellow-Jews who were at one in our respect for our Jewishness.

Moved by our immediately being able to converse in a friendly and intimate way, I got out of the barber-chair and walked over to the narrow, barred window of the fourth floor office. I peeked out of the window and looked in all directions, like a curious canary looking out of its cage.

In response to the doctor's asking me what I could see, I replied in a ponderous and cheerless tone of voice, "Graves."

"That's right," the doctor said in a matter of fact tone of voice. "To the right of our penal institution is the old Jewish cemetery. You can easily identify it by the ordinary tombstones, without crosses and the square alphabetical type of Hebrew lettering. On the left is the Russian, Greek-Orthodox Christian cemetery with the elaborate mausoleums, fancy ornamentation, cupolas and sculptures of the Madonna and the Nazarene, erected in Czarist times."

"No! I am not talking about those graves," I blurted out with a change of voice, as if I had suddenly gotten a sore throat. "You see," I said, stretching out my arms and pointing the index fingers of the right and left hands simultaneously in both directions, "those are regular graves, of regular people, who in their overwhelming majority lived a normal life and most probably died a normal death from old age, or perhaps an accident, or a fatal, incurable disease in the presence of their nearest and dearest, in their own beds in their own homes. What came to my mind while looking out through your window was an entirely different kind of graves!"

Miriam Moiseyevna put down the medicine bottles and walked over to the window with a puzzled expression on her face.

"Look please straight ahead, not sideways," I implored softly. "What do you see?"

"Straight in front of us is the tree-lined Proletaryatzky Boulevard," the doctor said.

"Right," I agreed. "What else do you see?"

"Well," said the medicine woman, looking intently out again. "All I can see at this time of the day when everybody is at work and there are almost no pedestrians are mountains of fallen leaves covering the sidewalk!"

"That's right," I replied. "You hit the nail on the head! Those heaped up multitudes of fallen yellow leaves reminded me of the other, entirely different category of graves which I wrote about in a lament before I was arrested."

"Do you happen to remember what you wrote?" Miriam Moiseyevna asked quietly, but with apparent interest.

"Oh yes! I remember every word of it. It is engraved in my brain forever, never to be erased. Sometimes, it becomes dormant for a while. But all that I need is an accidental cue, like a garbage collection team cleaning up the streets, or a dog-catcher lassooing homeless dogs, or a poor funeral procession without flowers, and the whole picture of destruction, death, and graves surfaces immediately."

"Would you recite for me this poem about those unconventional graves?"

"If you want me to."

"Yes, I do," the medicine woman plugged up the bottle and leaned on the wall opposite the barber chair.

> Falling autumn leaves
>   Turned my tree-lined street
> Into a botanical cemetery.
>   Prostrate on the cold concrete
> They lie there so bloodless, so pitiful
>   With the sickly, yellowish appearance
> Of famished, exhausted, jaundiced victims,
>   Like unclaimed, stiff little corpses
> On marble slabs in the morgue
>   Waiting for the city cleaners
> To do them a gracious favour
>   And perform their last rites.

Just like my fleshless, naked kinfolk
   On the Warsaw Ghetto sidewalk,
Piled up on one another
   Waiting to be gathered
By a rubbish push cart
   Of the anti-epidemic sanitation squad
To be buried
   In a collective, unmarked grave!

And just like then,
   Thirty months earlier,
The sky is innocently bluish,
   A dreamy azure canopy of benign mildness
With a decorative white silhourette
   Of last night's moon on the horizon
A well arranged beauty mark
   on the firmament.

Only a youthful grey cloud
   Conceives of the commotion in my soul
And forms itself into a question mark
   Why?

Why are such dissonant contrasts possible
   Between heaven and earth?
Why such a lack
   Of solidarity?
Why such deficiency of compassion
   In our environment?
In our life?
   Why? . . .

When I had finished, a moment of silence ensued, as if we were spontaneously honouring the memory of all the untimely deaths of the martyrs on
the Ghetto streets.

"It is very well written," Dr. Maimun commented.

"Well written," I repeated. "How strange," I mumbled to myself. "Is that
all she has to say about it?"

"Miriam Moiseyevna," I began, unable to restrain myself. "I am glad that
you liked my poem, but is that all it means to you? You don't seem to have any

awareness at all of the depths of my feelings on the subject. Do you know what has happened to the Jews of Europe? Maybe these are just mundane facts to you, and maybe this penal institution is simply the source of your income. But to me, I can tell you, this place is a Gehenna of stagnation and decay, a skid row behind a red brick wall!"

"Adam Yanovich, that was a very unfair thing to say! Although I was evacuated and did not personally go through the Nazi hell, as you did, I still feel the sorrow of bereavement very much myself, having lost a brother in the defence of Leningrad, and a husband in a Luftwaffe bombing of a military hospital behind the front lines, where he worked as an anesthetist. Believe me, my dear young man, I know very much what misfortune is and this is the main reason why I am so ardently dedicated to my grandfather Maimun's idea of alleviating human suffering. That's why I take the Hippocratic Oath so seriously as the guiding beacon of my medical career."

"I myself and Viera Rubinstein — the red-headed nurse who is also a widow as she lost all her family in Kirowgrad, and whom you got to know in the prison hospital — are in fact an unofficial two member order of Jewish Sisters of Maimonides, finding solace in helping the incarcerated with whatever we can. As medical workers, in order to be able to function under the most dire of circumstances, and to protect our sanity, we can't afford to become too involved emotionally. And thus we try to shield ourselves behind this alleged wall of detachment and of aloofness. So have a heart, Adam Yanovich, and don't tear down our weak defences. Don't knock our work! It is pretty difficult the way it is. Believe me, it is a very lonely and draining task to work in this institution, as you call it!"

"If you really want to contribute something constructive and good to fortify my spirit and strengthen my stamina, then why don't you tell me some more about my illustrious grandfather's life and works? You seem to be much more informed and knowledgeable with regard to his life and historical impact than I am."

I realised at once that I have been far too impulsive in reacting as I did. I was grateful to the doctor for so tactfully changing the subject and giving me another chance to talk to her, this time about the Rambam. I therefore tried my best to tell the doctor about the gigantic task undertaken by her ancestor who spent ten years wondrously codifying, in the most lucid and superb Hebrew, Jewish lore and law into a systematic and complete assemblage of jurisprudence, supplemented with his profound insights and intellectual comments pertaining to every single facet of Jewish life and its relation to history and humanity. I told her about the Rambam's work as an educator, a philosopher, a linguist, a psychologist, and an advocate of life-saving moderation, who understood the mysterious, biological processes going on in the human body, as well as the mental progressions transpiring in man's psyche. I told her about his program to reach out and to bring back to the fold all the confused, estranged, and alienated by emphasizing in his convincing and prodigious way the positive aspects of Judaism and the Jewish way of life in Torah and Mitzvoth as an ethical, meaningful, and gratifying set of ideas that one can hold onto as a genuine and satisfying *raison d'être* for all times and all seasons. I told her that the crowning achievement of all his prolific writing was his luminous formulation of the substance of the Jewish faith in thirteen principles which penetrate to the heart of every Israelite with touching and simple clarity.

"Yes, Miriam Moiseyevna! Your great ancestor spelled out the Jewish credo in a beautiful and moving declaration of eternal, everlasting loyalty to G-d almighty and to Jewish destiny. This has become the spiritual manifesto of our people in happiness and distress. Composers have been inspired to create soul-stirring music to his articles of faith and those songs were sung by many martyrs on the way to the gas chambers."

Miriam Moiseyevna obviously had the best of intentions when she equipped me with a score of garlic cloves, a fresh onion, and some salt to fight off a bleeding gum problem. She also gave me a bottle of home-made medicine for my stomach and intestinal tract, before returning me to my new location on the third floor. Yet as soon as the door was locked behind me she assumed the cool posture of an indifferent public official, uninvolved in the personal life of the detainee, and walked away without saying goodbye.

I was not disappointed and did not mind her sudden frigidity. After all, formally we were on two different sides of the fence. She was the medical woman on the NKGB payroll. And I was a suspected spy and saboteur under the harsh rigors of Paragraph 58. She had to appear uninterested in me so as not to jeopardize the chances of maintaining our doctor-patient relationship, with the possibility of keeping an eye on me and from time to time bringing me into her office for a check-up, a pep talk, and perhaps the treat of a home-made sandwich. Fraternizing with prisoners beyond the call of duty was quite a serious breach of discipline and could be seen in an extremely damaging light. If Colonel Nyekrasow or Captain Woronow had found out about our conversations in the doctor's office they would certainly, and without any sentiment at all, have pinned an additional accusation to my record for making a premeditated, perfidious attempt to ruin the atheistic morality of the Soviet populace, by clandestinely spreading demoralizing, clerical, and misleading religious superstitions.

Apart from the remarkable meeting with the prison doctor, everything remained the same for me. Obviously the prison authorities were in no hurry to conclude my case, as there were probably millions of cases more or less like mine all over the Soviet Union. Meanwhile, another cold winter was approaching; it was already December of 1944. I had been incarcerated for eight months already. Cold north winds were blowing around the prison yard, as well as penetrating every single crevice in the red bricks, window sills, and cracked glass frames of the unheated cells with their base concrete floors and cement block walls.

Slabosilnaya Kamera 369 was no exeption to the assault of the elements. I and my new associates were very lightly dressed and were in no position to withstand the cold, despite our supposedly privileged position as convalescent prisoners.

Cell 369 was much smaller than the hospital ward with an area of approximately sixty square feet. Ten individuals, a mixture of political and criminal prisoners, each occupied about six square feet of space. We were a really diverse group and the only common denominator between us was that we had absolutely no family or friends to help us, which made us completely dependent on the extra calories in a tablespoon of mashed potatoes that was added to our daily food ration.

There was, however, one exception: Hans Dietrich, a 23 year old ethnic German who had joined the Nazi police against the wishes of his parents, prosperous Kolkhozniks in the Odessa region. When the Germans were defeated he took off his uniform and came back home where he was immediately arrested. Hans Dietrich was an unusual exception, with a full sack of food hanging on a nail in the wall, right over his head.

What he was doing in the slabosilnaya kamera was incomprehensible. A six-footer, muscular with a red healthy face, he was placed in cell 369 by the warden himself, whose authority and decision-making were not subject to question. Perhaps it was a deliberate ploy to tease the starving inmates with the sight of mouth-watering food being consumed by someone else. Or, perhaps the warden was playing his own private joke on Hans by making him take his meals under the envious, begrudging gazes of half-starved people.

Dietrich did not care. He was not intimidated by the yearning looks of his salivating neighbours. He was quite unsentimental, a typical fascist who cared for no one else but himself. Defiantly, he sat down everyday, opened his sack, and gorged himself gluttonously with cheese and meat and honey and cake — supplied by his parents — without so much as a symbolic handout of an olive-sized morsel to all the others. Only Grishna Zarubin, a hardened criminal of Hans' size, sat subserviently next to him like a bodyguard getting leftovers after Dietrich finished eating.

My main worry at that moment was not the persistent lack of food, magnified by Hans' sumptuous feasting, but the lack of proper clothes and blankets to face the unavoidable winter. The nights began to turn cold, sucking the marrow out of our bones, in spite of the fact that, at sleeping time, we all lay one next to the other, cooped up like sardines in a can.

I and Pyetka, a fifteen year old juvenile thief from the city of Rostov, were the most unprepared in the way of clothes and we had to think of something. There were not too many alternatives. Just one difficult chance was available, in the form of an offer by the cell's 'dean,' the seventy six year old Dyadya Vasil. The little old man with the cataract covered eyes was willing to let us both move over to his corner under the window and sleep next to him, which meant the chance of covering ourselves with part of his large sheepskin, the size of a double blanket. Frail Pyetka accepted immediately, despite his tough underworld exterior. I still hesitated, because I knew that in the furry, woolly curls of the sheepskin there would be millions of uninvited little squatters — lice! Which was under the circumstances, more life-threatening, pneumonia or typhus? The dilemma lingered in my mind for quite a few days until a sudden frosty wind changed the morning dew into a glassy membrane covering the prison yard's grass patches with a white coating. It was a finger of heaven telling me not to speculate any more and risk my health. I accepted Dyadya Vasil's hospitality and the white little insects' bites. I found a little solace in the thought that fleas and bedbugs have an even more vicious sting.

Like Queen Esther in biblical days I no longer said anything about my Jewishness or the paragraph under which I was indicted. Neither did I ever try again to impress anyone with my stormy life-story. I had learned my lesson the hard way and had paid an enormous price for it. Anonymity, taciturnity, and keeping to myself as much as possible were now my policy.

I still took part in the social activities and games of the cell. Much story telling took place, mainly by two veterans of the Siberian labour camps who were professional larcenists, the twin brothers Ivanov. The siblings from Nikolayev, who looked just like each other, were gifted pilferers and excellent narrators, taking pride in their illegal skills and in their ingenuity at outwitting the establishment and surviving two three-year terms in the icy tundras of the far north where gold, iron ore, and coal were being mined by convicts from all over the country. Their graphic stories were colourful and interesting, portraying the hardness of criminal characters intertwined with the intransigence of nature. But always there was something else woven into their tales of glittering humanity: the self-sacrifice, heroism, and comradeship among the slave labour workers.

The Ivanovs' reminiscences were usually followed by loud daydreaming and fantasizing about the culinary delights of well done steaks, veal cutlets, shishkebabs, fried liver with onions and triangular dumplings filled with cheese or potatoes. Then came the main attraction of the day: the play of chance, the blackjack gamble for the ten tablespoons of mashed potatoes delivered at lunchtime. Slabosilnaya Kamera 369 was temporarily turned into a miniature casino with all the suspense of self-deluding expectations. The weak and enfeebled cell dwellers were now stimulated to an extraordinary degree by the ten-to-one chance of investing their extra spoon of starchy calories and perhaps collecting the tenfold winning prize of half a kilo of the angelically white, satisfying and delectable concoction known as potato-purée. Only when the illicit, short affair with chance was over did the eyes full of disappointment and hostility look in the direction of the winner who was stuffing himself inconsiderately with the nourishment of his losing peers. Yet, the cards were not thrown out, the game not abandoned. They were picked up carefully and returned to Sasha the cutthroat (a tuberculean Uzbek accused of slaughtering his wife), who had sacrificed the visor of his cap, from which the cards had been made. The next day the same scenario was repeated, usually with a new lucky man but always with a bunch of hungry, saliva-swallowing losers.

Whenever Pyetka, who was a born card wizard, won, he shared his loot with Dyadya Vasil and me, his so-called bedfellows. The Rostow kid, Pyetka, was a Russian street urchin. Loose-mouthed and vulgar with a tough, cocky exterior, he was in essence a lonely, orphaned boy who never knew his parents and who was raised in public institutions from which he ran away in search of family warmth and the feeling of belonging somewhere — anywhere. I could see the hidden qualities in him, his sincerity, loyalty, and gratitude to anyone who paid attention to him. Pyetka was in a dilemma about his future. His sixty-day sentence was due to end about two weeks after we first started to talk to each other. He needed someone to talk to.

"Well," I said to Pyetka boldly and candidly, "I know how badly life has treated you. You have been hurt, bruised and taken advantage of. Please allow me to be a modern day Joseph in foretelling your future path in life."

"Who was this Joseph?" the youth asked, intrigued. "In our schools we did not learn about him."

"Joseph is a biblical figure who landed up in an Egyptian jail thousands of years ago, falsely accused of making indecent advances to the wife of his boss."

"What happened to him?" Pyetka asked with increased curiosity.

"Joseph was innocent and believed that G-d would save him in his own mysterious way. In the meantime, King Pharaoh's staff members, the butler and the baker, offended his majesty, and were thrown into jail, into the very same cell Joseph was occupying. Joseph, who was a Zapadnik, a foreigner, just like I am, got to know them and with his sensitivity and wisdom he figured out what was going to happen to both of them. You surely know the adage: 'A guest for a while sees for a mile'!"

"This I know and understand," Pyetka replied.

"Well, that is what I meant by asking you to let me be your modern-day Joseph in forecasting your lot in life."

Pyetka was now one piece of inquisitiveness. "Good enough, that's okay with me," he declared.

"Let me see the palm of your hand," I said.

Pyetka gave me his hand. I looked at the hand which had been in many strangers' pockets and had taken many strange things. It was still the frail, undeveloped, delicate hand of a vulnerable, intelligent, young boy with bitter disappointments and sad experiences in life, who hit back at society by becoming a juvenile delinquent.

"Pyetka," I said, after a moment of intense palm-reading. "First it is my duty to inform you that your lifeline shows extraordinary longevity in years. You will live to become an old man and grandfather. Second, I am moved to tell you that your married life is going to be a success and you will have a harmonious family life, fathering half a dozen children. But the most important thing I see in your future is: a young doctor, an ex-convict who exchanged his razor blade for a scalpel and his spring-knife for surgical instruments, saving human lives and becoming famous in the medical field as a self-made man, who pulled himself out of the quagmire of crime and hopelessness by his own bootstraps."

A fortnight later, when Pyetka left for Rostov, he went via Dniepropietrowsk, carrying a letter from me to Wladek Starorzynski, who had married a Russian Jewish girl on Aryan papers by the name of Valentzova Maria, and who lived at #3 Korolenko Street. The letter was a plea to pull me out of the hellish predicament I was in. Pyetka gave me his word of honour that he would not only deliver the letter, but also stay in Dniepropietrowsk as long as it took to personally find someone of the Marrano group to start a petition to the National Kommisariat of Justice in Moscow to free Adam Yanovich Arendarski from any kind of guilt and finally open the doors to his overdue freedom.

Slabosilnaya 369 was different with Pyetka gone. In the choir of the cell's mature, thick voices, his ringing alto was sadly missed. It seemed that without the youthful pickpocket's reverberating laughter, argument, and uncouth comments, 369 was just an overcrowded, dingy, sick-room with coughing, yawning, scratching, starving, sinking, slowly expiring non-persons; except for Hans Dietrich who was gaining weight and feasting away on the goodies of his mother's parcels delivered to him every Sunday. Then, almost a whole week later, a new inmate arrived. On a Saturday morning, before kipiatok time, the door opened and a man in a fitted military uniform but with only one arm was ushered in, taking his place next to Dietrich's left side. As it turned out, he was a local Jewish boy and war invalid who had been locked up for ruffianism. His name was Siomka Gitlin. He kept no secrets and admitted that he had blown his top when, after coming back to Odessa from the military hospital, where his left arm, shattered by a Nazi missile, had been amputated, he found his parents' living quarters occupied by some unknown strangers. As a Red Guard Lieutenant who lost a limb in the patriotic war for Russia's survival, he felt morally entitled to reclaim his family's residence and demanded in a screaming, threatening voice, with a few bashed-in windows as demonstration of his seriousness, that the predatory squatter should get out and let him have the home of his annihilated father and mother back.

Unfortunately, the usurper of his parents' quarters and furniture was a high party functionary who immediately telephoned the militia. They arrived within minutes, arrested him, took him to an acting justice of the peace, read him his indictment and escorted him to prison to wait for his trial on a charge of unprovoked vandalism and damage to property.

I looked at the grimacing face of Hans Dietrich who was listening intently to Siomka Gitlin's conspicuous declaration of his impulsive aggressive behaviour. I felt instinctively that very soon a confrontation was definitely going to take place betwen the two. The fighting Jew and the unrepenting Nazi were, in the meantime peacefully lying side by side. There was, of course, quite a contrast between the two. Hans Dietrich was a personification of the trumpeted Nordic image, being blond and blue-eyed, with thin lips, a slim nose, and almost sandy white eyebrows. Siomka Gitlin was totally the opposite in appearance. A dark brunette with beer-brown eyes, prominent ears, full-blooded, thick lipped mouth, and a masculine nose, he was definitely not a prototype of the Aryan lineage. Gitlin did not yet know any particulars of Dietrich's past, and his weird, cruel-hearted behaviour towards his cellmates. But when they brought the evening soup, and he gave his portion to Grisha while as usual voluptuously stuffing himself with the home-made goodies of meat loaf, smoked kolbasa, a sausage and hard-boiled eggs, without so much as offering his fellow prisoners a sliver of anything, Siomka swiftly got the picture of what was going on.

"Priyatnovo appetito," he said sarcastically, wishing the rural boor *bon appetit!*

Dietrich lifted up his blue eyes and looked coldly at the smiling Siomka, without uttering a word. He must have known though, that Gitlin's smile was not a grin of admiration.

Later at night, Gitlin, who had been stationed for a time in Asia's Uzbekistan, moved over to skinny Sasha the cutthroat, and had a friendly conversation with him in his own native tongue. Nobody paid attention, considering it a normal bit of chit chat between two ex-soldiers who were still wearing their uniforms. This was no innocent conversation at all but a diversionary tactic to draw attention in the wrong direction. It was the beginning of a conspiracy to confiscate Dietrich's food reserves and divide them up among the cell-dwellers.

As usual, the following day was cold and nippy. The day started out quite normally with everyone doing regular chores, playing games, making plans for some hypothetical future, and chasing vermin. This was in fact no ordinary day, however, as everybody except Grisha and Zaraza (plague) knew that this night was the night for action.

The lights were turned off and the whole kamera went to sleep. I tried to stay awake so as not to miss anything of the miniature Robin Hood drama that was about to take place. From under Dyadya Vasil's sheepskin blanket I watched the contours of Hans' sack, hanging on the wall, until I fell asleep, mesmerized by looking at one spot for so long.

When I awakened I noticed in the darkness one of the Ivanow brothers getting carefully up and then standing on Siomka's belly as if on a step-ladder to remove the heavily loaded burlap pouch from the wall over Dietrich's head. A moment later he was already, with the sharpened handle of his spoon, cutting portions of meat loaf and bread, ripping broiled chickens apart into small pieces and handing them down the line to the quietly awakened inmates, who immediately started to devour them. Within minutes, everyone was involved in a gluttonous binge, chewing the stolen food at lightning speed: swallowing cookies, honey cake, pieces of butter, sour pickles, hunks of cheese, chunks of spicy sausage, apples, grapes, carrots, and onions.

Rather than leave whatever could not be eaten in Hans' sack we rather spitefully threw it into the parasha to render it unfit for consumption.

Grisha, Hans' subservient dependent first detected the muted commotion and alerted Dietrich to the fact that something was going on. But it was already too late. We conspirators were all back in our usual places, belching, breaking wind, and giggling, obviously content with the nocturnal gastronomical orgy.

Hans jumped up as if bitten by a snake, touched the empty wall space where his missing food reserves should have hung and started to scream hysterically, like a madman: "They stole my sack! They have taken everything I had! Guard," he lamented at the top of his voice, "Guard!!!"

A drowsy looking guard opened the cell-door indignantly asking, "What the hell is going on here in the middle of the night? It's 2 a.m. What is the shrieking all about?"

"They stole all my food supplies! The one-armed Jew Gitlin organized them against me," Dietrich complained in a not unexpected whining tone.

"You crazy maniac! So that is why you wake up the whole house?" the guard angrily rebuked him.

"But they . . ." Hans started again to explain.

"Shut up you nitwit!" the guard was furious. "One more peep out of you and I myself will personally drag you down to solitary confinement!"

When daylight began to seep into Slabosilnaya Kamera 369, I saw for the first time in my whole, stormy life an abjectly miserable scene of human degradation, disgrace and self-abasement. Zaraza, the ostracized informer who had been left out of the feast, scurried over to the parasha, stuck his hand into the feces, and fished out pieces of food. He found in the excrement an unfinished, large chicken leg, washed it off a few times with cold water, and ate it all up.

Siomka Gitlin did not remain in cell 369 for very long. Before he left, I had a heart-to-heart talk with him. I told him about my hellish experiences on the German side, and the unending nightmare of over eight months in Soviet incarceration. I gave him the addresses of my Marrano friends and fellow underground workers in Dniepropietrowsk, Dolgintzevo, and the village of Novoyezytye near Novy Archangelsk. I also gave him the address and name of the superintendent on Babela #31, where I used to live.

"Siomka," I said, "you will soon be set free. Please, I beg of you, don't forget me. Like me, you have travelled outside the Soviet Union, to Poland, Czechoslovakia, Hungary, Austria and Germany. You have seen the devastated ghettoes, the concentration camps, and the mass graves. Perhaps you too have felt the stench of the decomposing bodies of the victims. We have both lost family members in this horror. You are a G-d sent messenger to end my wretchedness. You have the rare chance to fulfill the tremendous mitvah of pidyon shevuim, the ransoming of captives, which is considered to be one of the most sacred duties of every Jew, superseding even the important obligation of feeding and clothing the poor.

"I beseech you: Go to Dniepropietrowsk, find Maria Valentzova, the wife of Wladek Starorzynski, or Klara Fuchs, the widow of Reuben Fuchs, alias Richard Lis. They know everybody and all the activities in which the Jews on Aryan papers were involved. Ask them please to go to the authorities and plead for my release. Ask them to sign petitions, send telegrams, do everything they can to get me out of this G-d forsaken place."

While I poured out my heart-felt pleas Siomka sat next to me, leaning on the cell wall, with his eyes closed as if better to absorb everything said. Then when it was all over, Gitlin reacted in a very peculiar manner.

"Adam," he asked softly. "What is the size of your shoes?"

I did not immediately grasp the connection between my predicament and my shoe size.

"Size 8," I replied mechanically, looking questioningly at the Jewish war invalid, trying to figure out what this was all about.

"You see, my friend," Siomka said: "I certainly do hope that you will very soon also be released from here. But just to be on the safe side, I would like you to have my high leather boots, in case you should have to travel someplace further. It is very, very important to secure your legs against frostbite and the Russian wintry cold. As for me, don't worry! I have another pair of leather boots in my aunt's place and I really want you to keep these as a memento of our extraordinary get together."

Now I understood everything perfectly well. *In case of further travel* was a subtle euphemism for the continuing possibility of my not being freed but sentenced to a labor camp in Siberia. The depressing possibility was probably instantly reflected in my face, because Siomka started energetically to cheer me up with Yiddish aphorisms like: "everything will work out okay; don't worry; and, there is nothing to be afraid of."

I cheered up a little and Siomka kept on in the reassuring tone of an older brother. Then, while pulling off his own boots, he said in his Russian Yiddish dialect, "Let me have your shoes!"

"Hmm," I thought, while unlacing my half-torn oxfords. "What a difference between Kowalenko's *Let me have your trousers* and Gitlin's *Let me have your shoes!*"

We swapped our footwear without knowing for sure if we would ever meet again. But we both knew that this memorable meeting of two non-criminal Jews behind bars had strengthened our self-esteem, reinforced our pride in being Jewish, and taught us a most valuable lesson in compassion and fellowship that would stay with us as long as we would both live.

In the morning, the warden himself unlocked the cell door and told Gitlin to pick up his things and follow him. An order had come to let him go home.

"Dosvidanya Rebyata! See you around guys! Keep well, Adam," Siomka roared, looking meaningfully in my direction as if reiterating his promise not to let me down in the effort to win back my freedom.

Cell 369 was again reduced to nine residents with four distinct life standards. Two thirds of the cell's inmates, including me, were continuously suffering extreme undernourishment. Grisha Zarubin was appeasing his desire for food with two payoks. Hans Dietrich was still luxuriously stuffing himself with Mama's newly supplied food parcels. And Zaraza, semi-conscious, with high fever and spells of vomiting, was hardly breathing after the earlier consumption of his marinated chicken leg.

Dr. Maimun, summoned by the guard, entered the slabosilnaya kamera and, without so much as glancing in my direction, walked straight over to the messed up figure of the sick man. Zaraza was sitting propped up in the corner with his head hanging down, his eyes closed and a whitish liquid oozing from his half-opened mouth. The medical woman took a close look at him and called in two guards with a stretcher to carry him over to the prison hospital.

"Who else feels ill?" she asked loudly.

"I do," I raised my hand. "I have terrible pains in my lower abdomen."

"That's from excessive gluttoning on the food he stole from me," Hans said, looking at me with open hostility.

"The Zapadnik stole food from you?" Miriam Moiseyevna asked in disbelief.

"Yea!" Dietrich insisted stubbornly. "It was him and the other damned Yid in uniform, that organized the after midnight holdup on my food parcel."

"Listen young man! No racial slurs are allowed here! You see and behave yourself, if you know what is good for you," the medical woman warned while motioning me to follow her. As soon as we reached the examination office, Miriam Moiseyevna put a piece of white material on the brown sofa and gave me a thorough check-up.

"Thank G-d," she said after a while with a sigh of relief. "There are no growths, no sign of any obstruction in the lower intestines. No accumulation of water in the abdominal cavity, because of diseased glands. It is all, I am afraid, a consequence of trapped gas, stemming unfortunately from an inadequate diet and little daily exercise. Your metabolism is simply rebelling against the conditions in which you live."

"Now, let us see what we can do about it," she said, serving me a large homemade cheese sandwich. "Adam Yanovich, I want you to know that I did not forget you, as you might have thought. As a matter of fact I thought quite a bit about you and all the things you spoke of last time. The Jewish way of life. The ethical conceptions of Torah, Talmud and Mishnah, gathered together and clarified by my illustrious ancestor. You opened up a whole new horizon for me. You see, our family moved from Egypt to Syria, to Turkey, to Teheran, to Baku, Leningrad, Moscow and Odessa. In the isolation of our wanderings and hardships and under the influence of changing times and regimes we lost touch with our traditions. We did religiously maintain the medical legacy, however. But now, since our unexpected talk, I am beginning to find my route back to the customs and traditions of our forefathers. For the last few weeks I have been lighting sabbath candles. I don't eat meat and butter at the same time anymore. I even improvise my own prayers to G-d almighty, and I feel terrific in my rediscovery of my own spiritual ancestry."

I looked at the medical woman with the silvery patches of grey in her brown hair, adorning an altruistic personality so passionately interested in recapturing her links with the vital Jewishness of mitzvoth and good deeds. All the hurt and chagrin at her fornot getting in touch with me in the last few weeks melted away from listening to the way she talked with reverence about past generations and the necessity of picking up where they left off, in order to continue in their footsteps. Telling her again about my misery in 369 seemed so irrelevant in the context of her touching and bubbly intoxication with her newly rediscovered faith that I decided to say not a single word about it.

I was obviously right in my decision, because a moment later Miriam Moiseyevna told me the good news that she had finally succeeded in switching me into another cell, the cell of the crew that ladled out the soup and handed out the bread for the entire fourth floor.

"Adam Yanovich," she said. "I cannot give you any more particulars but I am quite sure that from now on, you will not be hungry. Here are a pot and a spoon, so that there is no reason to return to 369 for whatever utensils you left there." Again, she handed me a fistful of fresh garlic cloves and told me to put them in my pocket. "Please don't be angry," she pleaded apologetically. "You must understand that I cannot see you as often as I would like. The risks are great, and I might jeopardize my whole career and chance to be of help to anyone. However, I can tell you that your general health is satisfactory, your youthful resilience pretty good. You have therefore the necessary prerequisites to overcome all stumbling blocks, and my sixth sense tells me that you are, G-d willing, going to make it as a free man to your destined goal in life."

"Before I take you back to your new, temporary abode, I would like to ask you something which is to me of tremendous significance."

"Go right ahead, Miriam Moiseyevna," I said in an encouraging tone of voice.

"On our last encounter when you kindled my imagination and awakened my dormant Jewishness with your summary about the gigantic contribution of my great ancestor, you emphasized his towering achievement in formulating the thirteen principles of the Jewish faith. Since I have no prayer book or any other liturgical texts I wonder if you can remember verbatim the content of them and could then perhaps dictate them to me, so that I can write them down."

"Oh yes I do," I said, smiling with pleasure. "I remember them word for word, after reciting them daily, come rain or come shine, on Ghetto or Aryan papers, for the last thirteen years since my bar mitzvah."

Miriam Moiseyevna excitedly grabbed a pad and pencil, looked at me with moist eyes of gratitude, saying, "Please kindly begin, but quietly! Because we are not really in the proper surroundings for doing this."

I bent forward in the barber chair and in a muffled voice I slowly recited to the NKGB doctor Maimonides' thirteen principles of faith.

CHAPTER 12

Graduation to Freedom

THE THREE numbers, four, five and nine, of Cell 459 added up to eighteen. In Jewish folklore, that was considered a good omen as the Hebrew for eighteen also means Chai: life. I certainly felt much more hopeful about my situation as I settled into the gloomy cell of the fourth floor caterers' team. It was a Garden of Eden compared to my previous cells.

There were only six people in the new cell, four of whom were involved in actually handing out the food. The fifth member of the cell was bearded and elderly, with the pious looks of a truly righteous man. Three times a day and before partaking in meals as well, he quietly washed his hands and said a prayer, obviously consoled by the thought that his connection with above could not be interrupted, intercepted, or even censured by the NKGB. Dobrodushev (good soul) was his name, very fitting for a man with a patriarchal posture whose looks and inner spiritual make-up complemented each other.

Dobrodushev was a scriptural scholar and an expert in secular literature. To him, books were just an elegant form of entertainment, and a vehicle of self-expression for gifted people in need of an emotional outlet. The Bible, however, is and was the indisputable, eternally living word of the Lord, guiding the human race away from the dark ages of cannibalism.

Two hours before lunch the quartet of cell 459 waiters started to prepare the bread in the very same recess under the stairs as the doctor's office was in, but on the other side of the balcony. A long table was used to cut the brick-shaped two and a half kilo breads into eight portions. Each part was supposed to weigh a little over three hundred grams. Occasionally, however, when the green curtain in front of the table was unveiled, one could see through the keyhole how unabashed thievery took place. In a tricky way, the bread was cut lengthwise, and then a one inch thick slice was cut away from the core. The two half breads were put together again and subdivided into eight sections which — after the illegal surgery — weighed only about two hundred and fifty grams each.

The skimmed off slices amounted to about twenty kilos of precious bread and, later in the evening, turnkeys toured the cells and struck up deals, bartering the stolen food for shirts, jackets, footwear, socks, military rubashkas, shawls, scarves, and anything else of value for which any bazaar client would pay a profitable black market price.

In the afternoon, a similar technique was used before the ladling out of the supper soup. Around four p.m., the working crew began to bring into cell 459 a dozen steaming huge pails of the evening meal, of which every inmate was supposed to get a whole litre in good measure. This was meant to be the most nourishing repast which the prisoners were awaiting the whole day. Yet, in the presence of a couple of guards — Dyadya Dobrodushev and the sixth newcomer to the cell — a sort of centrifugal procedure started, pouring successively from one bucket to another until the last two large pails were turned into one immense pot of a thick and rich mass of potatoes, beans, barley, vegetables, and little pieces of fish. This was the tithe the guards and the working crew arbitrarily took for themselves and some of which was given to me and Dyadya Dobrodushev, the octogenarian oldtimer.

Cell 459 was in fact an annex dining room for all the fourth floor guards. Individually and sometimes in pairs, they used to come in, fill up their dishes, sit down on the floor, and delight themselves with an enjoyable, free meal before going home. After all, it was still wartime. Everything was still rationed and scarce, with exorbitant prices for every food morsel to be bought on the black market. So it was no trifle to have such an additional source of good soup and bread.

After suppertime, when the job of serving the inmates was completed, the four crewmen came in, washed their hands, and sat down in peace and quiet to consume their own meal. They were muscular, tall men. Yet even after satisfying their own large appetites there was plenty left in the large bucket to treat me and Dyadya Dobrodushev to an added portion.

For the first time in almost nine months, my mind and body were comparatively at ease without the tortuous continuous absorption with the nagging thought of food. An inmate of cell 459 had no cause for worry about hunger cramps. He was secure with a good and plentiful diet as long as he was in the confines of the good cell with the lucky, symbolic Chai number.

I wondered whether Miriam Moiseyevna knew the sordid details of the operation which made cell 459 so opulent and self-sufficient. She probably had a notion of what was going on in the bread cutting room. Nevertheless, she was in no position to intervene and rectify all this without destroying herself in the process. So, she had little choice but to close her eyes and go on with her more important mission in life, healing the sick, without pursuing the additional tasks of crusader, reformer, and prosecutor.

"No wonder it took her so long to get me out of the slaboshilnaya kamera,"

I thought. "It must have been quite a struggle within herself, a real dilemma to decide which was more important: to be prudent and not to accept a favour from a corrupted official, or to circumvent principles and not allow a twenty-five year old Ghetto survivor to perish."

I was overwhelmed with gratitude to the medical woman for putting my life above the preservation of her immaculately clean personal record. Miriam Moiseyevna's image remained as untarnished as ever to me. In my book she was and remained a genuine Maimun, in the fullest sense of the word.

In order to justify my eating the organized 459 food, I resorted to historic sources depicting the awesome, terrible agony of hunger.

In the Book of Lamentations, read on the 9th day of the month of Av in the Jewish calendar, the anniversary of the devastation of both Temples in Jerusalem — the scriptural mourner describes the consequences of excruciating hunger when "the hands of the pitiful women have sodden their own children: They were their meat in the destruction of the daughter of my people." (Chapter 4, Verse 10) In contemporary times, I had been told that in Buchenwald and Maidanek, cannibalism took place as early as 1941. Emaciated starved camp inmates cut out hunks of flesh from their dead peers and kinfolk and ate them to stay alive.

In the Rozdielnaya prison I, myself, had almost stooped to the animal level of Zaraza in my willingness to do anything to pacify the terrible hunger and the abdominal spasms I was experiencing. I had just been transferred from my solitary nineteen-day confinement in the converted potato pit. The new, above ground cell was roomy and airy, with sweet, spring fragrances pouring through the broken window glass. It was like a climatic change from the sweaty and suffocating atmosphere of a tropical rain forest to the caressing coolness of the Swiss Alps. The side-effect was a swift return of the hitherto absent appetite, magnified a hundred-fold by a reactivated metabolism which screamed for food that was not to be had.

And then a young cat jumped onto the sill. It arched its shiny, furry back, and purred like a lost friend, pleased with the sunbeam's warmth. Intrigued by the curious surroundings, it stepped over to the inner side of the window frame. It was difficult to comprehend how such thoughts could even enter my mind, but the fact was that predatory, Stone Age instincts took over and I began to move towards the little cat which to my ravenous eyes looked like a roast. The cat detected danger, however, and catapulted back out to the yard as quick as a pebble from a slingshot.

Later that night I kept on thinking about the incident. A hodge-podge of different images, past and present, came to mind. There were pre-war Friday night meals in the rabbinical home of my father with so many invited guests and Chassidim; the Ghetto Sabbaths with nothing more on the table than stale bread and surrogate honey made from sugar beets; my sister Tamar's plentiful wedding banquet in the town of Cmielow and my eighteen month old niece Naomi's subsistence on watery farina without milk in Sandomierz-Tzosmer; the Warsaw juvenile, barefoot smugglers of produce and my own escapades into the Aryan side for protein, potatoes, and sugar. Then everything started to become vague, dim and hazy. I was falling asleep.

Even as I was falling asleep, however, I was still plagued by self-recrimination. I remembered a passage from the Book of Lamentations which partially consoled me: "They that be slain with the sword are better than they that be slain by hunger."

My dreams were also full of scenes of want, distress, and hardship. There was a series of scenes from the Umschlag-platz in Warsaw of Jews holding onto bread and marmalade handed out as reward for their volunteering to be deported. Then, from nowhere, appeared a book by Knut Hamsun entitled *Hunger*, with three exclamation marks in dripping blood and a footnote underlined with little swastikas announcing that the author had joined the Norwegian Nazi party. Then again a German Jewish refugee in *pince nez* glasses, grotesquely dressed in an expensive tuxedo, who had tried to sell me a Purim paper for ten Polish cents — a Purim journal as spiritual food for my soul!

An indelible experience of my years as a student was next. I saw myself on Elektoralna Street, still wearing the uniform of the only Jewish religious teachers' college in Poland. I was walking home from Menachem Begin's lecture given in the premises of the Jewish ex-army and war veterans organization (Brith Hechayal) dedicated to the idea of Jewish statehood. Suddenly, I was overtaken by a tide of screaming, ranting, banner-carrying hoodlums of the most extreme fringe of the anti-semitic radical party, promulgating as their main goal a Poland without Jews. Luckily, they did not know that the silver embroidered #3 on my left arm was the assigned insignia for pupils of this state-supported teaching college for instructors, where Hebrew in the Sephardic dialect was one of the official languages.

"Come on, colleague! We are going after Jews!" a tall hooligan with an iron bar tenderly embraced my shoulders and looked into my blue eyes. I, a rabbi's son, had successfully passed my first initiation test as an Aryan, which probably planted the idea in my mind of parading as a full-blooded Nordic when it was unsafe to be a citizen of the Israelite faith.

In the meantime, the huge band of ruffians, with me involuntarily entrapped between them, and armed with canes, knives, sticks, two by fours, and metal pipes, reached the Platz-Bankovy square and struck their first victim. He was a middle-aged man, elegantly dressed with a grey felt hat and grey coat. His screams for mercy and beseechings of the Nazarene and the Holy

Ghost did not do him any good. To the unruly attackers he had semitic looks. His features were Jewish and they beat the man — who happened to be a genuine Christian — into a pulp.

So much for our thousand year contribution to Polish life, I mused bitterly to myself in my sleep. That was the tragic consequence of our wanderings in the diaspora. A repetition of what had happened to us in Babylonia with its Jewish viceroy; in Spain with its Jewish Minister Don Itzchak Abarbanel; in Egypt where the Rambam had lived; in Germany and France with their Walter Rathenaus and Leon Blums, respectively. Our cultural, economic, and social successes were all ephemeral and short-lived, always ending in catastrophe, fiasco, and failure.

"Adamchick," Dyadya Dobrodushev was standing over me with his handkerchief, wiping the sweat from my forehead and helping me to get up. "You sighed, tossed yourself from side to side and even sobbed in your sleep," the good-hearted Dobrodushev told me. "You must have had terrible dreams!" The old man looked at me with concern.

There was nobody else in the cell. The crew was busy handing out kipiatok and Dyadya and I had complete privacy. It was a propitious time to confide in the benevolent, benign, Tolstoyan man who seemed to be so sincerely interested in my predicament and well-being.

I thanked him for his concern, for covering up my kipiatok can, that it should not cool off, and for his fatherly kindness in general. We sat down, shoulder to shoulder, and I told my older cellmate about my inner conflict, about my dreams and excursions into Jewish history and the vivid reliving of its traumas. I also told him about the way I was mistreated in the NKGB interrogation cell #3 on Babela Street, and the agonizing path of malnutrition and constant hunger until I got into 459.

Dobrodushev listened attentively and silently without interrupting. When I had finished telling him the story of my various adventures, he looked at me with visibly moist eyes of compassion and admiration.

"My son!" he said, in a choked, emotional voice, "the reason for your harassment, persecution and suffering is a very simple one. You do indeed belong to G-d's chosen people, and Satan can't take it! That is why he creates all this demonic violence and evil-doing to confuse you and break you. I am a Christian but I certainly believe in the G-d of Israel. I know that his covenant with your people is forever, and no one, not even the darkest forces, will be able to destroy it. I am a staunch believer in what our great Lev Tolstoy said about your fellow-Jews half a century ago, in 1891: *The Jew is a holy being who brought the eternal fire from the heaven that illuminated the earth and all living on it. He is the source and the new well from which all other nations have drawn their religions and beliefs. The Jew is the discoverer of freedom: The Jew is a symbol of eternity.*"

"Your father, mother, sister, brother-in-law, and all your annihilated family are saints who have sanctified the Lord's name on the altar of martyrdom."

For two weeks and two days, I stayed in the sheltered convalescent cocoon called 459. It was like a magic tonic for sixteen whole days. Physically, I gained many pounds. Mentally, I was restored to spiritual equilibrium. Then, the warden happened to walk by the open door of the working crew's cell and noticed me sitting on the floor, talking to Dobrodushev.

"What is the Zapadnik doing here?" he screamed in a rage. "Vanya!" The sergeant of the guards came running over. "How did he get in here?" the warden pointed his finger at me in obvious displeasure. "He is a 58 paragrapher and belongs to 369. Take him back there right away."

There I was, once again treading the dull sounding iron floor of the round balcony with the attached net to prevent suicide attempts. The sound of my feet on the metal stairs was like a pair of defective cymbals, producing strange chords and sounds. I was neither discouraged nor subdued. Neither did I feel relegated to some lower status by being called a 58 paragrapher. I knew that I was innocent and had the good feeling that my tortuous saga was soon going to end positively. My saintly father's promise had to come true. I was convinced of it.

As we entered the slabosilnaya kamera I suddenly realised that the sum of the three numbers of this cell (three, six and nine) was also eighteen, which in Hebrew is Chai: life. Once again I took this to be a good omen, and in truth it did feel as if I were coming back to a home of sorts, albeit a rather rotten and miserable home. Everybody was there still, as was the stench from the parasha, the vermin, the hole in the window sill, and the cavity in the lower part of the cell door which caused a constant, miserable draft. Except for Zaraza, of whose whereabouts no one knew anything, all the other 'boys' were in their usual places. The only noticeable change in the daily curriculum was the suspension of card playing for the extra starchy calories. Everybody now received at noon his own tablespoon of mashed potatoes, which came in very handy.

It was already the latter half of January 1945. With my increased weight I was less sensitive to the cold than before. Nevertheless, I was glad when Dyadya Vasil allowed me again to use part of his sheepskin as a night blanket.

Only one week later, the final turning point in my sojourn behind the bars of Odessa's main jail took place. Captain Woronow sent a special van to pick me up and bring me back to Babela. This was a moment that I had looked forward to for quite some time. I was sure that something extraordinary had happened to influence Woronow to pick up again where we had left off months ago. I wondered if perhaps Pyetka had made his trip to Dniepropietrowsk, found my friends and convinced them to do something to save me. Or perhaps Matway, the Cossack, had survived his ordeal in the suicide battalion, come back alive and gone to the Novoye-Zitye Kolkhoz to find Hruboshapka and start my defence. One thing, though was definite. Things had begun to move. Something decisive was in the offing. I would know soon enough.

Cell number 3 was almost empty with just three inhabitants all of whom were novices who had just started their investigative procedures. There was no sign of my past tormentors. It was as if they had disappeared into thin air. The new people — all locals — were very cordial and shared their provisions with me. They looked up to me as an experienced captive, a veteran prisoner with nine and a half months already served. Besides, I had not a stitch of European clothing any more. The working crew of 459 had bought my black flannel overcoat, woollen jacket and trousers, giving me in exchange a Red Army rubashka, khaki pants, and the greenish-brown outer garment of a regular Soviet soldier. With Siomka's high boots and cap, I looked like a genuine boyetz; a bona fide rank and file member of the Soviet Armed Forces who was therefore deserving of the preferential treatment given to a favourite son in trouble.

I did not talk too much; nor did I try to be too smart and show off my expertise in NKGB policy and interrogation tactics. In my given situation, I felt most comfortable with silence. Thus, I kept to myself, without saying anything unless I had to. Most of the time I tried to sleep and waited impatiently for the late-night hours when Woronow usually summoned his clients.

Contrary to past practices, however, the much anticipated call came in the afternoon of February 8th, 1945. Tolia came in and, without the cliched procedural warning about a bullet in the head for attempting to escape, led me into the office of the captain.

As I stepped over the office threshhold, I immediately noticed the absence of sternness on Woronow's usually solemn face. The captain was smiling amiably at me while leafing through some pages in a file lying in front of him on top of his desk. I picked up a chair, as I was already trained to do, and moved it back to the proper distance of about fifteen feet to give the interrogator a full view of me. But Woronow motioned to me to come over to his desk and sit down opposite him.

"Would you like a smoke?" he asked.

"Yes," I replied.

Woronow handed me his packet of Kazbek cigarettes. I took one and the interrogator lit it for me.

"Citizen interrogator," I addressed the NKGB man in the formal way that a prisoner under investigation was supposed to. But, before I managed to finish my sentence, Woronow benevolently interrupted me: "Adam Yanovich! Don't refer to me any more as citizen interrogator, but comrade interrogator.

I am going to set you free. You will be reinstated as a member of the Soviet society. You will receive full rights and become a man at liberty to do anything you please. Of course within the framework of law and order," he corrected himself.

I felt my heart beat spiralling upward and beginning to palpitate in overexcitement. The moment of truth had finally arrived, I thought, perspiring profusely all over my body as if a myriad of clandestine, tiny shower faucets had been let loose at me from all sides. I drew on the nicotine of my cigarette but could not calm my overwhelming emotions. My throat was choking. My temples and pulse were throbbing. My eyes became heavy as I tried to hold back accumulated tears. It was useless to play the strong silent type any longer. It was physically impossible to fight the convulsions of the soul. I could not exercise control any longer and burst into a spasmodic wail of joy and uninhibited sobbing.

Woronow gave me a couple of minutes to collect myself and then matter of factly told me about the order of the National Kommisariat of Justice in Moscow to cease the case and release me.

"You know Adam Yanovich, alias Amnon Alexandorvich Ajzensztadt, you are a one-of-a-kind man! An exceptionally lucky man! If I were not a Marxist and a sworn Atheist, I would say that G-d has certainly intervened on your side. It seems that you have the right friends in the right places, and at the right time. I have here in your dossier a deposition signed by Major Hershel Najdor of the Polish army, whose underground name under the German occupation was Wladek Starorzynski. He states that he knows you, worked with you in the same resistance group, and even takes responsibility for your personal integrity. It is pretty clear to me that he is the moving force behind all the telegrams and petitions, signed by almost half the citizens of Dniepropietrowsk, to the National Kommisariat of Justice asking for your release."

"Well, good for you! Your experience in our institution has probably been very educational and will surely last you for a lifetime. The only thing that still baffles me and which I would love to know about is this: How did Major Najdor, alias Starorzynski, find out about your predicament, and where you were detained?"

His voice had, once again, the ring of the incorrigible, coercive, and suspicious cop. I detected in it an obvious regret concerning the one who was getting away. I was by now quite composed, free from agitation and in full command of my senses. So, I shrugged my shoulders and remained silent. Woronow looked at me penetratingly, studying my pallid face. I did not back away, and I easily and wordlessly suppressed the fear that perhaps he might know something about the Dniepropietrowsk connection.

"Charasho!" the captain pensively said, after a short pause. "At this stage it really does not matter any more." He pressed the electric button on the desk.

Tolia came in, 'Yes, comrade captain?"

"Take Adam to the storage room and give him back all his possessions, the leather belt, the Omega watch, the knapsack, and everything he brought along to Rozdielnaya."

Tolia winked at me to follow him. At the door, Woronow's voice stopped us. "One moment! I am not finished yet with the paper work. So, Adam Yanovich, after you pick up your things you are free to go wherever you want to, Tolia will see to it. But you have to come back tomorrow before noon to get your official release document."

For the first time in ten months I found myself standing in front of the NKGB complex as an outsider, without a rifle pointed at me, without a guard watching me, without anyone telling me where to be and where not to be. I was a free man. No more kashtan, no more Marrano, no more Adam Arendarski, or Adamo Arendi. I was again Amnon Ajzensztadt, the rebbe Reb Zishe's son, the grandson of the Zaklikover Tzadik, the descendant of the Likutei Meril, the Panim Meiroth, and the Maharal of Prague.

A Ghetto dweller from Warsaw's Dzika-Gass, I was alive and well with all my faculties intact, all my vital organs still functioning normally, pale perhaps, bruised and lice ridden, but in one piece with no organic damage whatsoever. My father's promise and the calling I felt to perpetuate all that I had witnessed and experienced as a legacy for future generations had apparently pulled me through the gehenna of my life during the war.

I was intoxicated with my newly regained freedom and drank in the fresh winter air. I felt a child-like delight in plodding through the freshly fallen snow, leaving footprints like some celebrity might do. It was so enjoyable just to look at the beautiful gallery of human faces walking by me. I felt like shouting, whistling, somersaulting, and wallowing in the fluffy white feathers from heaven. I wanted to throw snowballs and let the whole world know that one downtrodden, maligned, and oppressed rebel had made it back to liberty.

My wild enthusiasm was suddenly dampened by the realisation that I had nowhere to go for the night. I had two choices, to go to my ex-neighbours on Babela Street and ask them to put me up for one more night or to make my way without delay to Siomka Gitlin's home at 17 Pushkina and see what happened when I got there.

It was only a fifteen minute stroll from 11 Babela Street to 17 Pushkina Street. I went to the superintendent and asked about Siomka Gitlin's place. The grey-haired janitor with the military moustache did not know anyone by the name. But when I described the one-armed lietuenant's looks the caretaker directed me to a fourth-floor flat on the left side of the building.

I ran up the stairs as fast as I could and rang the bell of an apartment with a recognizable little spot on the right door post suggesting that a mezzuzah was once attached there. It was indeed the right door, because a moment later I was locked in the steely grip of Siomka's right arm.

"Aunt Sarah! Come on in! The Jewish guy from Poland is here," he excitedly yelled into the kitchen.

A woman in her sixties came in, as if she had walked straight out of Vishniak's photo album. She had a wrinkled, creased face. The combination of her aristocratic features, the way she held her long-fingered hands folded, the wide wedding band, and the large coal black eyes expressing worry and past traumas made her look like a mixture of a Sarah Shernirer (the founder of the religious Beth Jacob school movement) and a biblical matriarch. Her melodic voice expressed tenderness, gentility, and at the very same time a special quality of strength and perseverance when she said, "Zdrastvuitye! Sholom aleichem!"

"Aleichem sholom!" I replied, bowing my head.

"This is the fellow on whose behalf I went on the Dniepropietrowsk mission!" Siomka interjected happily.

"I am very glad that you did go," Aunt Sarah said, with a smile.

"Well!" the lady of the house said energetically. "Let's make our guest comfortable. Siomka bring in the washtub from the attic. I am going to heat up some water."

"Amnon Alexandrovich, you will have to forgive us," she looked at me in a motherly way. We have no elegant amenities. This is an old building, so you will have to manage in an improvised, wooden fixture."

An hour later, the kitchen turned into a sauna-like sponge bath full of steam from the boiling water on the gas stove. Aunt Sarah discreetly slipped out and went to a next door neighbour while Siomka soaped and rubbed my back helping me to rid myself of ten months of prison filth.

"You know, Amnon," he said, while handing me a large towel and snow-white, clean underwear, "I have to tell you that I firmly believe that you have great, nay, tremendous zechus-oves (the accumulated merits of one's ancestors)."

"When I travelled to Dniepropietrowsk, I was a bit skeptical about your outlandish, bizarre story. A Rabbi's son in a German uniform. Modern Marranos, underground activities. It all bordered on the impossible. When I arrived at Maria Valentzova's place, however, and told her where I was coming from, whom I was representing, and the reason for my visit, it was like putting a match to a gasoline soaked torch. Maria Valentzova, whose real name is Mindl Valerstein, jumped up and started to cry: 'Oh my G-d! Adam Arendarski is alive!! Thank you dear Lord! He once saved my husband's life by warning him of a trap that Polish blackmailers had put out for him.' She did not know what to do with me. Quickly, she served me some food and tea before leaving for the ex-Gestapo building on Korolenk Street, which was now the headquarters of the NKGB. Yacek Polanski and Stefan Wrobel, your comrades in arms and friends, were now working there as watchmakers and precision mechanics. They had a bicycle at their disposal and at lunchtime instantly contacted Klara Fuchs, Richard Lis' widow, and Harry Horowitz. All of us met again the very same evening in Horowitz's place, which became my temporary home away from home. From there on, things began to roll with unbelievable speed. We edited a petition and started to collect signatures of people and neighbours and resistance fighters who knew you and your involvement in anti-Nazi activities."

"The next day, which was a lucky Tuesday, your personal friend, Major Hershel Najdor and Mindl Valerstein's husband, arrived on a ten day pass and devoted his whole holiday to your rescue. Within a week the petition with almost a hundred signatures and a precise list of your underground endeavours was on its way to Moscow along with a summary of the whole dramatic struggle of Dniepropietrowsk Kashtan Jews for their survival."

When we sat down to supper not only was I wearing Siomka's high boots, but his riding pants and his wintry green, Stalin-type tunic as well. Gitlin dressed me up from top to toe sharing his complete uniform with me. Aunt Sarah was as jovial as in the good old days when her husband, a composer and concert violinist, was still alive and playing his beautiful music. To mark the occasion, she lit some candles in her Sabbath candelabra which was a family heirloom, handed down from generation to generation, and used only for special events.

"Children," she said in a cheerful voice. "I would like to propose a toast, a combined plea, prayer, and benediction."

"Hear! Hear!" Siomka cried as together with me, he jumped to his feet.

Pouring home-made raisin wine into the goblets, she then stood up with the grace of a truly courageous woman and enunciated slowly in a clear, crisp Hebrew: "May the merciful one break the yoke from our neck; may he lead us uprightly and securely into our land."

It was the most beautiful and moving welcome speech that I could ever have dreamed of. It had all the ingredients, so close to my heart: religiosity, national identification, optimistic belief in the destiny of Am Yisrael and nostalgia for Zion and Jerusalem.

We three Jews had lost our families and our possessions, but not our human dignity to express our closeness to each other. As the unique celebration progressed, I was surprised and delighted to find out that Aunt Sarah Gitlin was a rabbinical daughter and ex-schoolmate of the eminent Odessan Vladimir

Jabotinski, and that Menachem Ussishkin, the prominent Zionist leader, had lived right next door to her parents and was actually, for a while, her Hebrew teacher.

"How about me?" Siomka humorously protested. "I am not just your common ordinary backwoods boy either! Maybe I was born 35 years too late to know personally all those giants of modern Jewish history. But, I do believe that I have a lot in common with one of the most fascinating and unforgettable heroes of our people."

"And who would that be?" his Aunt asked good-naturedly.

"Well! Since you are unable to figure it out on your own I had better tell you: Trumpeldor! Yes! Joseph Trumpeldor! The valiant Jewish officer who lost his left arm in Port Arthur, and later became the legendary hero of Tel-Chai. For sure there are a few geographic and calendar differences between him and myself. He lost his left arm fighting in the Czarist army. And I lost my left arm in the Red Army, in an even deadlier war against the Swastika demon. It all adds up to two limbs sacrificed for Matushka Russiya!"

Siomka was, by profession, a dental technician and Aunt Sarah had a degree in Semitic languages. Yet, their most important and unsung qualification was their self-sacrificing devotion to their fellow human beings. They were uniquely unselfish individuals willing to share whatever there was in the house, in the finest tradition of Russian Jewish hospitality.

After the borscht and potatoes, the chopped eggs and onions, the dessert of applesauce and tea, there followed a short after meal grace and lots of time for sharing memories and looking at family treasures. A prayer book, containing psalms, all five scrolls of the Song of Songs, Ruth, Ecclesiastes, Lamentations, and Esther, as well as explanations and texts for all the holidays, printed in Moscow in 1830, was one of the main exhibits. The brown, crumbling paper told its own story of a once cherished possession of pious, G-d fearing grandfathers and grandmothers, people who had used its large lettered pages of prayers with reverence.

There were, also, hand-inscribed ketuboth, marriage contracts adorned with beautiful graphics and biblical motifs in the style of the painter Marc Chagall. There were photographs of weddings, funerals, circumcisions, family gatherings, graduations, and army service, going back as far as the reign of Nicholas the First, when young Jewish boys, who became known as the Cantonists, were pressed into long years of pre-military apprenticeship under appalling conditions.

There were collectors' item editions of Pentateuchs, enriched with illustrative stories from Czarist times, and first editions of Yiddish translations of the classics printed by pre-war Soviet government presses. There were some posters of the Jewish anti-fascist committee in Moscow, and the first numbers of the Yiddish daily *The Truth*.

Siomka had his own collection of photographs of German atrocities and German prisoners of war. The captured Nazis no longer looked like Das Herrenvolk, cocky and tough, but like wretched beggars, unshaved, hairy, and dirty, subserviently pleading for a cigarette butt and a piece of bread.

I had nothing tangible to show. My father's colossal library was a thing of the past, either blown to smithereens in the Ghetto uprising, or hauled away by the thieving pseudo-scholars of the Third Reich. My own notes and pictures of the dramatic time when I was masquerading as an auxiliary member of all kinds of Nazi detachments, starting with the organization Todt and ending with the Luftwaffe, were in Woronow's dossier. I decided therefore to offer my hosts a poem which I remembered by heart.

"We will be very glad to listen to you," Aunt Sarah and Siomka assured me. I took a sip of the raisin wine and began:

> It is not easy, to be a lamenting poet
>   Walking around with an obsession to braid together
> New meaning and new life into words which are
>   Sad and age-old.
>
> It is like the Sisyphean task of an alchemist
>   Who tries and tries, experiment after experiment,
> To take kernels of sand, and turn them into
>   Nuggets of glittering gold . . .
>
> But sometimes, you are lucky and
>   The worn out, used up, sad words fall into line
> Like a tailor cut puzzle
>   Shapely in form, cheerful in thought
> Miraculously a comforting sentence is born.
>
> The reward is: euphoric
>   And you feel
> Like a nature-loving scientist
>   Who just made a breakthrough
> Creating the most beautiful flower of hope
>   From a prickly depressing thorn . . .

"Bravo!" cried Siomka.

"Gorgeous!" Aunt Sarah agreed. "Amnon Alexandrovich," she said. "Listen to me! Language is my field, so I definitely know what I am talking about. You are a talented man endowed with the capacity to mold and create images. You also possess a sense of rhythm and your poem builds up nicely to a fine conclusion. I only hope that very soon, while the memory of the events is still in your mind, you will sit down and write a larger work about all of your remarkable experiences."

Before going to bed, another glass of tea with home-made Russian preserves and cookies was served. Siomka and his aunt then invited me to stay on with them at least until the war was over.

"Where will you go in a country like Poland where all its Jewish citizens are annihilated?" Siomka Gitlin asked, with deep concern. "On my way home from Germany," Siomka continued, "I passed through the city of Lublin and I heard of ghastly things the Pollacks are doing to any Jews who dare to come back to their old homes. They ambush the homecoming Jewish compatriots and kill them mercilessly, just like the Nazis did! Stay in the meantime with us," he insisted. "You will be part of the family and later we will see. Why rush off into the unknown?"

While Siomka tried to persuade his ex-cellmate to remain in Odessa, Aunt Sarah fetched a blanket and milky-white, beautiful linen and proceeded to make up a bed for me on the living room sofa. This was a sight to behold! A sight I had not seen for a long, long time. After ten months of lying fully dressed on bare, dirty concrete floors, I was about to put on pajamas and lie down between clean white sheets, cover myself luxuriously with a fluffy down quilt and lean my head on a soft clean cushion without the fear of saying a Yiddish word, or a prayer, and without the necessity of having a loaded gun under the pillow. Most important of all, I had finally made it. I was free, with G-d's help, to make my own future.

"Have a peaceful night," Aunt Sarah and Siomka wished their guest before retiring to their rooms. Within minutes, I was falling asleep and was into the sphere of reveries. However, this time my dreams centred only around the present, dwelling on the subject of the Gitlins' proposal to join them as an adopted member of their family. It certainly was a tempting, almost irresistible proposal. After all the years of wanderings and homelessness, drifting from place to place, it would certainly be good to have a place I could call home. Especially when the home was to be shared with people like Sarah and Siomka. It meant security, belonging, and the precious, pure friendship of two wonderful Odessan Jews whom I already held in high esteem.

"What waits for you in Poland?" I heard Siomka's weighty and forceful argument. Nothing but tombstones and the possibility of being maimed or lynched by incorrigible Pogromchiks and vicious anti-semites, who willingly helped the murderers of our people in their final solution."

But the other more stern voice of my own alter ego warned me against that. "And what is going to happen if a member of your immediate family miraculously returns from a concentration camp, or slave factory, and there is no one to greet him, to say hello and lend a helping hand like the Gitlins gave you? Above all, what is going to happen with you sitting safely in alleged peace of mind in Odessa with your father's manuscripts rotting away in the damp Polish earth? And how do you know that when all the shooting stops, and things return to normal, that the Communist regime will allow you to get out of the U.S.S.R.?"

"The Gitlins are genuine, true friends, and they won't be hurt or insulted! They want you to be happy! They will understand and respect your decision to go back to your devastated city and look for remnants of your past with perhaps even the one in a million chance that someone did, just like yourself, come back miraculously from the ashes of devastation!"

In the morning, at breakfast, I told the Gitlins what I had to do. They were for a moment taken aback, but then sincerely wished me good luck from the bottom of their hearts.

"Have you got any money for the road?" Siomka pragmatically asked me. "You know that it is quite a few thousand kilometers from here to the Polish border."

"Well," I replied, a bit embarrassed. "Come to think of it, no, I don't! But I have a brick-shaped watch, so I will sell it in the bazaar, which should suffice to meet my needs."

"Oh no!" Siomka said. "The watch is of sentimental value to you. It's also an excellent timepiece which might come in handy for other unforseen complications." Hurriedly, he disappeared into his alcove and came back with two thousand Soviet rubles, which he handed to me saying, "This is my *bon voyage* gift to you."

"And when do you intend to start your pilgrimage back home?" Sarah asked tearfully.

"Well! Right after I pick up my release papers from Captain Woronow."

"That means today," she said, more to herself than to me, as if recollecting that she had things to do. "Excuse me, Amnon Alexandrovich. I must prepare something for your trip."

"Stay well, my friend." Once again Siomka embraced me, saying farewell with a mighty one-arm bear hug. "I would have walked you over to Babela Street. But, in twenty minutes I have an important appointment with a prosthesis specialist about an artificial limb and I cannot afford to miss it. Goodbye." The door closed behind his athletic figure and I heard him running down the stairs.

"Here is your knapsack!" Aunt Sarah was back from the kitchen and was also dressed to leave the apartment. "I made up a few sandwiches for you, boiled some eggs, and put in a jar of jam, a teaspoon, a large aluminum cup, a towel, and a couple of my late husband's clean shirts. Wherever you stop, there will surely be kipiatok, so mix it with some jam, and you will have a nourishing, gratifying drink." She said all this in the way that a mother instructs her son.

"I am going in your direction, not far from Babela, where I have a group of young Jewish students learning Hebrew. So if you don't mind, let's walk together."

"I would be delighted if you would honour me with your company," I said appreciatively.

We walked for a while in silence, with the nagging feeling of two true friends who are very fond of each other and are about to part, perhaps never to see one another again. At the corner of Engelsa and Babela, Sarah Gitlin stopped, kissed me on the forehead, and whispered in Hebrew, "Bon voyage, and may you have a safe journey." She then disappeared into the crowd of passersby.

At exactly eleven o'clock I was in Woronow's office. I greeted the captain but his face was stony and official, without a ray of congeniality or friendliness in it.

"Aha," he grumbled, "the Zapadnik Charasho. Here you are." He picked up a slip of paper with typed words on it. "Can you read Russian?" he asked.

"Da, Yes!" I said.

"So, go ahead! What are you waiting for? Let's hear what it says!"

Slowly I began to read, "Adam Yanovich Arendarski, alias Amnon Alexandrovich Ajzensztadt, was under NKGB investigation from the 10th of April 1944 to the 9th of February 1945. Discharged from interrogational detention due to discontinuance of case."

"That's it!" Woronow said. "Now, you have to go with this document to the militia's travel department, and they will issue you a travel permit back to Dniepropietrowsk."

"Comrade Captain! May I please have my notes and pictures back. They are important to me, as a symbolic reminder and factual documentation of the extraordinary saga I went through."

"You had better stop using fancy intellectual expressions like saga and documentation!" Woronow said, while giving me an icy look. "If you know what is good for you then lead a simple life! Talk simple, non-political talk, learn a productive trade, become a useful member of Soviet society, and keep the Jewish melodramatics to yourself! No, my dear fellow! You cannot have those pictures in German uniform and the Hebrew and Yiddish poems! They belong to the archives of the NKGB. Besides, whoever finds them in your possession will detain you again. And the second time you might not be set free at all. So, forget the past! That is my final word of advice to you. Also, watch your behavioural patterns, because, as I said, if you come back to us for some reason, you might remain here for a long, long while."

For the last time, I was in the lower numbers of Babela Street. I felt as if I had just experienced a cold shower and was a bit confused following the educational chat with the captain. Again, I took out my so-called graduation certificate of my ten months' course behind bars and looked at it closely. It was a cheap quality piece of paper from an ordinary note-pad, with rough edges caused by tearing it manually, without the use of scissors or office knife. Yet, it had the mighty round seal of the NKGB with the wreath and hammer and sickle right in the centre of it. Undeniably, this was an important piece of paper; and paid for in full, I thought. I folded it up and put it carefully back into my breast pocket before making my way to the militia's downtown headquarters.

At a newsstand I happened to see a tall, handsome colonel of the NKVD (National Commissariat for Internal Matters) border police units wearing a fitted, elegant uniform with the distinguished, golden five pointed star medal of a Hero of Soviet Russia! The adrenalin in my veins started to run amok. I suddenly realised that this man would really be able to tell me what to do in my predicament.

"Comrade Colonel!" I approached him a few steps away from the kiosk.

The Colonel turned his inquisitve brown eyes towards the strange, pale, young man. Now! my survival instinct dictated: go ahead and ask him!

"Comrade Colonel!" I repeated, "Are you of Jewish nationality?"

The Colonel smiled benignly and replied in a marvellous, pure Yiddish: "Yes, I am Jewish! And you don't have to strain yourself in speaking Russian. We can continue this conversation in our native tongue, Yiddish! Let's go up to the second floor in the next building," the military man said, "and we will have a bit of privacy."

A few moments later we were both on the staircase of an apartment building. "So what is your problem?" the Colonel asked.

Trying as best I could to control my nervousness I gave the NKVD man a brief synopsis of my whole life, including Ghetto, underground, masquerading as a German, jail — everything. And all of it I related in my Warsaw Yiddish dialect.

Once I had finished, the Colonel simply asked, also in Yiddish, "Show me what kind of papers you have."

"I took out Woronow's release paper and handed it to him. The Colonel read it quickly and commented again in a succulent Yiddish, "Is that so! You were in our hands and we actually let you go? You really must be a genuine righteous Jew!"

"So what am I supposed to do? I want to go back to Poland, to Warsaw. Maybe someone is still alive there."

The Colonel gave me back the release which I replaced in my breast pocket.

The NKVD man then walked up another flight of stairs, to make sure that nobody was eavesdropping on the conversation, and motioned to me to follow him.

"Listen!" he began again. "I am going to tell you how to get home. Do as I advise you and you will make it in no time. Don't go to the militia for a travel permit. Don't return to Dniepropietrowsk. Go straight to the railway station and take the first freight train going west to Zmerinka, Zytomir, Kiev, and Podvolochisk. They might arrest you for travelling illegally and without a ticket, but I guarantee you, the minute you show them your release document, they will immediately let you go free. If you have any money with you, don't keep it in your regular pockets. The hobos and other shady characters who will be travelling the same way will steal it from you. Put it into a handkerchief and bandage it — under your clothes — around your arms or legs where nobody can reach it without drawing your attention. Be especially careful to guard the release document like the pupils of your eyes."

I looked at the Colonel. The handsome, dark-complexioned officer was to me now like Elijah the prophet, disguised as an NKVD man. I felt the warmth, the sincerity, and the authenticity of his words coming from the depths of a Jewish soul. It was the unscathed and uncorrupted soul of Russian Jewry.

"Thank you comrade Colonel," I said.

"No, don't thank me! On the contrary, I thank you for giving me a chance to exchange a few words in the Yiddish language which I love so much."

The Colonel put his arm on my shoulder in a very friendly way. "You know! I just returned from Lwow Lemberg. I visited many Polish Jews there who are coming back from Partisan units, forests, marshes, and all kinds of other concealments and hideouts. They are all very excited about the idea of going to Palestine which will, in their opinion, soon become a Jewish state, a national home for the children of Israel, an independent, sovereign Jewish country for whose creation they are willing to fight and die."

Again, the Colonel looked inquisitively up to the next floor and bent over the bannister down to the lower floor. There was not a living soul around and he made his final statement: "If I did not have a father and mother living in Moscow, I would myself run away to Eretz Israel. Good luck!" he stretched out his right hand to me.

"Likewise!" I replied in traditional Hebrew, shaking the robust hand of the young Jew in the military uniform.

That same afternoon, on the 10th of February 1945, I found a cargo train loaded with hay and going westward. I was finally on my way back to the desolate, gloomy territories of Polish Jewry to search for survivors, dig up my father's manuscripts, perpetuate the memory of the fallen martyrs, and to start a new chapter in my twenty-six year old life, as far away from totalitarianism as possible.

GLOSSARY

GERMAN MILITARY RANK
ITALIAN EXPRESSIONS AND TITLES
RUSSIAN TERMS AND ABBREVIATIONS
EUPHEMISMS CONCERNING
JEWS ON ARYAN UNDERGROUND PAPERS

OBERSTURMBANNFUEHRER — Lieutenant Colonel of the S.S.

UNTERSCHARFUEHRER — Corporal of the S.S.

S.S. — Condensed form of Shutzstaffeln; "Protection Squad"

S.D. — Sicherheitsdienst; intelligence service of the S.S.

WEHRMACHTSGEFOLGE — Military label for auxiliary forces

SCHUTZPOLIZEI — Defence police

FELDWEBEL — Sergeant in the regular German Army

ORGANIZATION TODT — Nazy-Army Engineer Corps that built bunkers, bridges and highways

LUFTWAFFE — Nazi-Air Force

SOUNDERKOMMANDOS — Special squads

EINSATZGRUPPEN — Annihilation troops

UMSCHLAGPLATZ — Deportation station on Stawki Street in Warsaw

STREICHER, JULIUS — Editor of Nazi Hate Tribune "Der Sturmer"

HERRENVOLK — Master race

WLASOW — A former Soviet General, who organized armed units which fought on the side of Hitler's Germany in World War II

DUCE — Italian Fascist leader Benito Mussolini

CAPTAIN MINELLI — Commander of an Italian Battalion which deserted from the Russian Front

CARABINIERI — Italian police

SIGNORE — Mister

MOLTO-BENE — Very good

GRAZIE — Thank you

TRE STELLA — Three stars

VIVA L'POLONIA — Long live Poland

N.K.G.B. — National Kommisariat for State Security dealing with intelligence and counter intelligence

N.K.V.D. — National Kommisariat of internal affairs

KOMSOMOL — Communist youht organization for children, adolescents and young people aged 15-27

KHOLKHOZ — Collective, agrarian farm

NOVOYE ZITYE — New life

VOLGA — One of Russia's largest rivers eternalized in a famous national song

SZEWCZENKO — Honoured Ukrainian poet with many parks and gardens carrying his name

BABUSHKA — Grandmother

DYADYA — Uncle

GOSPODIN — Mister

DOSVIDANYA — Good-bye

MAKHORKA — Rough Russian tobacco

ZARAZA — Plague

GENERAL KOWPAK — Chief Commander of the Soviet Guerrilla forces in the Ukrainian forests

MARRANO — A concealed Jew hiding from the Gestapo like his predecessors in Spain who hid from the Inquisition in the Middle Ages

KASHTAN — A derogatory nickname for Jews on forged Aryan papers

ABRASHKA — A mocking, anti-semitic name for Jews in the Ukraine during and immediately after the war

INDEX